Material Spirituality

Expanding Philosophy of Religion

Series Editors:
J. Aaron Simmons, Furman University, USA
Kevin Schilbrack, Appalachian State University, USA

A series dedicated to a global, diverse, cross-cultural, and comparative philosophy of religion, Expanding Philosophy of Religion encourages underrepresented voices and perspectives and looks beyond its traditional concerns rooted in classical theism, propositional belief, and privileged identities.

Titles in the series include:
Philosophical Hermeneutics and the Priority of Questions in Religions, by Nathan Eric Dickman
Philosophies of Religion, by Timothy Knepper
Diversifying Philosophy of Religion, edited by Nathan R. B. Loewen and Agnieszka Rostalska
Collective Intentionality and the Study of Religion by Andrea Rota
Engaging Philosophies of Religion by Gereon Kopf, Purushottama Bilimoria and Nathan R. B. Loewen
Rethinking Religious Conversion by Jack Williams
Philosophies of Liturgy, edited by J. Aaron Simmons, Bruce Ellis Benson and Neal DeRoo
Art, Desire, and God, edited by Gereon Kopf, Purushottama Bilimoria and Nathan R. B. Loewen
Art Making as Spiritual Practice by Lexi Eikelbloom and David Newheiser
Rethinking Philosophy of Religion with Wittgenstein by Thomas D. Carroll
Reimagining Philosophy of Religion by Amber L. Griffioen

Material Spirituality

A Transcendental Phenomenology of Religion

Neal DeRoo

BLOOMSBURY ACADEMIC
LONDON • NEW YORK • OXFORD • NEW DELHI • SYDNEY

BLOOMSBURY ACADEMIC

Bloomsbury Publishing Plc, 50 Bedford Square, London, WC1B 3DP, UK
Bloomsbury Publishing Inc, 1359 Broadway, New York, NY 10018, USA
Bloomsbury Publishing Ireland, 29 Earlsfort Terrace, Dublin 2, D02 AY28, Ireland

BLOOMSBURY, BLOOMSBURY ACADEMIC and the
Diana logo are trademarks of Bloomsbury Publishing Plc

First published in Great Britain 2026

Copyright © Neal DeRoo, 2026

Neal DeRoo has asserted his right under the Copyright, Designs and
Patents Act, 1988, to be identified as Author of this work.

For legal purposes the Acknowledgments on pp. vi–vii constitute an
extension of this copyright page.

Cover design by Louise Dugdale
Cover image © Rawf8/iStock

All rights reserved. No part of this publication may be: i) reproduced or transmitted in
any form, electronic or mechanical, including photocopying, recording or by means of
any information storage or retrieval system without prior permission in writing from the
publishers; or ii) used or reproduced in any way for the training, development or operation
of artificial intelligence (AI) technologies, including generative AI technologies. The rights
holders expressly reserve this publication from the text and data mining exception as per
Article 4(3) of the Digital Single Market Directive (EU) 2019/790.

Bloomsbury Publishing Plc does not have any control over, or responsibility for, any
third-party websites referred to or in this book. All internet addresses given in this
book were correct at the time of going to press. The author and publisher regret
any inconvenience caused if addresses have changed or sites have ceased
to exist, but can accept no responsibility for any such changes.

A catalogue record for this book is available from the British Library.

A catalog record for this book is available from the Library of Congress.

ISBN: HB: 978-1-3504-1803-5
       PB: 978-1-3504-1807-3
       ePDF: 978-1-3504-1804-2
       eBook: 978-1-3504-1805-9

Typeset by Integra Software Services Pvt. Ltd.
Printed and bound in Great Britain

For product safety related questions contact productsafety@bloomsbury.com

To find out more about our authors and books visit www.bloomsbury.com
and sign up for our newsletters.

Contents

Acknowledgments   vi

Introduction: A Transcendental Phenomenological Understanding
of Religion   1

1   Material-Spirituality   23
2   Religiosity as a Religious Mode of Engaging the World   39
3   Thinking Religion within a Religious Tradition   57
4   What Makes a Phenomenon Religious?   81
5   Religious Experience and Materiality   101
6   Thinking Religion Cross-Culturally   121

Conclusion: Material-Spiritual Religion   139

Glossary   158
Notes   163
Bibliography   190
Index   203

Acknowledgments

Despite the preference for monographs in the corners of the academic world that this book inhabits, there are many conversations, ideas, discussions, and influences behind the scenes of this book. Among them, I would like to thank especially the members of the Society for the Phenomenology of Religious Experience (SoPheRE), which has been a very fruitful forum for me as I have been working out the ideas that would become this book. The encouragement of Olga Louchakova-Schwartz, Martin Nitsche, Michael Barber, and Peter Costello has been especially appreciated on this project. The International Network for Philosophy of Religion (INPR) has been another very helpful forum for me to work out these ideas. My thanks go especially to Emmanuel Falque, William Connelly, Domenico Cambria, and Pablo Irizar for all their efforts in organizing and hosting the INPR events I have attended in Paris, Perugia, and Montreal. I must also thank the participants of my Winter 2025 seminar "Material Spirituality: Re-Thinking Religion" for working through an early draft of this manuscript and offering helpful feedback: my thanks go out to Chris Christiansen, Alexander Ionut-Duma, Alayna Erickson, Mark Griffiths, Yosep Hong, Chad Maxson, Tyler-May Gruthusen, Ann Post, Daniel Shane, Benjamin Strachan, Sim VanderVinne, and Joe Watson.

I would like to acknowledge the support of the Social Sciences and Humanities Research Council of Canada (SSHRC), who provided a three-year Insight Grant in support of the development, writing, and completion of this book. The book could not have been done without that support, which is herein gratefully acknowledged.

More personal thanks go to Christina M. Gschwandtner, both for her immensely helpful and thorough comments on an earlier draft of the manuscript, and for her constant encouragement for me to pursue and then to finish this project. Chad Maxson deserves extra thanks also for his constant support of this project, and for helping me see some of the good that it could do. Mark Griffiths also gave feedback on an early version of the manuscript, and made numerous suggestions toward improving it. Thanks go out also to Aaron Simmons and Kevin Schilbrack for the gracious invitation to host this book in their series, and to Colleen Coalter, Aimee Brown, and the whole team at Bloomsbury for shepherding this project through the process of becoming a book. Anonymous reviewers of earlier drafts and proposals also deserve my thanks for helping the book become better than it would have been without their intervention.

The book has been immensely improved by the tireless work of Benjamin Strachan, my research assistant. Benjamin has caught and corrected countless mistakes, redirected me away from numerous dead ends, and made connections between this work and other areas that I would never have been able to make on my own. The book is much better for the role he played in it, and I thank him deeply for that.

Finally, thanks to Tanya, Hendrik, and Frankie for their patience as I worked away on another book project, and to the community at the Institute for Christian Studies for providing an intellectual and professional home for me.

Introduction: A Transcendental Phenomenological Understanding of Religion

Something is missing from the contemporary study of religion. It is not always easy to pinpoint, precisely, what it is, but its absence is felt in everything from the analysis of particular religious objects and rituals to broader questions about the nature of religion itself. In this book, I will attempt to articulate this missing element through the language of experience. In that terminology, I can frame my concern this way: the contemporary study of religion generally misses accounting for how religion affects how we experience the world. Instead, religion is almost always understood today solely in terms of the content, the "what," that we experience.

That is, religion is taken to consist of things that can function as the objects of our experience, like doctrines, concepts, practices, rituals, objects, and so on. Those things can affect our lives and our experiences: performing a meditative ritual in the morning can alter the mood with which I experience the world for the rest of the day, for example. But while meditating (especially in a particularly "religious" setting) is likely to be considered a "religious" practice, few scholars would hold that a person calmly engaging with others after meditating is thereby practicing something called "religion." Religion is almost solely understood in terms of things that can be the content of our experience, the "what" that occupies us: the concepts we are thinking about, the rituals we perform, the objects that hold our attention, the feelings we feel.

My conviction is that this content-based approach is too small a picture of religion. It misses the way that religion changes and transforms both people and the world by impacting *how* people experience the world in general. The primary aim of this book, then, is to explain how religion shapes our experiencing, such that we experience ourselves and the world differently because of it.[1] I will seek to explain that by situating our understanding of religion within a broader account of experiencing itself: only in looking at how experience is shaped and constituted in general can we come to appreciate the uniquely religious ways that religion shapes our experiencing of the world. Doing so will require a deep foray into transcendental phenomenology, as the method that, I will show, best lets us develop and talk about the conditions of experiencing.

A Quick Clarification of Key Terms

In saying that, I take as given a few key concepts that are, perhaps, worth making explicit here, at the beginning, to avoid any confusion. First, phenomenology, as I am using that term, is the philosophical exploration of *how* we experience (what we might call the "conditions of experiencing," provided we understand that these conditions are not simply logical conditions but are themselves conditions arising within experience[2]). This approach is different from the "phenomenology of religion" that happens in religious studies departments (or at least that happened there historically: think of figures like Eliade, Otto, Van der Leeuw, etc.) in two important ways: first, philosophical phenomenology[3] (as we can characterize it to help keep it distinct from "phenomenology of religion") has an obviously broader scope than phenomenology of religion in that it does not restrict the object of its analyses only to what we might call "religious" matters; second, philosophical phenomenology is necessarily transcendental in a way that phenomenology of religion is (mostly) not.

This leads us to the second key point of clarification: when I use the term "transcendental" I do *not* mean it as a synonym for transcendent. I understand that this is often how the term is used in religious studies,[4] but it is distinctly *not* how the term is used in philosophy—and especially not in philosophical phenomenology—and it is *not* how I will be using the term in this text. Instead, by "transcendental" I will mean those conditions that make experience possible, not simply in the logical sense (as in Kant), but as the conditions of experiencing that are operative in our experience. The transcendental refers to *how* we experience (as we have already said), rather than simply to *what* we experience. It says something about the nature of our experiencing rather than speaking primarily about the nature of what we experience in this or that instance; it speaks about affectivity rather than simply what affects us, or about intentionality rather than simply the things we intend. When it comes to religion specifically, transcendental phenomenology is concerned with how religion shapes our experiencing of things in general and is *not* concerned with whether the object of our experience must in some way transcend or be outside of the world (whatever we might mean by that). A transcendental phenomenology of religion is, therefore, an entirely different kind of analysis than a phenomenology of transcendence, of the type that seems to characterize classical "phenomenology of religion." To emphasize the point further: what we are interested in, in this book, is analyzing how we experience transcendentally; we are not interested in what we might call "experiences of the transcendent."

This leads me to a third clarification: when I speak of "phenomenology of religion," I mean, in general, the work done in the empirical study of religion inspired by people like Eliade, Otto, Van der Leeuw, and so on. This is different from the work done in what we might call "philosophical phenomenology of religion," which would include figures who tend to work in philosophy departments such as Jean-Luc Marion, Emmanuel Levinas, Jean-Yves Lacoste, Emmanuel Falque, and others, and which were the subject of Dominique Janicaud's ire in his infamous essay "The Theological Turn of French Phenomenology."[5] For those coming from that philosophical background, I think it important to signal clearly, up front, that "phenomenology of religion" has another meaning and refers to a distinct tradition in religious studies (that of Eliade, Otto, Van der Leeuw, etc.), and the usage in this book will follow that other meaning. Of course, the two traditions are not wholly distinct, and this book hopes to clarify that relationship in a particular way by focusing on the transcendental, the conditions and processes shaping how we experience, rather than the transcendent.

Finally, in outlining a philosophically phenomenological and transcendental account of experiencing, we will appeal to a particular (i.e., phenomenological and transcendental) understanding of spirit. This too requires clarification, in the context of the study of religion. For this account of spirit should not be conflated with the (ambiguous and largely intuitive) uses of spirituality that are operative in empirical studies of religion.[6] It differs from those accounts in two main ways: first, the account offered here is communal (or supra-subjective, in Husserl's terminology[7]) before it is individual (a re-evaluation of the "personal" nature of spirituality that is assumed in much of the current religious studies literature); and second, the account of spirituality offered in this book embeds us within a reality that is wider than just ourselves, rather than putting us in contact with an alternate or parallel reality (a re-evaluation of the "dualist" nature of spirituality that is at work in many notions of spirituality in the current religious studies literature).[8] These distinctions are marked by the use of the term "material-spirituality" for the transcendental account of spirituality under discussion. We can call this account transcendental because, as we will see, material-spirituality (as we will be talking about it here) is a condition of experiencing itself, whatever type of experiences we may be having (perceptual, religious, ethical, social, linguistic, etc.). Hence, spirituality cannot be reduced to religion, because the religious is only one (of many) ways that spirituality is expressed in human experience.

Casting our understanding of the religious within the broader framework of material-spirituality will give us some new insights into religion. That, at least, is the wager of this book. And the primary insight it will give us is that "religion" is not simply a thing that we experience, but first describes a dimension of our experiencing itself, a dimension that therefore shapes our experiences in our very experiencing of them, well beyond the realms of what we might normally consider to be "religion." In that sense, this book will endeavor to show that part of what is missing in the study of religion comes from its primary (and almost exclusive) focus on "religion" (as a noun, as a particular object of experience), which causes us to miss the religious dimensions of experiencing itself. In shifting our focus to talk more about the "religious" as an adjective or adverb, we will be better able to see the ways that the religious acts as a modifier changing the way we experience other things, perhaps even changing experiencing itself. This is not to say that all talk of religion must be entirely abandoned. If "religion" is a helpful umbrella term that picks out a particular object of inquiry that deserves to be picked out and described in that way (and my own inclination is to think that it certainly can be helpful in this regard), then it should continue to be used. My point here is simply to say: (a) that I think the term is more helpfully employed in its adjectival form, at least when viewed from the perspective of a transcendental phenomenological inquiry into *how* we experience; and (b) that, if one begins from that transcendental phenomenological perspective (as I will endeavour to do here), we might come to understand "religion" (the noun) in a different way, a way that will help us both expand the scope of what might count as "religion" and deepen our appreciation of the role that "religion" plays, or can play, in the lives of some of its practitioners. That is what is at stake in this book.

The Method of Inquiry: Philosophy and Phenomenology of Religion

This book is therefore interested in articulating how religion shapes our experiencing in a broad sense. To achieve that task, it undertakes a transcendental phenomenological investigation of religion and the role it plays in various people's experiences of the world. Framing it this way, the work done here takes place at the intersection of at least three distinct fields or bodies of knowledge: transcendental phenomenology (as a kind of philosophical method); philosophy of religion (i.e., the field in which religion is the subject of philosophical study); and religious studies (i.e., empirical studies that take religion as the object of inquiry). A contention of the book is that all three of these dimensions are necessary to capture the breadth of the phenomenon (religion) under consideration properly.

To begin to see why this is the case, we can look at some of the shortfalls of inquiries that have failed to account for all three of the dimensions outlined above. There has been a lot of work done in philosophy of religion, for example, that is carried out in a transcendental phenomenological way. We earlier called this the "philosophical phenomenology of religion."[9] This work has made significant contributions to our understanding of phenomenology and of experiencing (e.g., Marion's accounts of givenness[10] and the saturated phenomena[11]; Henry's account of Life[12]; Romano's account of the event[13]), and has included several interesting analyses of religious phenomena (e.g., Marion's account of the Eucharist[14]; Chrétien's readings of the Christian Scriptures and of prayer[15]; Lacoste's account of life as liturgical[16]). But these analyses seem to be compelling primarily to those within a particular religious tradition (Christianity, and mostly Catholicism), and even there, compelling mainly to those who not only share that tradition but also share a phenomenological background: Christina M. Gschwandtner, for example, has argued that Marion's account of the Eucharist seems to have little to say to the majority of people who participate in Eucharistic rites on a regular basis, in part because it provides us a view of the Eucharist that is "absolute and excessive [in] nature."[17] That is to say, this "philosophical phenomenology of religion," taking place at the intersection of transcendental phenomenology and philosophy of religion, yields excellent and stimulating philosophical insights—but how helpful is it in helping us better understand religion and/or religious experience?[18] While some religious experiences may be encountered as "saturated phenomena," many others are more mundane: although people sometimes experience a mystical unity with the divine, more often they are sort of bored listening to a sermon in a Protestant worship service, lose their train of thought in yogic or Zen meditations, or feel a resigned duty in giving alms and caring for the poor.

The philosophical phenomenology of religion, by and large, is missing a serious engagement with empirical practices of religion. This manifests itself, not only in the "excessive" nature of some of its conceptual claims ("excessive" especially vis-à-vis the regular experiences of religious practitioners), but also in the narrowness of its analyses, which are concerned (almost) exclusively with Christian and Catholic concepts, practices, and concerns. This is not necessarily a failure on its part, given that it is not, in general, claiming to do anything other than it does: provide phenomenological analyses of certain Christian practices, and giving Christian analyses of certain phenomenological movements. This only becomes problematic if we are interested in something else: a transcendental phenomenological analysis of religion itself (if there is such a thing).[19] In that sense, one probably more accurately calls it the philosophical phenomenology of Catholicism or perhaps of Christianity, rather than the philosophical phenomenology *of religion*.

The same is distinctly not true of the "critical"[20] philosophy of religion developed from insights into the empirical study of religion. This work, carried out by people such as Russel McCutcheon, Jonathan Z. Smith, Talal Asad, and Kevin Schilbrack takes place at the intersection of philosophy of religion and religious studies. It has been immensely helpful in reflecting on the meaning, significance, and helpfulness of "religion" as a concept for the empirical study of the various practices, ideas, objects, rites, and so on that (many) scholars seek to group under the name "religion." Through their critical reflections on the uses of the term religion across various cultural expressions, important questions have been raised about the nature of religion itself: is it a "genus" comprising various "species"? Does it require reference to some kind of super-empirical or super-human (i.e., transcendent) realities in order to draw its conceptual significance, or is it enough to refer simply to something in human life and practice? Is "religion" a helpful cross-cultural category, or is the concept itself inherently Western, and its application to non-Western cultures simply a continuation and implicit support of colonialism? Does "religion" actually refer to anything in the empirical world, or is it a concept that invents as much as it describes?[21] All these philosophical reflections have helped us better understand actual religious practices in a wider way, in part by helping us shift our understanding of religion away from epistemology and knowledge claims toward sociology, material practices, and affective power, and in part by helping us see just how different the various "religions" are, such that trying to think non-Western "religions" from within the conceptual framework of Western theisms, for example, risks missing something significant about the non-Western practices.

But something important remains missing from these analyses, it seems to me: a robust notion of experience and its implications for the study of religion (if there is such a thing). I do not mean that no one is interested in how various people engage with their own religious life, or that no one has done qualitative research into religious practice and religious practitioners. All of that has, of course, happened, and happened in spades. What I mean is that little, if any, thought is given to what it means that religious practices, for example, are not only performed, but *experienced*. While it is true that religious practices take place in the world (and not, for example, primarily in the minds of religious practitioners), something significant is lost if we think of them simply as actions taking place in the world. What is lost is not some super-natural reality or significance, but rather the impact of those practices being experienced by people with subjective capabilities[22]: those practices are lived through, and felt; they are shaped by prior experiences, and they in turn shape future experiences; they change people's moods, change people's behaviors, and have changed the world. Through these subjective capabilities, religious practices have impacts far beyond the scope of what we would normally consider "religion," and this is difficult to explain—difficult even to recognize—without a more robust account of experience, of subjectivity, and how the two interact.

This loss of the category of "experience" is significant, I am claiming, for our understanding of religion. In bemoaning its lack in "critical" philosophy of religion, I am not simply saying that I wish they were doing transcendental phenomenology instead. I am saying that something significant about our understanding *of religion* is lacking, if we cannot account for subjective capabilities and their influence on experience. One way this shows up, it seems to me, is in our difficulty in understanding religion in relation to other scholarly categories (like sociology, language, etc.). Too often we have been encouraged to think that religion must not be significant on its own but can simply be explained in linguistic terms ("religion is really just the study of semantics and meanings"), anthropological terms ("religion is really just the study of cultural practices"), or hegemonic terms ("religion is really just a manifestation of power relations"). But that it has impacts and effects in other cultural modalities need not imply that it is not itself a unique modality, impacting and affecting others (think, for example, of how political practices impact economics in profound ways, yet we would not say politics simply is economics or vice versa). Rather, what must be explained is *how* religion is able to impact, and be impacted by, linguistic, anthropological, sociological, and so on, realities. And I would contend that accounting for the subjective capabilities of people—that is, thinking of people also as subjects capable of experiencing and of shaping experiences—gives us one way to do that.

Another way this lack of experiencing shows up in critical philosophy of religion is in the circularity of its method. In general, critical philosophy of religion begins by looking at what does (and, in some cases, what does not[23]) count as religion, and then looking for commonalities between all the things deemed to be "religion" in order to come up with an account of what is meant by religion. This circularity—defining "religion" by looking for similarities between the things we consider religious—is normally taken to be logically problematic (it's why you are not supposed to use the term being defined in its definition). Critical philosophy of religion avoids this logical circularity largely by restricting itself in a linguistic way: we are seeking to explain our use of the term "religion" by looking at all the ways we use it and seeing what they might have in common. That linguistic restriction avoids the worst of the circularity only at the cost of leaving us unable to challenge in a fundamental way what we think counts, or ought to count, as religious. In other words, in talking only about how we use the term religion, we are not equipped to think differently about how we *might* use the term religion, nor about what function religion may be playing, whether we recognize (and name) it as such or not. Transcendental phenomenology helps us avoid this problem by opening us to consider, among other things, the role of prior experiences in shaping our usage of certain terms, the role of our hermeneutic presuppositions in our language and more broadly in our lives,[24] and the relationships between the various modalities or dimensions of our living.[25] Accounting for experiencing, that is, accounting for the role of subjectivity in experience and thereby accounting for the role of experience in various practices, is the task of transcendental phenomenology, and it has, we will see, something significant to contribute to our understanding of religion.

Of course, phenomenology has already played a huge role in our understanding of religion. It is not, I think, an exaggeration to say that the discipline of religious studies was founded in phenomenology.[26] The "phenomenology of religion" done by people like Rudolf Otto, Mircea Eliade, and Gerardus Van der Leeuw (among many others) was essential in establishing religion as something that could be studied empirically and scientifically. Their focus on people's religious experiences opened up data that could be studied empirically and so took the study of religion out of the realm of theology (talk about God or the divine) and into the realm of empirical inquiry (talk about human activities). Human actions, beliefs, and practices—rather than the divine—became the object of religious inquiry. Of course, the divine wasn't absent, especially from many of the accounts of the early phenomenologists of religion. But it showed up in people's *concepts* of the sacred, or in particular *practices* meant to invoke it, or in other various means by which humans sought to account for, admire, or engage with the divine in various ways across various cultures.

Yet this early phenomenology of religion lacked, for the most part, a serious engagement with philosophy, including with philosophical and transcendental phenomenology.[27] As a result, it accounted for human experiences, but lacked the resources to account for experiencing, and hence for the subjective capabilities we were discussing earlier. This was a phenomenology of religious experiences, but not yet a robust phenomenology of religious experience or of religious experiencing. It allowed scholars to take particular experiences seriously, and it began to postulate a few things about the nature of religious experience itself—although those were, for the most part, simply un-reflected-upon presuppositions about divinity, the sacred, and so on.[28] Critical philosophers of religion are, for the most part, critical of these early "phenomenological" attempts to think religion, seeing them as overly Western and monotheistic.[29] They lacked both a critical (philosophical?) distance and an understanding of the nature of experiencing itself. Which is to say, they lacked an understanding of transcendental philosophizing as it functions in phenomenology.

Clarifying the Transcendental Nature of our Phenomenological Investigation

Hence, transcendental phenomenology adds something important to our study of religion—provided it does not lose contact with empirical religious practices. Four things about this methodological approach are significant for the investigation that follows. First, and most basically, is the conviction that the things that we encounter are primarily *Sachen* [matters/issues] and not *Dinge* [things/objects]. A *Ding* is what it is in itself, that is to say, without regard for its relations to other things. *Sachen*, on the other hand, are what they are always in their embedded relationships to other *Sachen*. Karen Barad refers to phenomena as being necessarily "entangled," that is, caught up in webs of meaning that are simultaneously political, social, historical, cultural, linguistic, artistic/stylistic, and so on.[30] To engage with something as a phenomenon, you have to understand it as a *Sache* and not a *Ding*, and therefore account for how it is embedded in its world or culture. A phenomenon cannot be understand apart from that context.

Second, this "embedded" nature of phenomena is characteristic of phenomenality itself. That is, it is not just empirical phenomena that are "entangled," but so too are the various transcendental conditions that give rise to those phenomena and others like it. The embeddedness also of those conditions entails that the transcendental in phenomenology is not outside experience, but is generated within and so comes from experience, even as it also shapes and generates experience.[31] This is the fundamental distinction between phenomenological and Kantian types of transcendental philosophizing: Kantian transcendentals are *a priori*, and hence beyond or outside experience, normally because they are located in the structure of a subjectivity that is itself understood to be given *a priori*. The structuring of experience is, therefore, a one-way street for Kant: subjects constitute and shape experience but subjectivity itself is not, in its essential structures, shaped by the experiences that it shapes. Transcendental phenomenology, on the other hand, is interested precisely in how subjectivity itself is constituted or generated *within* experience[32]: transcendentals shape our experience, even as they are, in turn, shaped by those experiences. This is part of why I insist on distinguishing the transcendental so sharply from the transcendent: understood phenomenologically, transcendental conditions are not transcendent at all. They are generated within, and operate within, the world of experience: how we experience is shaped by what we experience, even as what we experience is also shaped by how we experience.

This is true also of subjectivity, a mode or type of the transcendental, as we will see in later chapters. Subjectivity is also generated within empirical circumstances, and as such is in no way God-like or transcendent, in either its distance from the world or in some postulated supreme and absolute freedom and sovereignty. This transcendent Subject is not what I mean when I talk about subjectivity.[33] For our analyses, we must remember that subjectivity arises in particular contexts, and functions differently in different contexts. As such, subjective ways of constituting or shaping experience—the various "hows" at work in our experiencing—are themselves conditioned and shaped by particular historical and empirical circumstances. Transcendental conditions—including subjectivity—are always situated, generated, and operative materially and historically.

This situated nature of the transcendental leads to the third methodological feature that is important to highlight for our investigation: there are different levels of transcendental analysis. Historically, phenomenology has distinguished four distinct levels of philosophizing at work in its analyses of the transcendental, four distinct ways that things/phenomena are "embedded" in a given situation. The most fundamental distinction on this score is one that we have already mentioned: the difference between the empirical (i.e., what we experience) and the transcendental (i.e., how we experience). But within the transcendental, within our experience of "how" phenomena come to be constituted in our experiencing of them, three further levels can be differentiated: the ultra-transcendental, the sensing-transcendental, and the quasi-transcendental. I will start in the middle, by talking about the sensing-transcendental. This refers to our different modes of sensing [*Empfindnisse*] the world. *Empfindnisse* (usually translated into English as sensings) is Husserl's portmanteau of *Empfindung* (sensation) and *Erlebnisse* (lived experiences).[34] The portmanteau refers to the way that these "sensings" are simultaneously a contact with the world (sensation) and a subjective living through of that contact. This implies a much closer connection between subjective life and the world than is offered in Kantian or Cartesian accounts of subjectivity. For phenomenology, we feel (or sense) the world in a way that is not simply a "taking-in" of what is "out there," but is already a connecting of our lived experience essentially with the world. We live (in and through) these sensings, and as such connection with, and immersion in, the world is essential to subjective life, as discussed above.

The plural form of sensings is crucial, for there is not one primary mode of sensing (self-reflection or rationality) but always a multiplicity of sensings, each of which engage subjectivity with the world. This multiplicity is itself twofold: there is a multiplicity of distinct sensings of a particular type (e.g., I see multiple different things at different times) and there is a multiplicity of types of sensings (e.g., visibility, tactility, aurality, linguisticality, sociality, etc.). These distinct types of sensings are in principle irreducible: no amount of tasting becomes sight; no amount of listening becomes touch; and so on. Yet their irreducibility does not leave them entirely unconnected with each other: we speak, see, touch, taste, and so on, the same world, and our experience is always informed by all these modes of sensing.[35] These sensings name, then, not primarily particular human practices (although we do, of course, perform acts of seeing, of hearing, of speaking, etc.), but distinct modes of being in contact with the world, each of which opens the world to us in new ways and new dimensions that cannot, properly speaking, be accounted for via other sensings: just as no amount of listening can give us the feeling of hardness or smoothness, so no amount of languaging can give us the (ethical) feeling of right or wrong or of social intercourse. While one can quibble about what exactly counts as a distinct mode of sensing, the general point is simply to recognize that every experience is informed by these modes of sensing. There is no experiencing that is not sensing.

But these sensings do not show up in our experience in this general sense. That is, we don't have an experience of "visibility"; rather, we always see things in particular ways or styles.[36] In that sense, the various modes of sensing the world—

in which any phenomena or experience we have is entangled—are themselves always embedded within particular historical traditions or institutions [*Stiftungen*[37]]: linguisticality shows up as English or Mandarin or Cree; vision shows up in the style of the artist or the scientist or the engineer; sociality shows up as this particular social norm or that one. And of course, each of those, also, is too broad: academic English differs considerably from Appalachian English; the painter sees the world differently than the sculptor or the dramatist; and norms for "professional" social interaction differ greatly for the classroom than for the boardroom than for the courtroom. Here, we see that empirical conditions have a great effect on how these transcendental modes of sensing operate, and so we can call this level—the level of *Stiftungen*, which is to say tradition or institution—a quasi-transcendental or empirical-transcendental level. It pays attention to the necessary embeddedness of transcendental modes of sensing within particular traditions that are both transcendentally operative (they shape *how* we experience) and empirically located (they are made up of particular, historical, concrete *whats*).

If *Stiftungen* describe how the transcendental exists or takes on being,[38] we have not yet explained how the various transcendental modes come to exist. This gives another distinct way that transcendental modes of sensing are embedded or entangled, now not quasi-transcendentally (i.e., embedded in empirical conditions) but ultra-transcendentally (i.e., embedded in something that itself gives rise to those distinct modes of sensing). Kant, as we said above, holds that transcendentals are entangled simply with the nature of the subject: it is the subject alone that makes the transcendentals what they are. This position, as we said, was deemed phenomenologically insufficient, and so others have tried to explain the transcendental modes in the context of other ultra-transcendental conditions: onto-genetic processes of differentiation in flesh (Merleau-Ponty) or in *différance* (Derrida); the destiny of different epochs of Being (Heidegger); responses to differing calls of givenness (Marion); different expressions of the self-unfolding of Life (Henry). The details of these differing ultra-transcendental accounts is not important at this time. Here, it suffices simply to show that *something* gives rise to the transcendental modes of sensing the world that come to us embedded in traditions/institutions, and that all three of these elements (ultra-transcendental, transcendental modes of sensing, quasi-transcendental) are included in our experiencing: we experience the world via distinct types of sensings that come to us embedded in both particular (semi-empirical, quasi-transcendental) traditions and in a larger (ultra-transcendental) context.

These, then, are the three different levels of transcendental analysis revealed by phenomenology: the ultra-transcendental, the transcendental modes of sensing, and the quasi-transcendental traditions. All of them remain transcendental, insofar as they are elements of how we experience, and as such are different from the empirical level of what we experience. But they are not different from the empirical in the sense of being different things or different kinds of things than the empirical phenomena that are the content of our experience.[39] Rather, these transcendental modes are the differing types of contexts in which the phenomena we experience are embedded or entangled, and as such they are part of our experience of those phenomena. In that sense, they are a crucial part of our experience, even if they are not distinct phenomena that could become the "what" of a distinct experience. Rather, they shape *how* we experience that phenomenon, *how* we are aware of it, and as such they influence or shape our experience of a particular phenomenon. As you read this book, for example, you experience the book visually (you see marks on a page) or tactilely (you feel marks on the page), but also linguistically (the marks mean something to you), socially (it is an academic work you are reading, not a novel or a poem), economically (the book has a certain value to you, which you may have had to pay money to acquire), and so on. These are the different modes of sensing at work in your current experience of reading the book. But your experience of the linguistic dimension of the book, for example, comes to you already embedded in the tradition of English, just as the social dimension of the book comes to you embedded in the tradition of the academic monograph. These are the quasi-transcendental traditions that contextualize how you experience the transcendental modes of sensing the world. And those modes come to you according to some pre-understanding of the world in general: they are gifts from God, or the products of evolutionary adaptations, or the results of a particular late-capitalist ethos of society. This is the ultra-transcendental context in which the transcendental modes of sensing are embedded. Accounting for the nuances and vagaries of *how* we experience is the task of transcendental phenomenology. You do not need to be aware of all of those nuances to understand what will follow—but the distinct levels of analysis will be crucial to my presentation of how religion impacts how we experience the world in general.

The fourth thing to highlight regarding transcendental phenomenology for our account of how religion impacts our experiencing is that "how" we experience things is expressively related to "what" we experience. For the most part, I am not consciously aware of, for example, the various traditions I am participating in in my experience of something. I am not consciously aware of English as the content of my experience of writing this book. Rather, I "live through" the English language while I am writing so as to "live in" the meaning contained in those (English) words.[40] But I do not simply ignore English either, for someone who does not know English would not be able to access the meanings that I am wanting them to access through my writing of these particular (English) words. This way we have of "living through" (but not ignoring) some things so as to "live in" others is what the phenomenological tradition calls "expression," and it is fundamental to our experience of the world and of ourselves.[41] We can say, then, that the various dimensions of transcendental analysis are mutually *expressive*: the ultra-transcendental conditions are expressed in the transcendentals, which themselves are expressed in the quasi-transcendental conditions/traditions, which are then expressed in particular concrete phenomena. In this sense, the phenomena are what they are, and can be understood as what they are, only by paying attention to the various ways they are embedded in (transcendental) conditions that shape them and give them their meaning. But so, too, the (transcendental) conditions are what they are only through the phenomena (and the other transcendental modes) that express them. Because the transcendental modes are not transcendent to the phenomena, they are generated in and through the phenomena that express them.

The Argument: Material-spirituality and a Transcendental Phenomenology of Religion

This brief (and perhaps therefore dense) foray into transcendental phenomenological method is my attempt to explain the details behind how I will proceed for those who care about those details. But the overall takeaway is this: properly understanding religion requires us to be able to account for the different (transcendental) modes of sensing by which we experience religious phenomena, and the quasi-transcendental traditions and ultra-transcendental context those modes of sensing (and those phenomena) are embedded in. Utilizing the tools of transcendental phenomenology, we will therefore be able to account for the role that experiencing—and therefore subjective capacities—play in our experience of religion in ways that the early phenomenologists of religion failed to do. This, in turn, will enable us to account meaningfully for experience (and experiencing) in our understanding of religion in ways that the critical philosophy of religion is largely unable to do. However, because the transcendental conditions and the phenomena are expressively related, those conditions must always be understood in the context of the religious phenomena that express them, and those conditions will be different in the context of different religious phenomena occurring in different quasi-transcendental conditions. Therefore, our transcendental phenomenological explorations of religion must be thoroughly informed by a variety of empirical phenomena of religion from a variety of different religious contexts and traditions in ways that philosophical phenomenology of religion has largely (to this point) failed to do.

Adopting this transcendental phenomenological approach to the empirical study of religion will therefore help us appreciate the role that religion plays in experiencing (in general) in ways that previous theories of religion seem largely to have overlooked. And by taking account of experiencing and subjective capabilities, it will also yield us an understanding of religion that will account, in more finely-tuned ways, for some distinctions in religious functioning (e.g., the difference between religious phenomena, religious traditions, and a religious mode of engaging the world) that are either overlooked or left implicit in many other theories of religion. The result of paying more attention to religion's embeddedness in experience will be a wider scope of application for religion in human living than was previously thought, in that it will be shown to play a role in all of our experiencing, and not simply in some particular types of experience. This will enable us to appreciate religious effects on things that (most) sociologists of religion would not consider to be "religion." In that sense, new things will be considered religious, precisely because we will have new ways of thinking the religious (i.e., as a dimension of our experiencing), a new way that emerges by tracing religious functioning through the various levels of our experiencing.

This new theory of religion is premised on the claim that understanding religious phenomena adequately on the empirical level requires understanding how these phenomena are expressive of distinct religious functions on the transcendental and quasi-transcendental levels, which themselves are expressive of the ultra-transcendental context in which they emerge and are generated. For this reason, our understanding of the religious must be situated within an explication of the ultra-transcendental context in which religious modes of experiencing and religious phenomena are generated.

This ultra-transcendental dimension is notoriously difficult to talk about, given its (phenomenological) distance from empirical circumstances. The level of abstraction at work in discussing the ultra-transcendental makes it hard to connect clearly to the concrete level of our empirical lives. My hope is that by tracing the ultra-transcendental context down through the various other levels—each time getting more concrete—a view of the religious will emerge that can resonate with those for whom religion is an important part of their lives (either as scholars or as practitioners).

But such a concrete view will begin in this book with ultra-transcendental explanations. Following a long line of philosophical phenomenologists, I will use the language of material-spirituality to describe this ultra-transcendental context. In the context of this book, then, material-spirituality refers to the fundamental and irreducible intertwining [*Verflechtung*] of subjectivity, history, culture, and materiality: subjective processes shape and constitute a world that also shapes and constitutes them. This claim was fundamental to our understanding of the transcendental as outlined above, and a proper account must be given of how we make sense of that claim, to better contextualize everything else that will follow from it. This intertwining entails that spirit [*Geist*] operates within subjectivity, as a kind of "subjective capability" to "make sense" of the world, to have a world of meaningful [*geistig*] things. But it also operates upon subjectivity, as a kind of generative spiritual [*geistlich*] force (a "mystical" force, Derrida will come to call it[42]) that shapes both subjects and the world in particular ways.[43] In that sense, spirit simultaneously illuminates how subjectivity functions and connects subjectivity inherently to the world, acting as a kind of movement from the subject to the world and from the world to the subject.[44] Subjects "make sense" of the world, then, only because they are themselves caught up in differing movements or forces of sense that generate and give rise to subjectivity, even as they are themselves generated and given rise to by the activities of subjectivity. This duality is what enables spirit to connect the transcendental conditions with their empirical expressions and so tie together also the various levels of transcendental analysis.

This spiritual force is operative within the world, not merely "on" pre-existing and wholly distinct material conditions, but *within* and as *material* conditions. That is why spirit is always material-spiritual, the expressive intertwining or entanglement of generative force and generated conditions. This spirit is, therefore, fundamentally phenomenological in nature: it (and not some sovereign, autonomous notion of subjectivity) is a matter of what makes experience itself possible. It is not equated with spirit in a dualistic sense, in which spirit is sharply distinguished from the material. Spirit is not something done *to* materiality; it is a material movement—provided we recognize that materiality is not simply physical or chemical, but is also historical, cultural, semiotic and meaningful.

Acknowledging and explaining this spiritual-material nature of things will provide the ultra-transcendental context in which the various modes of experiencing (including religious experiencing) become possible. Chapter one provides such an acknowledgment and explanation, by demonstrating that experience is essentially material-spiritual. First it explains that experience is both individually lived-through and communally shared because it necessarily engages people with the world. It then argues that material-spirituality names the necessary intertwining of subjectivity, history, culture, and materiality that makes such experience possible. This notion of material-spirituality is then compared to other notions of spirituality at work in the contemporary study of religion to show that material-spirituality functions (ultra-)transcendentally but not transcendently.

As an ultra-transcendental context of experience, material-spirituality engages people with the world in a variety of different ways that we earlier called transcendental modes of sensing the world. Chapter two moves further into the explicit engagement with religion by arguing that one of these transcendental sensings is a uniquely religious mode that we will call religiosity. Just as visibility opens both a visual quality to things (i.e., things can be seen) and a distinct subjective process (i.e., we can see), so, too, religiosity opens both a new dimension to phenomena and a new kind of subjective process that accesses or engages with that dimension. After dealing with some objections to the very possibility of a religious mode of sensing, the chapter explores what type of subjective process religiosity might open up. Broadly speaking, it characterizes religiosity as an experience of the connectivity inherent to material-spirituality conceived as a necessary intertwining of subjectivity, history, culture, and materiality. It then outlines several different ways this connectivity has shown up in various experiences and traditions, to show that such a mode of sensing the world seems to be operative in a variety of different peoples and cultures. As such, we can distinguish religiosity (as a concept or category) from any of its particular expressions in various different traditions. And this broad category or concept of religiosity also functions transcendentally but in no way requires transcendence. As such, it avoids the criticisms levelled by critical philosophers of religion against earlier accounts of religion put forward by the phenomenologists of religion.

Chapter three then furthers this non-transcendent account of religiosity by showing how our thinking of religion (including the category of religiosity) always occurs in the context of some religious tradition or other. Because religiosity opens up a distinct way of accessing phenomena via a distinct subjective process, people accessing phenomena via that process would yield a consistent or recognizable way of being in the world, the same way that visibility gives us a visual way of being in the world, a way that includes both seeing (as a subjective capacity) and being seen. And as this religious way of being in the world was enacted in various different social, historical, and cultural contexts around the world, different traditions of religiosity have emerged throughout history, each of which experiences or engages with religiosity differently (again, similar to the way that painters see the world differently than scientists do, or Inuit people see snow differently than people from warmer climates do). This is because these traditions are not to be understood simply empirically (via the phenomena they have produced), but also quasi-transcendentally, via the way they shape how subjectivity engages the world religiously. This religious engagement is twofold: first, religiosity is done differently because of how it engages with other modes of sensing the world and the various traditions arising from those various modes; and second, religiosity changes how those other modes are engaged with as well. This means that the religious dimension to our experiencing is not confined to religiosity but begins to impact various (perhaps all) the ways that we engage with the world. The chapter then explores secularism as a kind of case study of a quasi-transcendental religious tradition, outlining how secularism arose out of, and inevitably altered, the Christian religious tradition, in two notable ways: first, its insistence on, but also mutation of, the transcendent nature of religion; and second, its claim that religion must be rigorously separable from "non-religious" domains of life. Not only has this shaped contemporary views on things ranging from religion to the university to the labor market (as Michel Henry shows in *Barbarism*), but it has also had an oversized role in our contemporary scholarly understanding of religion. As secularism is but one religious tradition alongside many others, how religiosity functions in that tradition will not be how religion functions in all religious traditions. This opens the door to new ways of understanding religion, without dismissing the secular approach (which remains rooted in transcendence) as incorrect.

In focusing on the transcendental and quasi-transcendental effects of religiosity in Chapters two and three, respectively, we will see that experiencing itself is marked by religious effects in a variety of different ways. Indeed, it can seem that all phenomena are therefore marked, in some way, by religious effects. Chapter four pursues this question by showing how quasi-transcendental effects come both from phenomena and from subjective activity (because those two things are fundamentally intertwined in the material-spiritual understanding of experience). This means that religious effects impact experience both via subjectivity and via phenomena, suggesting that perhaps all phenomena are indeed religiously marked in some way. However, this does not mean that all phenomena are equally marked by religious effects. As such, some scholars, especially those with more empirically minded concerns, might find value in distinguishing some phenomena as more religious than others, while other scholars, especially those interested in exploring transcendental and quasi-transcendental effects, might find more value in looking at the religious nature of all phenomena. By detailing the various ways that phenomena are marked by religious effects—empirically, quasi-transcendentally, and transcendentally—this chapter makes clear how such differing approaches to religious phenomena need not render the category of religion useless, as some scholars have contended.

If Chapter four explores the implication of our material-spiritual approach to the study of religious phenomena, Chapter five explores the implications for our understanding of religious experience. To the extent that it talks about experience at all, the secular-Christian approach to religion tends to equate religious experience with mystical experiences of transcendence. Given the various empirical, transcendental, and quasi-transcendental effects that religiosity has on our experiencing, this seems too narrow an understanding of religious experience. Drawing on insights from philosophical phenomenology of religion, this chapter explores two alternatives to the secular-Christian approach to religious experience: a "sacramental" model, in which materiality is essentially marked by religiosity, and an "event-al" model, in which religiosity exercises an insistent function, changing material conditions by working upon subjectivity. Although both those approaches still seem to harbor some vestiges of transcendence, some elements from each are brought forward into a material-spiritual account of religious experience. This account focuses on the transcendental and quasi-transcendental effects of religiosity, thereby showing how experiencing itself has a religious dimension to it. This means that accounting for that religious dimension is crucial to providing a thorough understanding of both a particular phenomenon and of experiencing itself.

Chapter six then picks up the question of how to account for that religious dimension by suggesting three distinct but related approaches to the study of religious effects. The first is a phenomenology of religious phenomena, which seeks to account for the various effects that a particular phenomenon has, empirically, transcendentally, and quasi-transcendentally. The second is a phenomenology of a religious tradition, which seeks to account for the unique "style" that a particular religious tradition gives to how its adherents experience the world. The third is a phenomenology of religion, which seeks to account for the very categories of religious experiencing itself, such as religiosity, religious traditions, and religious phenomena. The chapter argues that all three approaches are best served by drawing on insights of the others. This renewed, transcendental phenomenological approach therefore gives us a way to speak meaningfully of religion and religious effects across different cultural traditions, thereby offering a model for cross-cultural religious studies that does not fall prey to the colonial critiques of traditional secular-Christian accounts of religion that remain rooted in transcendence.

Finally, the book's conclusion seeks to summarize and make explicit the conceptual tools for the study of religion that have been developed through the arguments contained in the book. These tools have helped us articulate the distinction, but also the relation, between various elements of religious analysis that previously were used in ambiguous or confused fashion: the "religious" dimension of experience as opposed to distinct religious experiences; religious philosophy as opposed to philosophy of religion; phenomenological analyses of religious experience as opposed to a transcendental phenomenological philosophy of religion; empirical experiences of religion as opposed to the transcendental effect of those experiences; these are just some of the distinctions the book has sought to bring to clarity. In doing so, the book shows how the insights of the transcendental approach to phenomenology bear directly on the empirical study of religion in ways that create a more robust awareness of the role of empirical experience (including individual experiences, but also historical and social constitution, politics, sociological trends, etc.) in the emergence of a transcendental (although not transcendent) understanding of religion, as well as a more robust understanding of the way that religion can play a transcendental role in the constitution of individual and communal experiences. To properly account for religion, then, we must be aware of: (a) its empirical expressions; (b) the ways it structures the experience of those for whom it operates transcendentally; and (c) the necessarily intertwined relationship between those two facets. What emerges, then, is a call for a renewed quest to understand religion as an empirical, sociological, philosophical, and transcendental force that must be sensitive to the way that these things are expressed differently in different cultures without losing the sense that there remains a significant reason to talk about, and understand, those various expressions alongside each other. The cross-cultural study of religion is a necessary step in understanding both religion and individual religions.

Through this argument, the book will demonstrate the different ways that religion impacts our experiencing of the world in general. In doing so, it provides insight both into the study (and practice) of religion and into our understanding of experiencing itself. As such, my hope is that this book proves helpful both to scholars of religion and to phenomenologists.

1

Material-Spirituality

Experience is essentially material-spiritual, and this can change how we think about religion. This is the fundamental claim of this chapter. Yet almost every word in the first phrase of that sentence requires further elaboration, if the claim is to be meaningful in any significant sense. "Experience" and "spiritual" are both terms with such a wide range of definitions in both phenomenology and the empirical study of religion as to have become almost meaningless, and "material" is often understood in quite reductionistic ways that lose any important connection it could have to the concept "spiritual." So all of these must be clarified in this chapter to establish the basis for our arguments concerning the importance of experiencing for understanding religion.

Experience

To that end, let us begin with experience. Taking this as our starting point makes sense methodologically, given the phenomenological nature of the investigation. Philosophical phenomenology has revealed to us many important facets of experience. The first, as discussed already in the introduction, is the distinction between what we experience and how we experience it. These are not two distinct elements of experience but are always connected. This point can be made in more technical ways, but overall it is quite simple: in experience, someone (the subject of how we experience) has an experience of something (what we experience).

The nature of this "experience" requires further elaboration, as, ultimately, does the nature of the relationship between the someone and the something. But given that there is someone experiencing, experience must have an essentially personal component. Philosophical phenomenology discusses this via the notion of *Erlebnisse* (lived experiences), which allows us to see there is a *lived* or living nature to experience: it is not enough for there to be the empirical fact of what is happening, there also must be a living-through component essential to the nature of experience. This simply means that when I experience, the experiencing of the I is a crucial component of the experience. It is why we say that a person experiences, but a camera does not, even if both were aimed at the same thing. This living dimension of experience is what we equate with the felt or affective components of experience[1]: this is our *feeling* of things, not just in the sense of the emotions we have about them, but the ways that I, personally, am affected by the world[2] in ways that are compelling and, indeed, quite "incontestable" to me.[3] Indeed, who could question *my experience* of something, for who could have better access to how I experience something than I do? This is something I took a while to appreciate: after I first got married, my wife would sometimes say "I'm cold." More than once, I responded "No you're not"—and she just gave me a look like I was an idiot. What I meant, of course, was something like "You shouldn't be cold, because it's not that cold out" or "I wouldn't be cold in such a situation," or something along those lines. But saying "No, you're not cold" is a ridiculous thing to say to someone, precisely because cold is an affective experience, and no one has better access to an individual's affective experience than they do. My wife was living through her cold-ness, and I was in no position to contest that.

Of course this is not all there is to experience. In mystical experience, for example, the lived nature of experience as *Erlebnisse* is more or less universally acknowledged: unless we think the mystics are simply charlatans or fraudsters, we do not contest that someone had experiences that they encountered in the ways they describe. But while we may not contest that Augustine had an experience at Ostia, or that Rumi felt something that he took to be the divine, there are certainly people who would challenge whether they experienced anything other than a personal and individual hallucination. For in addition to the private, affective part of experience, there is also a shared, communal, and interpretive component to experience. While some people try to reserve the term "experience" only for the personal encounter and leave the rest to a separate act called "interpretation,"[4] transcendental phenomenology has long maintained that every experience is essentially hermeneutic, that every seeing is a seeing-as.[5] This, too, is included in the claim that, in every experience, someone experiences something. The fact that experience is always "of something" means that there is necessarily a shared component to experience: experience is never *just* a "living through"; it is always a "living through" of something that is, in principle (and usually also in fact) shareable. There is a "what" to our experience that can be shared with others: Augustine and Rumi share their experiences with us via language, communicating what they have experienced to others, who can understand their experience and perhaps have a similar one themselves as a result of this communication. For even if we do not experience the divine in the same way as Augustine or Rumi did (with something like a perception), we nevertheless have a (linguistic and conceptual) experience of those same things when we read their accounts, and so we can understand their experiences and integrate them, somehow, into our own lives and thought processes.

From this quick example, we see another crucial element about experience: we can experience the "same" thing in different ways. That is, although experience is always someone experiencing something, that "something" is experienced in a multiplicity of ways, even within one and the same experience. Transcendental phenomenology discusses this first via Husserl's notion of *Empfindnisse*, which we discussed already in the introduction. This is the sense of living experiences [*Erlebnisse*] of sensation [*Empfindung*], which are usually referred to as sensings. And these sensings, as Husserl and especially Merleau-Ponty point out, are necessarily multiple: we can have visual sensings, tactile ones, aural ones, but also linguistic ones, social ones, affective ones, and so on.[6] All these give us different dimensions of our experience of the same thing. These different dimensions can be grouped together in one experience (in experiencing my dog at this moment, I simultaneously see my dog walking, hear her groaning as she lays down, smell her, conceive of her as a dog, and have affection for her), or can be added on as different experiences: if my dog is far away and I'm looking the other way, I probably first hear her; once I turn my head, I add a visual experience to that auditory one; and as she draws nearer, I gain an olfactory experience as well.

Now, these types of sensings are themselves shareable, although not in the same way as the content of my experience. That is, while others can also see, smell, touch, and so on, my dog, and all of us recognize it as the "same" dog, it is also true that we recognize a certain sense in which we share visibility, tactility, linguisticality, and so on, not in terms of us having the same vision, but in terms of all of us accessing the same visibility, which includes both the shared visible world (we see the same dog) and the shared capacity for vision (we both see). It is this shared access to visibility (and other types of *Empfindnisse*) that transcendental phenomenology explores in the sensing-transcendental dimension.

However, as mentioned in the introduction, this shared capacity is itself differentiated, not simply individually (I live through my visual experiences in a way that you do not, and you live through your experiences in a way that I do not), but also in shared traditions [*Stiftungen*]. That is, it is not just that you and I may see things differently as individuals, but also that the painter sees the world differently than the scientist, as Merleau-Ponty famously discusses.[7] We talk about the world differently in English than we do in Cree, and this difference is not merely perceptual (we make different sounds), but also conceptual (we mean slightly different things, with different connotations, different affective valences, and so on, when we say the word "dog" than when we say "atim," which can also mean horse, or beast of burden). Or—to get ahead of ourselves a bit—the Christian experiences God differently than the Muslim experiences Allah or the Hindu experiences *brahman*. While there is a sense that the Christian, the Muslim and the Hindu are having the "same" experience (in the same way that both the painter and the scientist are "seeing"), as Otto and other early phenomenologists of religion emphasized, it is also true that that "sameness" of experience is experienced differently in and because of the different traditions.

Let us refrain from pursuing that larger religious point for now (although that is where we are heading, in subsequent chapters). For now, we are simply clarifying that we have both different ways of experiencing and different experiences, each of which has a component that is individually lived-through and a component that is shared (or, at least, in principle shareable). What is left to explain is the relationship between the individual, lived-through components and the shared/shareable components. This explanation must be twofold. On the one hand, we must account for how an individual can tie together different experiences (both in the sense of temporally different experiences and experiences of different types of *Empfindnisse*) into one experience: how does my sight of, smell of, affection for, and so on, my dog get united into one experience of my dog, and then get connected also with previous experiences I have had of the "same" dog? On the other hand, we have to account for how my experience of my dog is shareable with someone else's experience of the dog, such that we can recognize that each of us are experiencing the "same" dog, even if we may experience it differently (delivery people may not share my affection for my dog, for example).

The first explanation is given, at least in most Western philosophy after Kant, via the notion of subjectivity. There is something called "subjectivity" that enables people to combine various facets or elements of experience together into one unitary experience. Just as visibility allows us all to see the visible world (or see the world as visible), so subjectivity allows us to experience the world as *the* world, rather than having fractal experiences of a multiplicity of worlds—a visible world, a tactile world, a social world, and so on. In its most basic sense, this is what subjectivity is: the capacity to have unitary experience, rather than be adrift in the multiplicity of experiences. In other words, for our purposes, subjectivity should be understood simply as the capacity to have a single stream of experiences for the one experiencing.

There seems, therefore, to be an undeniably individual nature to this subjectivity: I unite various experiences together into *my* experience. Yet over-emphasizing this individual nature leads to unhelpful reifications (subjectivity becomes the Subject) that make answering the second problem posed above difficult: for if each of us is a separate, distinct substance known as a Subject, how are we able to share our experiences in any meaningful way? If the answer is simply via language and concepts, we are left to struggle with the question of how we can ever know if what we experience is the same as what other equally separate and distinct Subjects experience: are we sharing experience in any real sense, or are we simply functioning beside each other as synchronized monads, as Leibniz maintains?[8]

This problem dominates much of Western philosophy in its Modern period, giving it its stereotypically epistemological focus. Phenomenology's response to this problematic is unique. Like Kant, phenomenology is interested in understanding the conditions of experience. But while Kant treats these as *a priori* (and therefore logical) conditions that make experience possible, phenomenology is interested precisely in seeing them as conditions *of* experience, which is to say, conditions that not only hold *for* experience, but which also arise *from* within experience. This leads to differing accounts of subjectivity: for Kant, subjectivity (as a capability) is given with and as the (transcendental) Subject, *a priori* and outside of experience. For transcendental phenomenology, however, subjectivity is itself generated within experience.[9] Although Husserl did not always realize the full implications of this, the tradition of transcendental phenomenology eventually comes to see that this makes subjectivity a process that enables us to engage the world in a unique way, akin to visibility, tactility, and so on, while impacting all of them.[10] Yet if subjectivity is part of how we experience, but does not name who experiences, then we are left to account for how subjectivity itself is possible. That is, if subjectivity is not the (ultra-transcendental) explanation for how we are able to have experiences and experience, then where does experience arise from?

The answer is that experience arises from a background,[11] horizon,[12] or milieu,[13] that gives rise both to subjectivity and to the other modes of engaging the world. This background is "material-spiritual" or "spiritual-sensuous,"[14] not insofar as it combines two distinct elements together, but as it is the common background out of which both materiality and subjectivity emerge and are able to be differentiated. In that sense, materiality and subjectivity are connected before we are able to separate or abstract them: we can distinguish seeing from what is seen only because both emerge in visibility; we can distinguish touching from what is touched only because both are generated in tactility. The material-spiritual is the background out of which those modes of engaging the world emerge, and which, therefore, those modes of engaging the world necessarily express.

This returns us to the question of the relationship between the "someone" who experiences and the "something" that they experience. Insofar as subjectivity is a process that expresses its material-spiritual milieu, it is not yet the "someone" who experiences. Rather, subjectivity is a particular way that "someone" is necessarily engaged with the world. Those who are taken up in the process of subjectivity—that is, those who are able to function subjectively—are, therefore, necessarily themselves also situated material-spiritually. They are individuals who have arisen or been generated in the same material-spiritual conditions that gave rise both to the world and to the various modes of engaging it (visibility, tactility, subjectivity, etc.).

Husserl[15] (and Michel Henry after him[16]) name this primordial material-spiritual condition the Earth and distinguish it from the world (as what we encounter with our sensings) and the (life)world that we live in and engage with daily.[17] This distinction is characteristically phenomenological, not ontological. That is, it does not name three distinct things (as if there were other "worlds" behind the one we experience everyday), but rather three ways of looking at or experiencing the (same) world: ultra-transcendentally (Earth), in the mode of transcendental sensings (the world our sensings enable us to experience) and quasi-transcendentally (the lifeworld we inhabit daily, filled with the meanings and sense particular to our distinct historico-empirical situations), as we outlined already in the introduction.

The upshot of this distinction for our purposes in this chapter is that the purported problems of knowing and engaging the world that hounded modern philosophy disappear for phenomenology. In clarifying these as phenomenological rather than ontological distinctions—that is, differences in our experiencing of things but *not* a difference between distinct things—we are enabled to see that subjectivity is not ontologically distinct from the world but is phenomenologically connected with it (as both arise from the same shared milieu we are here calling the Earth). So while the Kantian (and likely also the Cartesian) Subject are given *a priori* and therefore outside of the world of experiences, subjectivity (in the phenomenological understanding) is not: it is generated in and through the same material-spiritual processes that give rise to the world. And therefore the problems that the Subject may have in knowing and engaging a world understood as ontologically distinct from itself do not arise for subjectivity, precisely because it is not ontologically distinct from the world, but always phenomenologically engaged with it.

Further, in shifting from Subjects to subjectivity in this way, phenomenology is able to say that it is not Subjects as such that know the world, but people (or other types of experiencers) who know the world via subjectivity and via the other modes of engaging and knowing the world (such as visibility, tactility, etc.). And experiencers arise and are generated out of similar material-spiritual processes as the ones that give rise to subjectivity and the world, which is to say, experiencers, subjectivity, and the world all emerge—as distinguishable things— from the material-spiritual background of the Earth. Because of this shared material-spiritual emergence, people (qua experiencers) can therefore engage the world materially and subjectively.

The concrete implications of all this will emerge over the rest of the book, but the overall point is simply this: experience is both individually lived-through and communally shared because it necessarily engages experiencers with the world.[18] This does not mean that all experiencers will have the "same" experience, even when looking at the same thing, however. This is because we engage the world in a multiplicity of ways, including the various sensings we have and the various traditions by which we enact those sensings. This multiplicity of ways of experiencing does not mean that we cannot share our experience, though, as these ways of experiencing are all rooted in the same background or milieu that gives rise to them, to the things we engage in our experience, and to other things that can function subjectively, even if that background or milieu is encountered or engaged with in different ways. So both what we experience and how we experience are material-spiritual, and this material-spiritual basis enables us not only to experience things ourselves, but to be able to share that experience with other material-spiritual beings.

Material-Spiritual

We have therefore shown that experience is material-spiritual. Now it remains to clarify what, exactly, that means. Rather than defining material and spiritual separately, however, it makes the most sense to define them together, because the claim is that their differentiation is in fact a secondary abstraction. In actuality, materiality and spirituality are connected, and neither, therefore, can be understood apart from the other.

Of course, in one sense, that claim is patently false. Materiality can not only be understood as distinct from spirituality, but it often has been understood that way, at least in Western circles over the last few hundred years. Particularly, following Descartes (or perhaps Cartesianism),[19] Western thought has understood materiality in purely physical (or purely biological or purely chemical) terms. In this sense, something could be considered "material" to the extent that it had physical extension—and, at times, precisely *only* to that extent. Desks and chairs are "material," but concepts and ideas are not (although the books by which those ideas are disseminated are).

This reductive account of materiality as physical extension was often paired with an account of spirituality as an "ideal plane above and beyond history."[20] In that sense, spirituality was taken to be supernatural, as opposed to the natural world of material things: whereas materiality was physical extension, spirituality was immaterial, non-extended, and took place outside the material world.[21]

It is precisely this kind of oppositional *definition* (and not simply an oppositional relation) that phenomenology strives to avoid with its characterization of the material-spiritual. Therefore, the material-spiritual is not simply physical or non-physical, but is about the inter-relation between those things (and others as well: history, culture, etc.). Let us take as our starting point in this explanation the phenomenological notion of spirit [*Geist*]. Already for Hegel, this is non-oppositional, an activity of bringing itself to consciousness, an "activity of coming to itself, of producing itself, making itself actually what it is in itself potentially."[22] In this sense the activity of knowing and the content of what is known are together in a certain way that Hegel calls "freedom," but also "self-supporting, absolute real being."[23]

This togetherness of knower and known has two related elements to it. On the one hand, there is a particular force [*geistlich*] that works in and upon (and perhaps as) subjectivity, constituting subjectivity precisely by taking it up in a movement that exceeds it, moving subjectivity beyond itself to the world.[24] This movement taking subjectivity beyond itself does not originate in subjectivity, but is something that subjectivity is caught up in: we "make sense" of the world only because we first receive that ability to "*make* sense" *from* the world. Think, for example, of the way that the very categories by which we engage and interact with the world (concepts, linguistic terms, but also styles of seeing, of touching, etc.) are things we receive or inherit from the traditions we are a part of, even as they are fundamental to our very ability to engage and interact with the world. Robin Wall Kimmerer, for example, talks about how the Potawatomi people's view of the world primarily as animate is inscribed in their language: "The language reminds us, in every sentence, of our kinship with all the animate world," in part through the fact that the Potawatomi "use the same words to address the living world as we use for our family. Because they are our family," and in part through their verb-based language in which "[t]o be a hill, to be a sandy beach, to be a Saturday, are all possible verbs in a world where everything is alive."[25]

This alteration of our experience because of our concepts and language is true in ways that are both philosophically rich (think of the different understandings of "being" at work in, say, Aristotle,[26] Nāgārjuna,[27] and the Potawatomi people[28]) and in ways that are much more mundane (consider the various different words and corresponding ways of thinking about and engaging with snow and ice in Inuit cultures[29]). But it seems an inescapable fact of our reality as we currently understand it that the ways we think about and engage with the world are, at least in part, determined by the (linguistic and other) traditions we are a part of. And thinking of this as resulting from a (spiritual) force highlights the sense that this is something subjectivity *receives* or is taken up in rather than an ability subjectivity simply *possesses* on its own.

In this sense, we can think of spirituality as a kind of animating or driving force that pushes subjectivity to engage the world around itself in "productive" or generative ways. Which is to say, spirituality is transformative, shaping and changing subjectivity and the world, leaving behind itself sense-filled and material traces of its activity. This animating and transformative notion of spirituality is therefore always historically and culturally situated, precisely because the force that pushes subjectivity to engage the world is itself (materially) productive. In making sense of the world, we not only draw on but also (re-)produce concepts, linguistic terms, and other objects of subjective processes (i.e., phenomena of visual, auditory, tactile, social, etc. types). Hence, the other side of spirituality as animating or driving force is the notion of spiritual products. These products are necessarily marked, in their essence, by their inherent relation to subjectivity: it is part of what a chair (for example) is that it has been produced in a particular (cultural and historical) style by a being that is functioning subjectively.[30] For it is clear that a chair's material structure is heavily influenced by cultural factors: the material out of which it is made varies both between cultures and between historical time periods, and does so in typical ways (chairs from fourth-century Rome tend to be made of marble, those from thirteenth-century England of oak, while those from the Song Dynasty in China tend to be made of bamboo or rattan). Furthermore, it is not just how the chairs look that is culturally influenced, but the very existence of chairs themselves seems to be thoroughly cultural: without the intervention of humans refashioning plants or stones into other materials, and then refashioning those materials into particular shapes that are then distributed via complex economic exchanges and in accordance with complex social mores, there would be no material entities called "chairs" at all. The ideas of the artisan, the economic desires of the tradespeople, and the tiredness of the chair owner are all in some way wrapped up in the reality of the chair. The chair is, therefore, a product of the "spirit of the times" in which it was made, and therefore can be considered a "spiritual product," the result of the "spiritual force" that pushes humans (in their subjective capacities) to engage with the world, not simply passively (by taking in sensings) but actively (by living and producing in the world).

From all this, we can conclude three ways that spirituality is inherently material. First, it is always located in particular historical circumstances, that is, in particular times and places that influence and shape how spirit functions in those circumstances. Second, spirituality is always productive, generative, and transformative of material conditions (objects, abilities, etc.) that are themselves tied to the particular historical circumstances in which spirit finds itself. And third, its productive capacity leads to both processes and outcomes that are themselves material: both how we live and what we produce in our living are material. In this threefold sense, spirituality is inherently material, and we can perhaps come to see "culture" as the name we give to this material-spirituality in its concrete, empirical existence.

But what is meant by "material" here? At this point, it should be clear that material is clearly more than simply physical extension, although that may be part of it. Materiality, in the material-spiritual sense, recognizes that physical extension is in the actual world, and as such is never simply physical but is also always caught up in historical and cultural reality. In the actual world (and in the life-world), material never simply takes a position in some Newtonian abstraction of absolute space. Rather, materiality concretizes and actualizes various productive relationships with subjectivity: chairs, for example, concretize artistic creativity, economic exchange, and social mores alongside their physically constitutive parts and their internal chemical make-up, and they do so necessarily. Furthermore, this is true also for the "natural" world, which necessarily expresses its relations to the spiritual life of subjective processes: not only is the "natural" world always the potential object for spiritual activity (things to be seen, to be touched, to be talked about, etc.), but it is also part of both the material-spiritual milieu out of which subjectivity arises and the lifeworld in which we all live. This point is widely acknowledged in non-European cultures: in Mi'kmaq legend, for example, the cultural hero Kulskap lives in a cave on a certain mountain, and that mountain therefore holds a spiritual significance for the Mi'kmaq people as part of their communal identity and connection to the land. But this point remains true even in the colonizing cultures of Europe: when that same mountain was renamed "Kelly's Mountain" during colonization, this shows a similar (although certainly not identical) weaving of that physical place into the history and self-understanding of the colonizing British people.[31] Indeed, thinking the opposite, that there could somehow be "natural" parts of the world entirely unaffected by (human) spiritual activities, is to deny that humans impact the world. No part of an ecosystem is unaffected by the other participants in the ecosystem. This is a material reality.

And that material reality is, essentially, also a spiritual reality in the phenomenological sense described above, in that spirit, in both its activities and its products, is part and parcel of the same material-spiritual world as is materiality.[32] To think materiality only as physical extension (or only as biological activity or chemical basis) is to forget its necessary immersion in spirit. And to think spirituality only as "supernatural" is to forget its necessary immersion in materiality. Hence, our invocation of the material-spiritual, a hyphen that does not tie together two otherwise disparate things in an arbitrary connection, but rather a hyphen that marks precisely the necessary expressive intertwining of two relata that are what they are only in their mutually co-constitutive and co-generative relation: spirit only is what it is in its relation to materiality and vice versa. The material-spiritual therefore names the necessity of the relation between spirit and material, a relation that intertwines subjectivity, history, culture, and materiality in an inseparable bond.

Material-Spirituality and a Preliminary Turn to Religion

Thinking through this bond for all the facets of experience is the task of transcendental phenomenology. And thinking of its implications especially for the study and practice of religion is the task of this book. Before we venture down that path, however, let me first address two potential misconceptions that could arise about this account of material-spirituality. The first pertains to my use of the terminology of spirituality. It may be contested that, whatever I mean by spirituality in talking about material-spirituality, it simply is not what the term means in the study and practice of religion and therefore has little or nothing to contribute to our understanding or practice of religion. Indeed, this is a common response I get when I present this material at conferences, both philosophical and religious. "That is an interesting idea," people will say. "It simply isn't 'spirituality.' You should just call it 'culture' or something like that."

On the one hand, I could simply concede the point. As we will see, the implications of material-spirituality for religion have little to do with the language of "spirituality" as it is employed here. This is not some trick of language, where I am trying to smuggle in religious implications by using a religious term ambiguously. So, in some sense, little is at stake, for me, in this objection.

On the other hand, the objection seems misguided, in at least three ways that perhaps merit some consideration here, to better understand material-spirituality in relation to other contemporary accounts of spirituality. First, the presumption that there is, in fact, a stable and unambiguous use of "spirituality" at work in the study of religion (or any other scholarly discipline, or even, I would suggest, in the cultural "common sense") is eminently contestable. In fact, spirituality is a term with an almost notoriously unfocused and ambiguous usage in contemporary discourse. Kenneth Collins claims that the language of spirituality "is largely amorphous, lacking definitional precision," although "it often refers vaguely to some interior state or heightened awareness or perhaps to participation in a project, however conceived, greater than oneself."[33] Walter Principe agrees that there is a "fluidity" or "vagueness" to the term spirituality.[34] Philip Sheldrake contends there are at least four major different *paradigms* of what is meant by spirituality within the Christian tradition alone,[35] to say nothing of its potential uses and meanings in other traditions, while Chinedu Nweke claims that "spirituality suffers even greater complication as a concept"[36] than does religion, a concept for which one famous text notoriously outlines forty-eight different uses.[37] There simply does not seem to be a clear "what we mean by spirituality in the study of religion," and so the use of spirituality being described here cannot fall outside of that commonly understood usage. Because there is no commonly understood usage.

Second, within the panoply of possible meanings of spirituality, there is a nexus of scholars who claim that spirituality is a name for the deepest driving forces of one's life as manifest in one's immersion in one's tradition. In this sense, the account of material-spirituality offered here—a culturally situated driving or animating force that shapes and transforms experience—does not seem entirely out of line with (at least some) contemporary uses of spirituality. Sheldrake, for example, suggests that, "despite the fuzziness" of the concept of spirituality, "it is possible to suggest that spirituality refers to the deepest values and meaning by which people seek to live."[38] Principe claims that the most general possible account of spirituality might be something like "the way in which a person understands and lives within his or her historical context that aspect of his or her religion, philosophy or ethic that is viewed as the loftiest, the noblest, the most calculated to lead to the fullness of the ideal or perfection being sought."[39] Elsewhere in the same edited volume, Sandra Schneiders suggests that spirituality deals with "the life of the person as a whole, including its bodily, psychological, social, and political dimensions,"[40] and John Macquarrie contends "that fundamentally spirituality has to do with *becoming a person in the fullest sense*."[41] While none of these are the *same* definition of spirituality, all of them point to an account of spirituality that has strong resonances with the account of material-spirituality being offered in this chapter: the deepest driving force of subjectivity, one that comes embedded always within particular social and cultural traditions and one that impacts the whole scope of human living. The account of material-spirituality offered here, therefore, does not seem entirely out of line with (at least some) contemporary uses of spirituality. While it may be unique or different, it is hardly so unrecognizable as to have no value for discussions of spirituality or to be unrecognizable as a use of the term spirituality.

The accounts of spirituality that enable us to say this, though, might then lead us to be sympathetic to the last claim of the objection, namely that material-spirituality is simply a fancier (and perhaps unnecessary) word for culture. The third step of my response to this objection, then, is to show why this is incorrect. While we have already suggested above that culture is a name we might use to refer to the concrete reality of material-spiritual functioning, this does not mean that the material-spiritual is simply equivalent with culture, as we use that term. Especially in academic contexts, culture tends to refer exclusively to what we, given the distinctions we have made in the introduction, would call "empirical" practices and institutions. Culture is about what people do in its historical and social significance. But what I am calling material-spirituality is not simply empirical, and as a result it has effects and impacts that are not simply empirical. Material-spirituality is the ultra-transcendental milieu that explains our ability to sense the world in various ways. Accounting for it therefore has implications, not just ultra-transcendentally, but also on the level of transcendental sensings, provided we think those things differently if they arise from a material-spiritual milieu than we do if they exist simply as capacities of the Subject, for example. Further, the differing results or products of those sensings open us to see the quasi-transcendental role that *Stiftungen* (traditions) play in the various "styles" by which we experience or engage the world. As a result, material-spirituality has effects that are quasi-transcendental, as well as ultra-transcendental and on the level of transcendental sensings. Thinking of empirical results as phenomena that are necessarily expressive of traditions, which are themselves expressive of particular sensings, will also impact how we understand the empirical level, as we will ultimately see in Chapters four, five and six. In that sense, our account of material-spirituality leads to results that are not simply empirical (although there may also be empirical results), and as such cannot be strictly equated with culture, as that term has come to be understood.

Of course, one could, I suppose, think "culture" in different ways, ones that are not exclusively empirical. Michel Henry seems to do as much in *Barbarism*, where he explains culture as the embodiment of a genuine expression of Life (his name for the ultra-transcendental dimension).[42] In this discussion, he approaches different types of culture ("such as art, ethics or religion" but also "cultures of food, shelter, work, erotic relations or relations to the dead"[43]), which, could, perhaps, mirror, at least structurally, the different modes of engaging the world on the level of transcendental sensings. However, this is not, it seems to me, how culture is normally understood, and certainly not in religious studies.[44] And it certainly does not function, for Henry, on the ultra-transcendental level. So while there might be a case to be made for referring to some functions of material-spirituality as "culture," it is not itself simply the same as culture, and certainly not as culture is usually used and described in religious studies. Hence, for the purposes of this book—where we are explicitly interested precisely in the various types of (ultra- and quasi-) transcendental effects material-spirituality allows us to consider—it would not suffice to simply refer to what we are calling "material-spirituality" as "culture."

In describing the material-spiritual as ultra-transcendental, though, we perhaps open ourselves to another objection, especially in relation to religion. This would be the objection that the material-spiritual is simply another name for the transcendent reality (sometimes called God, divinity, the sacred, the numinous, or the holy) around which early phenomenologists of religion tried to organize the study of religion. Many scholars have recently contended that that notion of the transcendent is the product of Western thought and religion and therefore can only serve as the basis for the study of religion more broadly if the latter becomes a colonialist project, in which the study of "religion" simply means the application of Abrahamic concepts and understandings to non-Abrahamic traditions. Does material-spirituality merely smuggle in these same Abrahamic preconceptions under different terminology?

This is the second misconception I think it is important to avoid, in order to understand properly the relation between material-spirituality and religion. While of course material-spirituality, arising within a transcendental phenomenological approach, is itself the product of traditions that are broadly Western in character, I do not think it is the product of Christian (or more broadly Abrahamic) theological assumptions.[45] Certainly, the material-spiritual is not simply another name for God or divinity. The material-spiritual is transcendental (in at least three distinct ways), it is *not* transcendent. There is nothing beyond the world or outside of experience at play in this account of the material-spiritual. In that sense, it is fundamentally different, it seems to me, than the "super-empirical" accounts of the transcendent at work in Western-centric religious studies. In calling it transcendental, I mean that the material-spiritual is not an ontological reality. It is not a being, nor a dimension of being. In good (Husserlian) phenomenological fashion, it brackets the question of its ontological reality, instead focusing on the role it plays in experiencing. The material-spiritual is a dimension of experiencing, not a claim about what exists. And this dimension of experiencing is within experience, not somewhere else. Hence, material-spirituality is neither a logical nor a theological speculation about the "necessary conditions of possibility." It is simply a claim about what is going on in our experiencing: experience is inherently material-spiritual.

That said, precisely because it does not make a claim to ontological reality, it also makes no claims precluding the possibility of such super-empirical ontological realities. This is important to point out because, if it did preclude such possibilities, it would seem unable to take seriously at least some parts of some religions, especially the Abrahamic ones that seem to require some notion of ontological transcendence. Material-spirituality is not saying we have this type of material-spiritual experiencing *instead of* having experiences of divinity, the sacred, and so on. Rather, it is saying that, if we are able to have experiences of transcendent realities, those experiences—qua experiences—would need to be material-spiritual. We would need to engage them with some modes of sensing, and those engagements would need to take place within the context of particular traditions.

But the account of material-spiritual experience discussed in this chapter also enables us to say that we do not *need* to have experiences of transcendent realities in order to have something we can meaningfully call "religion." Instead, religion can be understood as arising not from *what* we experience, but from *how* we experience. As we said earlier, material-spirituality enables us to engage the world in a multiplicity of ways: visibility, tactility, but also linguisticality, sociality, and other modes of sensing that differ from the "five senses" of naïve empiricism. The question before us now is whether religion can be understood to emerge from such a distinct mode of sensing, a religiosity on par with visibility, tactility, linguisticality and sociality as a distinct way of sensing or engaging the world, opening us to experience the world in new and different ways. If this were to be the case, then we could talk of a meaningfully religious dimension to our experience that is not defined by the content of *what* we experience but by a particular way of sensing that is part of *how* we experience.

Material-spirituality also teaches us that, as people experience the world in one of these sensings, their experiences are necessarily productive: visibility enables both seeing and phenomena that are seeable; linguisticality yields both speaking and phenomena that can be spoken, and so on. It is not, of course, that the subjective capability (seeing) enables the objective correlates (seeable things), nor vice versa. Rather, the world-as-visible simultaneously opens up both dimensions. Similarly, then, a religious mode of sensing (religiosity) would open up both a distinct subjective capability and the ability to encounter things in the world in that way. The product of those encounters would be religious phenomena, encountered or experienced in a uniquely religious way. In both producing and engaging with those phenomena in particular ways rooted in previous historical and cultural communities, religious traditions or styles would emerge, akin to the differing visual or linguistic traditions [*Stiftungen*].

The account of material-spirituality outlined in this chapter, therefore, suggests a way of thinking religion that is not grounded in notions of the transcendent. Given the many problems that arise for the global study of religion rooted in such Abrahamic conceptions, this new way of thinking religion could prove helpful to the study of religion, both comparatively (i.e., when thinking religion across and between different cultures) and within particular traditions. We can call this new way of thinking a transcendental approach to religion, and it requires a meaningfully unique way of religiously sensing the world. It is to this that we must turn in the next chapter, to begin to truly explore the religious implications of the fact that experience is, necessarily, material-spiritual.

2

Religiosity as a Religious Mode of Engaging the World

We are now in a position to look more closely at what it would mean to experience the world in a fundamentally religious way. We have made clear already that this is not simply a matter of what we experience (e.g., experiencing the world in a way that also includes "super-empirical"[1] objects). Rather, the question is whether the material-spiritual nature of our experience expresses itself somehow in a uniquely religious way of experiencing.

That material-spirituality expresses itself in multiple ways of experiencing is easy for almost anyone to understand: we see the world, hear the world, touch the world, and so on.[2] Each of these modes of sensing the world open us, simultaneously, onto the "same" world "differently": it is the (same) world that we see, touch, hear, and so on, but seeing the world adds a fundamentally new and distinct "flavor" to our experience than does touching the world or hearing the world. None of them can be reduced to the others without something significant being lost. This is easy to see in relation to the five senses of naïve empiricism. However, transcendental phenomenology has shown us that these different modes of experiencing or engaging the world are not limited to the five senses. Merleau-Ponty, for example, talks about linguisticality as something akin to visibility and tactility.[3] Michel Henry talks about "art, ethics, or religion" as distinct expressions of (material-)spirit.[4]

Let us examine some of these other modes of sensing to get a better idea of what it might look like for there to be a "religious" mode of sensing. Some of these other modes of sensing also strike us as quite intuitively plausible. For example, the first of those mentioned by Henry, which we can call the aesthetic, is not overly difficult to understand: we experience the world aesthetically, and this aesthetic experience cannot be reduced to the other senses (such as visibility or aurality), even though those other senses may be present and even significant in and for our aesthetic experiencing. This is because experiencing the world aesthetically adds something new to our experience: we no longer just see the world, but we experience it also *as beautiful*[5] (or as harmonious[6] or as allusive,[7] or in whatever way the core meaning of the aesthetic way of experiencing the world is understood). And beauty is not reducible to visibility, because we can also experience music as beautiful (aurally), or a poem as beautiful (linguistically), or even, in some cases, a mathematical formula or a well-designed play in football as beautiful. So, the aesthetic is not reducible to the other modes; attempting to do so would lose the ability to experience things as beautiful (or harmonious, allusive, etc.). But neither is the aesthetic completely distinct from the other modes. Rather, it combines with other modes of sensing the world to add yet another element to our experience: in addition to experiencing the world as visible, aural, tactile, and so on, we also now experience the world as aesthetic.

Henry claims that spirit is also expressed ethically. For this to be the case, "ethics" would have to refer not to rules or principles governing "proper" behavior, but rather to a unique mode of experiencing the world: as "good" or "evil," perhaps, or as "just" or "unjust." In this sense, as with the aesthetic, ethicality, as a mode of sensing the world, would open us to a new dimension or way of experiencing the world: in addition to what it looks like, sounds like, tastes like, or "beauties" like, we would now engage the world also according to what it "ethics" like, that is, the way we encounter it also with a dimension of justice or injustice.[8] This, too, opens a new dimension of our experiencing, and not simply a new way of thinking. In that sense, justice (like beauty in the aesthetic mode) is not simply something we reason to, but something we sense and engage directly in the world, the same way that we do not reason to but sense visibility or tactility. This does not remove the possibility also of reasoning about justice, nor even that, in reasoning or thinking more carefully, we might come to the conclusion that our initial sensing was incorrect and must be modified. That we can be wrong about what we take to be just or unjust does not mean we do not experience things as just or unjust, any more than being wrong sometimes about what we (think we) see means we do not actually see things. In fact, quite the opposite: perhaps we can only reason about what is just or unjust precisely because we are able to experience things as just or unjust. That is, perhaps our feelings of justice do not follow from our conclusions about justice, but vice versa: perhaps someone can convince us something is just or unjust only because we first have "intuitions" or "feelings" about the un/just. This ability to intuit or feel justice and injustice would be the ethical mode of sensing (ethicality, on par with visibility, tactility, etc.).

If we can concede the possibility of modes of sensing the world beyond the five senses of empiricism, we are then able to ask whether there could be a distinctly religious mode of sensing the world, and if so, how we might characterize it. That is the purpose of this chapter: to make the case for a distinctly religious mode of sensing or engaging the world, a religiosity on par with ethicality or aestheticality. The first step in building this case will be to show that such a thing is possible—that there is nothing inherently contradictory or ridiculous about suggesting we sense the world religiously. Then, we will try to articulate what it might be like to experience the world religiously. This articulation will endeavor to paint as widely applicable a notion of religiosity as possible, and as such will not, as much as possible, commit itself to any particular religious assumptions about what it might be to experience the world religiously.[9] In doing so, it will paint a picture of religiosity as an experience of our connectivity with the world and the phenomena within it. Given this account, we will see that empirical phenomena can be experienced or sensed in this way, hence showing both that this religious mode of sensing occurs and that transcendence is not necessary for it.

The Possibility of Religiosity

The best place to start attempting to show the possibility of a distinctly religious way of sensing the world, it seems to me, is by acknowledging that vast numbers of people in the world claim to actually have such a religious mode of sensing. If by "religious mode of sensing" we mean a distinct way of experiencing the world that is uniquely religious, then it seems that literally billions of people have claimed to have this over the course of human history. I do not just mean that people have claimed to have religious beliefs, nor that people have participated in religious rituals. I mean that people have claimed that their religious commitments and participation have, in some important way, changed how they experience the world around them.

This does not strike me as a controversial claim. Various Buddhist traditions hold that the world is experienced as *maya* or illusion; although the depth and impact of this illusory nature varies, the world is to be experienced as "not what it seems to be."[10] The conception of *Tat Tvam Asi* found in several monistic Hindu traditions also shapes how its adherents experience the world. In this case, the world is seen as not being entirely distinct from people, but as in some way unified with them: "Believe, my son: the finest essence here—that constitutes the self of this whole world; that is the truth; that is the self (*ātman*). And that's how you are [*tat tvam asi*]."[11] Similarly, the sense of the world as created shapes how practitioners of Judaism and Islam experience the world, never simply as "just there," but always as inherently meaningful and in some way showing God's purpose. In Christian traditions, the notion of "love" is often understood as a gift, sent by God,[12] to shape how people experience and engage the world and phenomena within it, including other people.[13]

This brief summary is neither exhaustive nor nuanced, but it should be sufficient to establish the claim that practitioners of various traditions within, at least, Buddhism, Hinduism, Judaism, Islam, and Christianity would claim to experience the world differently because of their religious commitments. Given the vast number of people who would be included under these umbrellas, it seems to me that we have billions of people claiming that they experience the world differently because of their religion, and as such the existence of such a religious mode of sensing the world should be seen, on its surface, not only as possible, but as plausible. Although billions of people could be wrong about this, it seems to me that we would need compelling evidence to contradict their claims.

Now, there very likely are people who would wish to contest their claims and this conclusion. For there are certainly also a not-insubstantial number of people in the history of humanity who would claim not to have such a religious experience of the world. If this is a mode of sensing the world, why do so many people (seem to) not experience it? This objection is not as problematic as it might at first seem. After all, not every individual person throughout history has been able to see, but we do not therefore question whether visibility remains a valid and important part of the experience of the world for those who are able to see. That people have different abilities to experience or sense the world is not a compelling objection to the fact that (at least some) people seem to experience or sense the world in a particular way. That some people do not experience the world religiously, therefore, does not, on its own, rule out the possibility that others do, precisely because no mode of sensing the world has to be universal in order to be efficacious on experience.

Someone might protest further: "yes, but at least I know what someone means when they say they see something. What do you mean when you say we experience the world religiously?" While I grant the force of the question, here, again, I find it less than compelling as an *objection*. For while I may know what someone means when they say they see something, that is because I myself am a person who sees. But could someone who has never seen truly be able to understand what it means to see? Would we be able to explain to someone what vision is, without appealing to any prior experiences with visibility? This seems highly unlikely to me, especially given our earlier claim that the various modes of sensing are irreducible to each other, and hence precisely cannot be fully explained by recourse to the other senses. That someone may not fully understand what others mean when they say they experience the world a certain way does not itself entail that other people are not, in fact, experiencing the world that way. While someone who has never had a sense of sight may not have a real understanding of what it means to see, they do not therefore doubt that other people experience the world that way. Because people who are blind from birth are able to acknowledge that other people see things, so too people who do not experience the world religiously should be able to acknowledge that other people seem to experience the world that way.

Perhaps one might claim that religion is not like visibility because everyone with vision tends to see the same things and describe them the same way, but this is not the case for the religious mode of sensing. Therefore, religiosity is not really a mode of engaging the world like visibility. Now, it is true that the religious sensings that we outlined earlier were quite different: experiencing the world as "not what it seems" is not the same as experiencing the essence of the world as the same as one's own individuality, nor are either of them the same as experiencing the world as creation nor as loving the world. How can we account for this vast difference, if there is indeed a religious mode of sensing the world?

First, I think we have to clarify the claim that "everyone with vision tends to see the same things and describe them the same way." The first part of that claim—that everyone with vision sees the same things—is of course only true if they are looking at the same things. What I see out my window in rural Alberta in January is not what someone living in urban New York sees looking out their window in January, nor what someone living in Morocco sees looking out their window in January. When we look at different things, we see different things. So one possible explanation of the various descriptions of religious sensings are that the different religious traditions are experiencing different things.

This aligns slightly with the criticism I would have of the second claim in the objection—that every person who sees describes the same things the same way. We saw in previous chapters that Merleau-Ponty claims that we always experience the world from within particular traditions, each of which has its own "style." His most famous example is that the painter sees the world differently than does the scientist. This could be because they are looking at different things: perhaps painters look at their canvas or the natural landscape that they are painting, whereas scientists look at their laboratory or the experiments they are performing. In that sense, the styles offered by the different traditions impact what they are looking at, because different traditions will necessarily look at different things (painters at canvases, scientists at laboratories). But I think Merleau-Ponty's point is different than that: the traditions we are part of not only shape what we see, but more profoundly they shape *how* we see. A painter and a geologist may look at the same mountain and see very different things: contrasts in color, the interplay of light and dark, the gleam of the sun in the case of the painter; rock formations, various mineral veins, and the types of flora and fauna they can support in the case of the geologist.[14] In that case, to say that everyone with vision who is looking at the same things would describe them the same way seems false, for I would certainly get different descriptions if I asked the painter and the scientist to "describe the mountainscape you see before you." But I would also likely get different descriptions if I asked the painter and the geologist to look at and describe the play of colors or the rock formations, given the differences in familiarity each person would have with what they are being asked to look at. Even when called to look at the same thing, they would see and describe differently.

The same could be true, then, in the case of the (possible) differences in religious modes of sensings[15]: perhaps their purported differences are attributable to them experiencing different things and/or to their experiencing the same things differently, as a result of the different styles caused by their differing traditions. If one then also takes into account the historical and sedimentary nature of traditions—that what happens in the past shapes us in the present, which in turn becomes the past that shapes future presents, and so on—and remembers also the intertwining of material and spiritual, then this explanation becomes even more likely. After all, if people's descriptions of the "same" phenomenon were only slightly different to begin with, over time those slight differences could lead to different foci, which would in turn lead to different practices that would further entrench the differing foci, helping some traditions experience some elements of the world or the phenomena more than others (like the painter experiences color and light more than a geologist does, because they have been trained to pay more attention to it). That is to say, even if the descriptions of Buddhism, Hinduism, Judaism, Islam, and Christianity might have been only slightly different originally, those differences would have been magnified by the thousands of years of history that have followed from those origins, and the very different cultural circumstances in which those years unfolded.

And those cultural circumstances also point to another factor that could explain the possible differences in description of the same mode of experiencing. For although we can now see that even vision is maybe not as unitary and "the same" as the objection first assumed, the differentiation is even more pronounced if we talk of modes of sensing like linguisticality or aestheticality. For language, it is clear that particular languages are different: no one doubts that English and Mandarin are very different, but this difference is not just in semantics, vocabulary, or syntax: perhaps even our understanding of how language functions or what language is could itself be quite different, depending on the linguistic tradition we are a part of. Linguists from Indo-European backgrounds articulate the nature and structure of language quite differently than linguists from Asian, African, or Indigenous backgrounds. The emphasis on the subject–predicate structure, for example, is not as universal as Western languages might at first suggest, and hence the notion of language as "symbolic representation" may seem more obvious to Western linguists than to those of other cultures.[16] That they might understand the nature of what it is to function linguistically quite differently would not undermine the fact that both English and Mandarin are functioning as languages.

What, then, is the value of looking for similarities, if even the structure and function might be quite different? Why talk of "languages" and "linguisticality" at all, and not just speak of English, Mandarin, Cree, and so on? This is a fair question, and one that is not new for the study of religion. In relation to the material-spiritual nature of experiencing, I think the reason to still speak of and look for similarities is because what we are describing, in terms of religiosity, is a distinct way of experiencing the world that, in turn, opens up new possibilities for experience. Linguisticality opens up new possibilities for meaning-full experiences, even if we might understand "meaning" differently in different linguistic traditions. Visibility opens up new possibilities for visual experiences, even if we might "see" differently in different visual traditions. And paying attention to these new modes of experiencing—speaking of "language" and not simply English, Mandarin, and Potawatomi—therefore helps us better understand both our own experiences and the role that various phenomena play in them.

This is not to downplay the danger of too quickly universalizing our experiences, turning "my" or "our" experiences into "the human experience." That is a danger we need to be aware of, in both religion and transcendental phenomenology. But there is also the possibility that we come to see new connections that we did not previously notice, and in doing so give a new flavour to our experiences, and perhaps new ways to understand them. At times, when we try to explain a way of sensing, we come to see other things as fulfilling that sensible function that we may not have previously recognized as such. Explaining language as "symbolic representation," for example, allowed some people to start considering mathematics as a distinct kind of language, which itself gave rise to breakthroughs in computer programming and artificial intelligence. Although, traditionally, most people would not have thought of mathematics as a language akin to English or Mandarin, it can be considered to work that way, given certain understandings of language. So, too, it seems that attempts to explain religiosity could end up helping us see new things that might fulfil this religious function that would not have traditionally been considered to be "religion," insofar as they do not appeal to any kind of super-empirical realities.

Articulating Religiosity

Let us not get ahead of ourselves. We will return to this point about what might function religiously later. For now, let us try to articulate what we might mean by this religious mode of sensing. In doing so, we acknowledge: first, that we do so from within particular traditions that might influence how we understand the nature of religiosity (a point we will return to in later chapters); and second, that our attempts at articulation must therefore balance between specificity (which will more clearly align with how religiosity actually operates in particular religious traditions or according to particular religious styles but will therefore apply less broadly) and abstraction (which will apply more broadly to various traditions, but which will therefore not align as clearly or neatly with how religiosity functions in any one particular tradition). In order to make the case for the possibility of a religious mode of sensing against those who might deny this possibility, the discussion in this section will veer toward the abstractive side of this balancing equation. That is, we will try to discuss religiosity in broad enough terms to be plausible to a variety of different religious traditions, even if, in so doing, we will not quite capture what religiosity feels like to practitioners in any one particular tradition. As such, we will not seek to determine once and for all the nature of religiosity itself, bolstering our suggestion against all possible opponents. Rather, we will simply outline one way that one could plausibly understand the notion of religiosity in a general way. Hopefully this approach will reveal something important to us about the nature of religiosity itself.

To do this—and to try to mitigate as much as possible the effect of starting from within a particular tradition or other, and most specifically to try to avoid starting from the assumptions of Abrahamic religious traditions, whose problematic impact on our understanding of religion are well-known for scholars in religious studies—I propose to think of religiosity primarily in terms of the unique way it expresses our material-spiritual condition. Starting from this standpoint in experiencing is consistent with the transcendental phenomenological method I am seeking both to employ and to develop in this book. It should also prove widely applicable, if our analyses in the last chapter were correct that experiencing itself is inherently material-spiritual.

My contention here is that religiosity expresses particularly well the connective nature of material-spirituality. That all experience is rooted in material-spirituality entails that all phenomena (i.e., experienced things) are located in material-spiritual conditions; if they were not, we would not be able to experience them as phenomena. This means that material-spirituality provides us ways to think and to experience the connection between phenomena and phenomenality, between (material) things and our (spiritually motivated) experiencing of them. This connectivity is different than the unity that characterizes subjectivity, as it was explained in the last chapter. Subjectivity is about uniting phenomena and phenomenality together in *my* (or one's) experience. In that sense, it is not interested in the connection between phenomena in themselves, or between phenomena and phenomenality in themselves, or between different modes of phenomenality in themselves. Instead, it functions primarily to tie things together *for me*. As such, it opens up a new dimension of experience (individuality; mineness). But this is different from experiencing the connection between phenomena and phenomenality in themselves. Because subjectivity is focused on how I connect things, it therefore functions as if I am the centre of the connectivity. In that way, it loses the sense that there are connections outside and beyond myself, connections that might even include and incorporate myself into them. Seeking connectivity beyond subjectivity, then, would provide us ways to speak of forms of connection that are not subject-centred, even if they might also function within subjectivity.

Material-spirituality is the ultra-transcendental name I have given to that which connects phenomena and our experiencing of them with things and experiencers.[17] And that connection is not simply speculative or rationally constructed—it is itself part of our experience. Religiosity is—I am suggesting here—the name we give (or should give) to the mode of experiencing that lets us experience this connection. In that sense, religiosity is our experiencing of the connectivity that binds us (*religare*[18]) together, not simply within our own particular religious traditions but more broadly with the world, with other humans, and/or with the cosmos itself. Religiosity therefore opens a new dimension to our experiencing: just as ethicality enables us to experience the world as just (or not) and visibility enables us to experience the world as see-able (or not), so here religiosity enables us to experience the world as connected (or not).

This sense of connectivity ties, as we said, phenomena to phenomenality. As such, it is often experienced subjectively as a kind of radical coherence in which I experience that I, too, am one with the world. This is the core of religiosity as a mode of sensing the world: a way of experiencing the connectivity or coherence of ourselves with the wider world. The nature of this connectivity varies across different religious traditions, as mentioned earlier, but the commonality is that there is some experienced (and not merely posited or reasoned to) sense of our connection with the world. There are, of course, other types of connections and coherence that we might experience, but they are not all religious in this sense. Logical coherence, for example, is something that we can experience (positively or negatively, that is, as something that is present or something that is notably absent). But while there may be a religious dimension to that coherence for some people (a point we will return to below), most of the time it would not be a religious connection or coherence. Religious connectivity is an experience of the binding together or coherence of things in a non-limited sense: it is not just that certain things are seen as connected in a local or limited way or according to one particular set of criteria or other, but that there is an experience of my own (or our own, in more communal traditions) being-connected with the world in a way that exceeds the parameters of a certain situation. To see a particular set of premises as logically coherent is not, therefore, religious. But to see logic or rationality as the tie that binds the world together (as in some accounts of *logos* theory) and so to experience one's understanding of a certain point in philosophy or mathematics as connecting one with some kind of overarching principle of intelligibility would be religious. Similarly, attendees of a concert often experience a sense of togetherness, not just with others in attendance but in some way with the "world" itself, a sense of immersion or participation in something bigger than themselves and their current situation.[19] Similarly, many people experience a sense of oneness and connection with the natural world as a whole when they hike or camp[20]; experience a deep connection with a community that exceeds the present when participating in parades, festivals, and other holiday activities; or even feel a deep sense of cosmic connection when performing particular tasks in a "flow" state.[21] These would all be examples where religiosity as a mode of sensing is at work in an experience.

Particularly poignant examples of this experience of connectivity could be characterized by what we might now call "mystical" experiences, in which one has an overwhelming sense of connection to a cosmic principle (be it a divinity or the cosmos itself). Indeed, in much of the current literature, "religious experience" is almost entirely interchangeable with this kind of mystical experience. But these are only extreme cases of a sensing that is operative in other experiences as well. I need not be consciously aware of this "cosmic" connection for it to be operative in my experiencing: I do not have to be consciously thinking "logic is what ties the world together" for that to be a significant element of my experiencing of things. Most times, in fact, the religious dimension of our experiencing is likely to be sub- or pre-conscious: one *experiences* the connectivity or coherence, but one need not be reflexively aware of it.

Hence, there can be gradations of religiosity in our experiencing. Just as visibility is present both in experiences in which visibility is the primary or leading mode of engaging the world (looking at a landscape through the window of a car, for example) and those in which it plays a secondary role (like reading a book, which heavily relies on visibility for non-Braille readers, but which is itself characterized primarily by the linguistic function: we read in order to inhabit meanings, not simply to see marks on the page), so too might religiosity function both as a leading function for particular experiences, and as one type of sensing alongside others in other experiences. In other words, not all religious experiencing needs to be overwhelming in order to be religious.[22] More subtle forms of this type of experiencing of connectedness can be found in various experiences. People who experience a religious dimension to their concert-going, for example, would not likely characterize it as the primary focus of their experience: they are there primarily to listen to the music, though they do report also this sense of connectivity as a palpable part of their experience.

I am claiming that religiosity is the mode of sensing that enables us to experience this sense of connection or oneness with things beyond oneself. It is a unique way of experiencing or engaging the world that many experiencers have, and not merely a fanciful wish, an irrational emotion, or a reasoned conclusion. It is a distinct way of experiencing or engaging the world, leading to distinct kinds of sensations, just as the "feeling" of seeing something is not reducible to the "feeling" of hearing something or of tasting something.

This sense of experiencing our connectedness with things beyond ourselves is not necessarily an experience of transcendence. However, insofar as we feel this as an experience of connection, there is a real sense that what I am connected with is both within me and beyond me. This is sometimes characterized by language of being "immersed" in a wider reality; sometimes it is simply characterized by solidarity and connection. In all those cases, there is a sense that what I am connected with is not experienced simply as beyond myself, but as in some meaningful way being within myself as well, even if it nevertheless exceeds me and can never be reduced to me. In that sense, my relation to that which I feel connected to in religiosity is never a transcendent, super-relation (characterized by sharp boundaries holding things apart: the natural versus the super-natural), but rather what I, following other phenomenologists, might call a supra-relation[23]: that which exceeds its relata, while nevertheless shaping or structuring them from within. Husserl thought, for example, such a supra-relation characterizes the relation between the individual and its community as a "supra-subjective" relation: communal influences shape and structure subjectivity in fundamental ways, and so are found within subjectivity, though those forces also, of course, exceed subjectivity and the individual subject.[24] Similarly, the Dutch religious philosopher Herman Dooyeweerd speaks of "supra-theoretical" prejudices that are not themselves strictly theoretical, though they shape and structure our theory implicitly.[25]

This "supra-" relation is characteristic of many of the religious modes of sensing we outlined near the beginning of this chapter. The Hindu notion of *tat tvam asi*—"that you are" or "that's how you are"—is the most explicit example: the essence of the individual person (*ātman*) is identified with the essence of the whole world (*brahman*), yet without reducing *ātman* to *brahman* or *brahman* to *ātman*. Similarly, we can see the notion of love (especially in the form of *caritas* or *agape*) in Christianity as comprising this kind of supra-relation: qua gift of God, love is not wholly contained within any particular person or relationship, but exceeds it, going so far as to be identified with the essence of God itself.[26] At the same time, this love is the very mark of the transformed Christian individual. Hence, this love is neither merely immanent within Christian practitioners nor does it simply transcend them; rather, it bears a supra-individual relation to them.

In this supra-relation, these religious forms of engaging the world provide us accounts of how we are connected to the world and other phenomena within it: God's love (which is within me) connects me to God, to my neighbors, and to the rest of the world which, qua creation, is also full of the love of God. Because *ātman* is *brahman*, we are connected inherently to *brahman*, which itself is in everything, thereby connecting us to everything. The apparent connections and differentiations we (think we) see in the world are simply *maya*, understanding the nature of which will better equip us to see our real connection with other things (although the nature of that "real connection" varies in different Buddhist traditions).

This is not to say that it would be impossible to have transcendence with this account of religiosity. Some traditions could conceive of the connection at work in religiosity in transcendent terms (a point we will return to in the next chapter). The point here is simply to state that it need not be construed that way in the functioning of religiosity.[27] In that sense, my use of "religiosity" is not religious because it evokes any kind of transcendence. What makes it religious, and therefore worth calling religiosity rather than something else (like "connectivity," for example), is that I think the various traditions we currently recognize as "religious traditions" are best understood as arising in response to the results of religiosity. These experiences of connectivity have been articulated differently in different languages and different cultures, leading to differing concepts (God, *brahman*, *maya*, etc.), doctrines, practices, and, even, differing understandings of the religious. This differentiation goes all the way down: I am not claiming that God and *brahman* are simply different translations of the "same thing," or different words for the same phenomenon. Nor am I claiming that the connection that some people feel with the world as creatures in creation is the same connection that others feel with the world as *maya*. The various religious traditions can each be considered a "religious" tradition not because they share the same content or are about the same things (because I do not think they do or are), but because they arise as distinct traditions (or *Stiftungen*, in the phenomenological sense) in response to the unique mode of experiencing or sensing the world that we have here called religiosity. The phenomena that each tradition has generated (doctrines, concepts, practices, objects, affective complexes, etc.) have in turn contributed to the ongoing generation of those traditions, revising and restructuring the tradition, its phenomena (including its conceptions of itself and of religion), and how experiencers shaped by that tradition are able to experience religiosity. Just like the painter and the geologist see differently because of the differing traditions they have been apprenticed into, so too might the Christian and the Buddhist "religion" differently (if we can turn religion into a verb here, the active form of religiosity). Indeed, this might explain why there are so many different definitions of religion—because religiosity religions in so many different ways.

Implications of this Account of Religiosity

There is some way to go yet to clearly establish or explore some of the claims made in the previous paragraph. I will do that in subsequent chapters, but before

I do, I would like to highlight a few important implications that have arisen in our conversation about religiosity thus far.

First is the non-transcendent nature of religiosity. As religiosity is not necessarily about transcendence, it means that the focus on religiosity would open us to see things as religious even if they are not about super-empirical entities. This opens new possibilities for the study of religion, in that things that previously were not considered religious (because they did not pertain to super-empirical realities) might now be considered religious, insofar as they focus on our connectivity with the world. While expanding the scope of religion is not a good in and of itself—it is better to consider as religious only those things which are meaningfully religious—it is good if it helps us better understand either some phenomena or experiencing itself. That is, one can agree with the concern that "if everything is religious, nothing is,"[28] but disagree that the way to draw the line between the religious and the non-religious is to draw lines between different *things*: this "thing" is religious, that "thing" is not. Given the account of religiosity as a mode of sensing alongside other modes, and given the suggestions that multiple modes of sensing are involved in any experience of any phenomenon (a claim that will be explored in greater detail in the next chapter), perhaps the same things could have components that are both religious and not, in the same way that reading a book has components that are linguistic (like trying to understand the meaning of the words) and those that are not (like the tactile feel of turning the pages or scrolling the pdf, the visual perception of the marks on the page or screen, etc.). In that sense, not only can new *things* be considered religious that were not previously considered to be religious, but new religious traditions leading to new styles of religiosity might also now be able to be considered in ways they were not before. Some evolutionary theorists have posited biological life as the connectivity tying us all together. Thinking through a lens of religiosity allows us to see a potentially religious dimension to some evolutionary theory. Similarly, some capitalist theorists maintain that value as determined by the law of supply and demand is what connects us all in this globalized world picture. Might this thereby constitute a religious dimension to capitalism? Perhaps. Of course, not every connection needs to be a religious one, and the question of religiosity is a question of experience and not a question of theory. If some people experience biological life or capitalistically determined value as the tie that binds, then we seem to have a reason to consider a potentially religious dimension to those experiences, even if what they are experiencing is strictly empirical and not at all super-empirical. The point is not to claim that biology, evolution, or capitalism are primarily religious institutions, or that they somehow smuggle religious ideas or implications into their premises; rather, the point is simply that those things might have a religious component to how they are experienced at least for some people, and if they do, then having the tools to recognize, acknowledge, and make sense of that is better than not having those tools.

The previous paragraph already made reference to the second implication I want to highlight: the non-objective nature of religiosity. This is the claim that religiosity is not about what we experience, but how we experience. This is different at least from substantive definitions of religion, and potentially also from functional definitions of religion.[29] One criticism of functional definitions is that they have "become sprawling, overly inclusive, and unwieldy,"[30] and as such "there is not much within culture that cannot be included as 'religion.'"[31] Once "everything becomes 'somehow' or 'implicitly' religious," then the concept of religion seems to be useless or "futile,"[32] no longer a helpful conceptual tool because it does not distinguish anything. This expansion of our understanding of religion seems problematic only if religion has to be circumscribed or defined by its objects (the "whats" that we experience). That is not our approach here. Even if every phenomenon might have a religious element to it, that would not make everything religious, in the same way that not everything is visibility just because (almost?) every phenomenon has a visible element to it: acknowledging that we can see a tree does not entail that trees are simply "visible" things which must be understood primarily (or exclusively) in terms of visibility. Trees are visible—but they are also tactile (they can be touched), economic (they can be bought and sold, given a value, etc.), legal (they can be owned, and people can be liable for them and their repercussions), aesthetic (they can be beautiful), and so on. Adding religiosity as one further possible dimension to things does not seem to risk making religion "futile" or "unwieldy"—it simply opens us to a new dimension of analysis and of experience. Even if every "thing" in culture might have a religious dimension to it, this still need not make everything religious in the way that reduces the effectiveness of religion as a tool for analysis.

Thinking of religion as an analytic tool reminds us that the use of religion as a conceptual tool is always strategic: it is done for some purpose or other, or to achieve some end or other. This is why Peter Berger can claim that definitions are best evaluated not in terms of their correctness, but in terms of whether they are "more useful or less so."[33] This begs the question: useful for what? Here I am willing to concede the possibility that sociologists or anthropologists of religion might have different goals, and therefore require different tools to achieve those goals, than do philosophers of religion. If definitions of religion are entirely strategic, then it is possible that what works as a definition of religion for a transcendental philosophical phenomenologist of religion (like myself) might not work for those with other interests in religion. That makes a good deal of sense to me, and I can see that thinking of religion primarily in terms of things or objects might be useful for an anthropologist of religion, for example. However, I would hesitate to affirm a situation in which uses of the term "religion" were wholly ambiguous or unconnected between different disciplines. In such a case, philosophers of religion would have nothing to offer sociologists or anthropologists of religion, and vice versa. I noted in the introduction that, in many ways, this seems to be the case today, and I think it inhibits our understanding of the phenomenon of religion.

The problem is not irresolvable. Our accounts of the religious can be slightly different, given our different purposes and needs, as long as they are not inherently ambiguous or inconsistent. My hope is that the account of religiosity as a mode of sensing offered in this chapter can be developed and clarified in ways that can also meaningfully speak to sociologists (e.g., through an account of religious traditions as shapers of experiencing and not simply as collections of doctrines, practices, etc.; see Chapter three) and to anthropologists and cultural theorists (e.g., through an account of religious phenomena as empirical "things" necessarily embedded in, and generated within, religious traditions arising from experiences of religiosity that are expressive of our material-spiritual situation; see Chapter four). It is possible that sociologists or anthropologists need to focus on religious phenomena or religious traditions, while I, as a philosopher and phenomenologist, prefer to focus on religiosity or on the material-spiritual. This need not mean we have nothing to contribute to each other's work or to the shared project of understanding religion, provided our accounts of the religious can meaningfully cohere. Showing such a coherence will be the project of the ensuing chapters.

Before turning to that, however, there is one last implication of the account of religiosity developed in this chapter that I want to highlight: that religiosity, as a mode of sensing, must be distinguished from our concept of religiosity. Just as a theory of vision is not the same as seeing (although it tries to articulate what seeing is), so a theory or philosophy of religiosity is not the same as religioning, although it is trying, as best it can, to articulate what religioning is as a mode of sensing the world. While this may seem obvious in the case of vision, I fear it is not always obvious in the study of religion: we sometimes treat our theory of religion as if it was the thing that we are studying, to the point that failure to agree on the theory has led some prominent theorists to wonder whether there is anything religious at all in the world.

While I understand the nature and purpose of that criticism (namely that we risk turning what we are studying into our account of it, and therefore missing what is unique or interesting in the various differences at play in religions), I think we should be careful about equating our theory of religiosity with the mode of sensing that we are trying to articulate by that name for at least two reasons: first, problems with the theory are not necessarily problems with the sensing; they might just be the indication that we need a new theory. That is, should the account of religiosity I offer here prove problematic, that need not mean that there is no such thing as a religious mode of sensing. It could be the case that there is such a mode of sensing, and I have just articulated it poorly.

It could also be the case that I articulate it well, and people still find it problematic. This points us to the second reason to emphasize the difference between religiosity (as a mode of sensing) and the account of religiosity I offer here: articulations of religiosity are necessarily phenomena generated from within some particular tradition(s) or other(s). While the account we strove for in this chapter tried to be as abstract as possible to show the broad applicability of an account of religiosity, it could not itself be from nowhere and therefore applicable everywhere. Rather, it was itself necessarily rooted in particular traditions, at least one of which (transcendental phenomenology) I have tried to be quite explicit in articulating. Yet its being consistent with phenomena in one particular tradition might make it less consistent with phenomena from other traditions, precisely because traditions have developed differently. As we said earlier, the more we try to make a concept abstractly fit across multiple traditions, the less it is able to fit snugly within any of them. The more we fit an account or concept to the phenomena within a particular tradition, the less likely it will be applicable in other traditions.

In terms of the cross-cultural study of religion, then, are we doomed either to colonially put our definition onto other people from outside or abandon entirely any meaningful talk of "religion" or some other category through which we might see similarities worth noting amid the differences? I hope not, and I will endeavour to show where this hope comes from in subsequent chapters. I will suggest instead that perhaps all we can do is talk about how religiosity works for us, and then talk with others to see how religiosity works for them, while acknowledging that our differences may not be the result of one side being "right" and the other "wrong," but could merely result from being different: different things we are experiencing, different styles we experience by, or some combination of them. A full account of religiosity would need not only to be abstract (to be widely applicable), it would also need to encompass the entire scope of possible different styles of religiosity. It was not possible to provide such an account in this chapter, which had the much more modest goal of helping people see an intuitive plausibility in religiosity as a mode of sensing the world. I will not provide such a robust and rigorous account of religiosity later in the book, either. The point of this chapter was to argue for religiosity as a possible mode of sensing the world, and to lend credence to this as a way of thinking the religious. If this notion is taken seriously, the kind of cross-tradition conversation to flesh out this picture of religiosity could then emerge. My hope is that it will.

Before it can do so, I think we will need to flesh out this account of religiosity in relation both to religious traditions in general, and to the particular religious tradition(s) that are currently dominant in our understanding of religion. It is to this that we now turn.

3

Thinking Religion within a Religious Tradition

Last chapter we highlighted the need to distinguish between religiosity (as a mode of sensing) and the account of religiosity that one provides, which is a particular phenomenon arising within a particular tradition. At stake in this distinction is the nature of the difference between transcendental modes of sensing the world, quasi-transcendental traditions, and empirical phenomena. To better understand both the account of religion in general that I am trying to highlight in this book and the contemporary understandings of religion that dominate in the academic study of religion, it is necessary to further clarify this difference.

Two Ways of Understandings Religious Traditions

The difference is a difference of *how* they function in our experiencing of the world, and not a difference in *what* is experienced. That is, religiosity is not a different thing than the traditions by which we experience it (say, Christianity, Buddhism, Islam, Judaism, etc.) nor than the religious phenomena we encounter (beliefs, objects, rituals, etc.), just as the traditions themselves are not a different thing than the phenomena that express them. Christianity is experienced through beliefs (in the Trinity, the full-divinity and full-humanity of Christ, the expiation of sins, etc.), objects (crucifixes, churches, prayer books, etc.), rituals (prayers, festivals, holy days, worship rites, liturgies, etc.), and so on. It is neither something other than those things, nor is it reducible to those things. Rather, qua religious *tradition*, Christianity names the perdurance of certain typical beliefs, objects, rituals, and so on through time as a (relatively) coherent whole.

This notion of a religious tradition is usually understood in strictly empirical terms: we look at the various phenomena that characterize a particular tradition, and that is what makes the tradition what it is. Buddhism is the name given to a particular set of beliefs, practices, objects, and so on. Daoism is the name given to another particular set of beliefs, practices, objects, and so on. This strictly empirical understanding of religious traditions is immensely helpful in and for comparative religion as a mode of studying religion, but it does not yet account for the (quasi-)transcendental effects that those empirical phenomena have.

By quasi-transcendental effects I mean the ways that particular empirical phenomena impact how experiencers experience the world. Earlier, we talked about how an artist and a geologist would see the same mountainscape differently because they are an artist or a geologist. Their disciplinary training not only changes the set of beliefs they hold (artists know about chiaroscuro, geologists about sedimentation), the objects they engage with (paintbrushes, clay, and/or studios; rocks, hiking shoes, and/or specimen collection bags), and the rituals they undergo (compiling a portfolio or finishing an artwork; passing one's comprehensive examinations and publishing articles)—it also seems to change how they inhabit particular modes of sensing (like visibility). That is, being an artist or a geologist does not seem to add a new or distinct mode of sensing,[1] it simply impacts or affects how people experience in and through other modes of sensing (i.e., it makes people see or hear differently).

We can, therefore, talk about traditions in strictly empirical ways or in quasi-transcendental ways. The strictly empirical way focuses exclusively on empirical phenomena: in art, that would include paying attention to works of art, famous artists, time periods, and so on. In doing so, we often find further sub-traditions within a tradition (in art, that would include painting, sculpture, music, theater), and sub-traditions within those sub-traditions (e.g., Impressionism, Surrealism, Shanshui Hua, Kalamkari in painting; Greek tragedy, Sanskrit drama, Kabuki in theater). This approach to traditions is interested primarily in understanding and appreciating how what happens today takes a position in an ongoing unfolding of the tradition, and so is part of an ongoing and ancient conversation (e.g., the tradition of art).

All of this would explore the history and current practice of that tradition, but it would not yet look at how being immersed in a tradition affects how those immersed in that tradition experience other things. To begin to look at that—to start to see how an artist sees the world differently than a geologist—we could still speak of art as a tradition, understood now precisely in this quasi-transcendental way: our interest would be the ways in which being entangled with the phenomena of art affects *how* someone experiences, rather than simply looking at how being entangled with the phenomena of art affects *what* type of art one produces. This sense of tradition seeks to explore the quasi-transcendental effects on subjectivity, influencing how subjectivity inhabits various transcendental modes of sensing the world in different ways.

This distinction in ways of understanding a tradition is important because we need to think of religious traditions also in this quasi-transcendental way. That we already conceive of religious traditions in the empirical way does not, I think, need further explanation: we clearly do. If we commonly account for religious traditions empirically, why should we think we need to also account for these quasi-transcendental effects? Let me use the example of white evangelicalism in the United States to try to highlight how a religious tradition seems to have broader effects on how people experience the world that cannot be easily explained by other means. It is well known that white evangelicals in the USA are more likely to have voted for Trump. This could easily be explained by looking at moral issues (such as abortion and questions around sexuality and gender) and positing that one party simply embodied those values better than others. What interests me from this quasi-transcendental perspective is that white evangelicals are more likely even than other Republicans to believe certain conspiracy theories that seem to have no inherent connection to their religious beliefs or practices, such as the claim that there was widespread voter fraud in the 2020 election (74% of white evangelicals in the USA agree with this, compared to only 54% of Republicans overall) and that there was a "deep state" working to undermine Trump and his supporters (67% support among white evangelicals, only 52% support among Republicans overall).[2] Here we see statistically significant differences, not just in beliefs, it seems to me, but in how these people are inhabiting the social mode of sensing the world: white evangelicals show themselves to be less charitable in their reading of social situations and more likely to see nefarious motives at work beneath the surface.

Some scholars try to explain these data in purely sociological terms by talking of the insularity of white evangelicals vis-à-vis other groups.[3] There are certainly empirical data to support that sense of social insulation, but why should that feed into these conspiracy theories and a more wary approach to social interactions? If white evangelicalism is more socially isolated than other religious traditions, this is certainly not for reasons inherent to their religious beliefs or their traditional religious practices. Given their own emphasis on evangelism (i.e., sharing Christianity with those who are not already Christian), we should expect them to be more engaged with other groups, not less so. Indeed, other data show that some of these differences in how white evangelicals inhabit sociality are not easily explainable by recourse to their empirical religious beliefs or practices: in another poll concerning human rights (inspired by the Black Lives Matter movement), white evangelicals were significantly less likely to support human rights for groups outside of themselves than were non-white evangelicals.[4] This suggests that it is not simply their religious beliefs or practices that are shaping their beliefs here, because those are largely shared with non-white evangelicals. But that same poll also shows that the differences cannot be explained away solely by recourse to race, as white evangelicals were also significantly less likely to support human rights for other groups than were white non-evangelicals. So, there is something about how people are formed in the particular sub-tradition of white evangelical Christianity that exceeds the mere phenomena of their religious tradition (as not all evangelicals feel that way), but yet is somehow tied to that tradition (as they also differ significantly from white non-evangelicals).

I will not endeavour here to explain the details of how or why white evangelicalism has these effects. Others have started to try to do so in other places,[5] and although I find some of their analyses intuitively compelling, they seem to be missing precisely the quasi-transcendental character that I am trying to explain here. They can say *that* white evangelicalism clearly supports Trumpism, and can historically trace *why* that has arisen, but they cannot yet, it seems to me, account for *how* white evangelicals not only think and act differently, but really seem to experience the social world differently than other people.[6] My point here is not to try to establish either the habits of white evangelicals or to clarify precisely how those habits can be traced to their participation in white evangelicalism. This is merely an example to make intuitively plausible the claim that participation in religious traditions impacts how people experience the world in a broader way, and we therefore ought to seek to understand religious traditions as having quasi-transcendental effects as well as empirical effects.

Religiosity and Religious Traditions

We are defining these quasi-transcendental effects as altering how people inhabit the various transcendental modes of sensing the world. How does this align with the argument in the last chapter that there is a distinctly religious mode of sensing the world, and that religious traditions in some sense embody this religious mode of sensing in distinct ways?

The answer is quite complicated, phenomenologically. I will try to be clear here, without losing the forest for the trees. Because all the modes of sensing arise out of the material-spiritual condition of experience, they are connected to each other, even amidst their differences. So, although visibility and tactility are distinct modes of sensing, they are connected: we can, generally, see what things will feel like ("that looks soft!"), even though the seeing of something fuzzy is not yet the feeling of softness. Similarly, having different meanings (in the linguistic mode of sensing the world) will often impact how we see things (for example, the different words for snow and ice in the Inuit language mentioned in the last chapter) or having the capacity for beauty (aestheticality) will impact how we see or hear things as beautiful or not (for example, as people's appreciation of jazz music enables them to hear what would otherwise be quite discordant notes as beautiful or compelling).[7] These examples show that the distinct modes of sensing open us onto the "same" material-spiritual world, and as such they never work alone.

This working together means that subjectivity is always immersed in multiple traditions at the same time. If every mode of sensing gives rise to traditions, and the various modes of sensing also work together in our experiencing, then our experiencing always participates in multiple traditions at the same time. Aestheticality gives rise to various aesthetic traditions; linguisticality gives rise to various linguistic traditions; sociality gives rise to various traditions of social mores; and so on. These traditions intersect in various cultures, which are simultaneously linguistic, aesthetic, social, and more. How one inhabits a particular tradition, therefore, is impacted by how one inhabits other traditions at least as much as how one inhabits a particular tradition impacts how one experiences a particular mode of sensing. If the artist sees differently than the geologist, it is also the case that the Chinese Shan Shui artist sees differently than the French Impressionist. Both articulate and experience their relation to art and to the world differently. The intersection of traditions alters both how we experience the world and how we experience each of the modes of sensing.

This intersection of traditions means that, although religious traditions arose (qua religious traditions) in response to religiosity, their (quasi-)transcendental effects are felt in all the transcendental modes of sensing, not just religiosity. Adherents of different religious traditions therefore religion differently—but they also see differently, speak differently, have different social mores, and so on. Hence, it is not simply the case that religious phenomena are always embedded in cultures that show different linguistic, social, and so on mores; more broadly, I am claiming that subjectivity functions differently in all the modes of sensing because of the impact of religiosity (and because of the impact of the other modes of sensing as well). This claim can be discussed abstractly or philosophically, at the level of how religiosity, as a mode of sensing, impacts visibility, tactility, and so on as modes of sensing. Furthermore, it can also be discussed in relation to particular concrete situations: how *this* religious tradition affects *this* community's abilities to see, to mean, to touch, and so on. When we do the latter, we are examining the quasi-transcendental effects and so are dealing with the religious community in this quasi-transcendental sense.

For example, we said in the last chapter that some Christian traditions experience religiosity as love: their immersion in Christianity opens them to love the world in a way that, they claim, would not be possible without that immersion. This is different, we said, from how Buddhist or Hindu traditions might experience religiosity. We can now see that how this love is articulated and experienced will also be different for various Christian (sub-)traditions. If traditions are always intersecting, then Christian traditions in different times and places will always be impacted by the other traditions that their adherents are immersed in: Christian love in a majority Christian culture in thirteenth-century Normandy might look very different from Christian love in a minority Christian culture in twenty-first-century Mali and from Christian love in a post-Christian culture in twenty-first-century Canada.

As such, the idea of a "Christian Tradition" seems to break down, at least if we want to identify a tradition by a stable and unchanging type of content. But that is not what I am seeking to do here; rather, I am using the term "tradition" as a translation of the phenomenological notion of *Stiftung*, to trace a style or way of experiencing the world, a style that is generative and hence always changing. But that it is changing does not mean that it ceases to remain itself, any more than I cease to be myself since I am much different now than I was as a 5-year-old child. Thinking religious traditions in this phenomenological and quasi-transcendental way allows us to trace a thread of tradition through these differences, precisely by tracing one (historical) thread through various knots and tangles with other threads. We find these individual threads always already woven together into various tapestries and fabrics that we analytically try to unravel into their constituent parts. Such analyses are always the product of acts of abstraction and reflection, and we must be cognizant of the ways that the individual threads themselves are altered by our pulling them out of their various weaves. We cannot assume that religiosity (for example) is simply the "same thing" in the various religious traditions that (seem to) express it, or that a religious tradition is unified and monolithic across its various historical, geographical, racial, and cultural differentiations. Nor should we assume that talk of religiosity is always and only a creation of the scholarly imagination. Rather, religiosity is expressed differently in various religious traditions, which themselves are expressed differently in different empirical circumstances and in connection with different expressions of other transcendental modes of sensing the world.

This complex interweaving of religiosity and religious traditions makes it difficult to trace out religiosity or a particular religious tradition from its various concrete expressions. Difficult, I would argue, but neither impossible nor undesirable. It is possible to do this insofar as a religious tradition contributes something different to the intersection of traditions than do other types of tradition, and this difference can be articulated and paid attention to, even if the difference it makes is not the same difference in every situation. What Christianity contributes to thirteenth-century Normandy, for example, might be very different from what it contributes to twenty-first-century Mali, but it is contributing something in each case. What it contributes is itself quite varied: it has political implications, but also social, ethical, linguistic, and aesthetic implications (to name a few). Those implications themselves can be understood empirically (*what* new political concepts emerge, because of Christianity? What ethical injunctions arise?), but also quasi-transcendentally (*how* does subjectivity function differently, because of the role of Christianity as a *Stiftung*?) and transcendentally (*how* do linguisticality and sociality function differently, because of religiosity?). That there are so many implications of so many different types creates a lot of ways of tracing religious influence. My argument here is simply that we can and that we should include also the variety of quasi-transcendental effects in our analyses of religious influence.

If it is therefore possible to trace the thread of a religious tradition through its various alterations, it is also desirable to do so because religious traditions do appear to have an effect, even if those effects are varied both between traditions and within traditions. One might wonder why, if the effects are so varied, there is any need to speak of, for example, a "Christian" tradition at all (quasi-transcendentally, at least)—why not simply speak of the effects of particular sub-traditions, or even the effect simply of individual subjects? While we might see value in speaking of Christianity or Buddhism as differing accounts of religiosity (which might be relatively stable), the more local and concrete one gets, the more we see variety instead of sameness. Why bother referring to the effects of "Christian love" in thirteenth-century Normandy and twenty-first-century Mali when what is meant by that term is, perhaps, very different in each instance? This is a fair question, one that faces anyone working intersectionally: why speak of "Black" experience when what it is to be Black is so different in different times and places? Why speak of "male" experience when that is so different for heterosexual, cis-gendered males in sub-Saharan Africa than it is for gay, trans-gendered males in South Beach? Obviously we do not want to ignore the differences in any of those cases—but there seems to be something worth hanging on to in the general sentiments (Christian, Black, male) for reasons of both continuity (i.e., to trace a historical line from thirteenth-century Christianity to twenty-first-century Christianity) and experiential accuracy (i.e., "Christian," "Black," or "male," all may be important self-descriptors for individuals or communities in the various locales). Even if each means something different by it, both the cis-gendered and the trans-gendered male identify in some important way as "male." Our understanding of masculinity is richer when we trace it through its permutations, and do not simply let one (current or historical) definition define what it is to be male for all times and all places.

So, too, there is value in our understanding of religiosity and of the various religious traditions by tracing them through their various permutations and not allowing one to simply define the term for all others. This value holds for our understanding of religiosity, of the various religious traditions, and for our understanding of unique, empirical situations: the "Christian" flavor of our concepts, for example, may prove significant, even when we want to sever them from their "Christian" tradition, as we know from post-colonial critiques of religion as a concept.[8]

Secularism: A Case Study in Religious Tradition

To see why this is the case, it will be helpful to look at the role of secularism in our current understanding of religion. This will do two things: first, it will provide a concrete example or case study of how a religious (sub-)tradition maintains important connections to its historical tradition, even when it wants to sever those connections, thereby helping us see the import of tracking a tradition through its various permutations. And second, it will begin to bring to light some of the assumptions shaping the current academic study of religion, thereby setting the stage for arguments I will pursue in more detail next chapter.

My claim in this section is twofold: first, that our current understanding of religion in the Western academy is largely dominated by secularist assumptions; and second, that those secularist assumptions emerge from a particular religious tradition and continue to bear the marks of that tradition. As such, secular understandings of religion constitute one understanding of religion from within one particular religious tradition. They are, therefore, religious phenomena, a fact that has been lost on some scholars of religion who fail to adequately account for secularism as a religious tradition. Secularism should be part of our collective understanding of religion, but I see no compelling reason why it should get to dominate that conversation, especially in terms of the cross-cultural study of religion.

Neither of the claims in the previous paragraph are particularly new. Talal Asad has argued both that our current understanding of religion is largely dominated by a particular assumption that is "part of a strategy (for secular liberals) of confinement [...] of religion"[9] and that that assumption grows out of "a particular history of knowledge and power" that he articulates via a "brief sketch of transmutations of Christianity from the Middle Ages to today."[10] This suggestion that secularism arose out of a broadly Christian tradition is argued for at considerable length also in Charles Taylor's *A Secular Age*.[11] The connection between secularism and Christianity is not just a historical accident: there is something essentially Christian and kenotic about secularism's assumptions, as Gianni Vattimo has argued.[12] The "rejection" of the supernatural at work in secularism is the product of particular conceptions of God/religion that are being rejected[13] and particular intersections of the Christian religious tradition with other traditions that have enabled this rejection.[14] For this reason, we can see secularism precisely as a religious (sub-)tradition that emerges in the unfolding of the religious tradition of Christianity: it is not simply that secularism emerges in a society that had at one point been Christian, but that the quasi-transcendental effects of Christianity upon subjectivity in Western cultures were a necessary element of the emergence of secularism. Without using this phenomenological language, Asad, for example, shows that mutations of Christianity caused by its coming into contact with both Enlightenment rationalist philosophy and other cultures and religions enabled subjects to experience religion primarily in terms of individual belief and positive emotional affects, particularly in light of pain and suffering.[15] This, in turn, allowed religion to be individualized and privatized, something individuals could do if they chose to, but which had no shared, communal impact. The ability to think religion as Secularism would, therefore, not exist as we know it, except as an outgrowth of Christianity in its quasi-transcendental function as a religious tradition.

This is not to reduce secularism merely to beliefs (or not) about God. That would be to treat secularism as a religious tradition in the merely empirical sense, pertaining to particular phenomena (in this case, beliefs about super-empirical entities). We are trying to show, rather, that secularism is a religious tradition in the quasi-transcendental sense of shaping how subjects experience the world in ways that are importantly connected to religiosity. However, as mentioned last section, that a tradition is importantly shaped by religiosity does not mean it is only shaped by religiosity or religious experiences. Quite the opposite: we have been trying to make clear that religious traditions always function at the intersection of various other traditions (social, linguistic, etc.) and that they precisely do *function* there, which is to say, they do something significant that cannot be explained away without missing something important in the emergence of phenomena. That was the main point of our turn to secularism: to show that something important is missing from our understanding of secularism if we do not understand it as growing out of the Christian religious tradition. This is simply to point out that religiosity, as one mode of sensing the world, is caught up and implicated in various experiences, and therefore religious traditions exercise quasi-transcendental effects on subjectivity that must be accounted for if we are to understand experience in general. All of cultural life is not reducible to religion—but there may be a religious dimension to all of cultural life.

Of course, what we mean by "religious" in that statement cannot be reduced to some "transhistorical and transcultural phenomenon"[16] or essence. If religiosity always works alongside other modes of sensing and religious traditions always work at the intersection with other types of quasi-transcendental conditions, then religion always operates within the historical and cultural unfolding of human activity. To use phenomenological language here, we can say that religion is always part of experience: it is always caught up in the interplay between subjectivity (which, remember, cannot be reduced simply to individual subjects but also has supra-individual effects) and world.

Affirming this religious interplay between subjectivity and the world is, I would argue, not necessarily to reject transcendence as such. It is merely to reject a particular form of transcendence, one that, it is worth noting, seems to be inherently secular in nature. The search for transhistorical and transcultural phenomena is a mark of secularism, and not simply of Christianity or Abrahamic monotheisms (although, as argued above, secularism is itself an outgrowth of Christianity, and so there is a connection to a certain "style" or sub-tradition of Christianity at play here). Returning to our earlier claims about the individual and privatized account of religion that emerged in post-Enlightenment Christianity, we can now understand how those connect directly to secularism, in Taylor's famous explanation of secularism in terms of a disenchanted world and a buffered self.[17] A disenchanted world is one in which non-empirical forces (which is to say forces that are neither psychological nor physical) cannot have any causal power. A buffered self is one that has drawn a sharp line between self and other, such that what is "in" me (usually understood in psychological terms) is radically distinct from what is "outside" of me (usually understood in physical terms). Hence, in the disenchanted secular age, there can be nothing beyond myself that can make me do something "from within": gravity and other physical forces may work externally on my body, but there can be no spirit or demon that could possess me and make me think or want something. The individualized and privatized "faith" of post-Enlightenment Christianity has morphed into a disenchanted world and a buffered self—neither of which would have been imaginable to earlier forms of Christianity, to say nothing of their inexplicability to other religious traditions.

Yet secularism did not break entirely with Christianity, either. Its Christian roots left it unable to reject such non-empirical forces *in toto*. Instead, such forces were weakened (to use Vattimo's terminology) and denuded of (almost all) efficacy. If there are such super-empirical things, secularism holds, they cannot act within subjects (because we have buffered ourselves, making a strong distinction between self and others), nor can they act causally in the world (because the world is disenchanted, not home to such things). They cannot, we could say, act within subjectivity nor in and upon empirical phenomena. All that is left for them, then, is to "exist" (if they do at all) somewhere beyond the world. As such existence can neither be experienced empirically nor traced by its causal effects (because it cannot have any), that existence cannot be experienced directly. It can only be inferred: we can think *about* such things, take them as the object of our thoughts by a mode of non-evidentiary belief that will come to be characterized by the word "faith." This is, as Asad points out, "the only legitimate space allowed to Christianity by post-Enlightenment society, the right to individual belief."[18] Precisely because these super-empirical things can have no actual force in the world, secular politics is committed to letting people hold whatever religious beliefs they want "in private," precisely and only as long as those beliefs make no impact upon the shared public world. Again, such a claim—that one's religious conviction would have no impact upon the world or upon our shared life together—would have been scarcely imaginable to earlier forms of Christianity or to other religious traditions.

Hence, a new way of understanding transcendence is opened up by this secularist development of Christianity: the transcendent is that which exists wholly and entirely beyond the world of experience. Insofar as the inner working of the subject was also thought to be radically separate (i.e., buffered) from the world, this made the beliefs of the subject the perfect (perhaps only) place to encounter these super-empirical entities, whose transcendence came to be marked by that same kind of radical buffering: it's not just that these entities may have exceeded the world in some fashion (while still operating within and being functional upon that world), but they are understood as existing entirely outside or beyond the world of experience. They were "somewhere else"—and this somewhere else was understood precisely to include the assumption that they were not "here." This mark of the transcendent or supernatural as having no efficacy on the world of experience and as not operating within the world would, again, have been quite foreign to both earlier modes of Christian functioning and to other religious traditions. This is a distinctly secular development of the Christian religious tradition.

Of course, if one rejects the sharp distinction between self and world (as non-secularists largely do, and as phenomenology clearly does, and as Asad seems to urge us to do), then it becomes difficult to make sense of the claim that something could be thought about without having an impact on the world. Only a buffered subject could believe that its own acts of thinking or believing were anything other than activities that take place within, and therefore have effects upon, the material-spiritual nature of the world as experienced. As such, the notion of "private" religious beliefs that would have no impact on "public" affairs is shown to be an inherently secular-Christian formulation: it presumes a disenchanted world and a buffered self. But so too is the broader search for "transhistorical and transcultural" essences or phenomena, at least where that "trans-" is understood as transcending in the particular, secularist sense outlined above: if one searches for something that is unchanged and unaffected by history and culture, one seems to be pursuing a secularist project. Hence, the search for super-empirical realities, in the secularist sense of transcendent realities, can be an essential definition of religion only as religiosity functions within the secularist religious tradition. It is, therefore, not a transhistorical or transcultural definition of religion at all, but a very historically, culturally, and religiously determined one: a secularist one, produced in western culture in the periods roughly between the eighteenth and twenty-first centuries.

Thinking Religion Today within a Religious Tradition

The implications of this claim for our understanding of religious phenomena will be explored in the next chapter. For now, let us stay focused on the relation between religiosity and religious traditions. It should be noted in that regard that, for Asad, this attempt at a universal definition of religion is not problematic merely because it is secular. What makes it problematic is that it seeks the impossible: a "transhistorical and transcultural" definition of something that, in both its details and its emergence, is itself rooted in a particular history and culture. That is, the problem is not that it is secular, but that it pretends to be something other than the product of its particular (secular-Christian) religious tradition. Specifically, in pretending to offer transhistorical and transcultural accounts of religion, secularism loses its own sense as a religious tradition that thereby has quasi-transcendental effects on subjectivity and on phenomena. Instead, it purports to offer understandings of religion that get beyond any religious tradition, treating religion only, as it were, from "the outside," transcendent (in the strong, secularist sense) of any particular culture or tradition. Once re-contextualized as a historical and cultural definition of religion, secularism's understanding of religion should be able to play a role in our understanding of religion and religious function: it is how religion functions in one particular (i.e., the secularist) religious tradition, where it seems to have produced a series of effects that are now crucial to the contemporary Western understanding of religion.

Unfortunately, this secular approach to religion seems to have an oversized role in contemporary academic understandings of religion, at least in the West. This oversized role is not simply found in the fact that many still hold that belief in transcendence in the secular sense is an essential mark of religion. The empirical study of religion, at least, has largely moved beyond an obsession with cognitive claims: religion is not understood as pertaining simply to what we believe, but is now clearly understood to be about what we do (rituals, practices), the things we interact with (the "material turn"[19]), and the effects they have on us and the world (the "affective turn"[20]). Of course, these are not mutually exclusive: religious people have beliefs about their practices, the objects they interact with, and the effects all of those phenomena have on themselves and on the world. It is also true that believing and being-affected are practices we do, and that beliefs are, therefore, objects (or at least phenomena) we interact with. All of this complicates the equation of religion with beliefs about secularly transcendent realities, and much of this complication is now commonplace in the empirical study of religion.[21]

Where secularist assumptions still seem to function unacknowledged is in the assumption that religion can (and should) be isolated as an object of study, without also recognizing the role it plays in our experiencing, including our experiencing of religion. That is, it is secularist to think that religion can only be a *what* that we study, and never part of *how* we study.[22] To equate secularist assumptions only with cognitive claims or beliefs is to forget that, qua religious tradition, secularism has had quasi-transcendental effects on subjectivity, and therefore on our experiencing of the world, including on our experiencing of religion.

Michel Henry has outlined some of these impacts on experiencing in his book *Barbarism*. There, he outlines how a "spirit" of barbarism[23] impacts how experience itself unfolds in those cultures where the spirit of barbarism reigns. This barbaristic spirit is characterized by the "abstraction of Life"[24] (which is Henry's account of the ultra-transcendental conditions of experiencing itself), which manifests itself in a kind of wilful forgetting of subjectivity.[25] This forgetting or isolating of subjectivity from the world has close connections to the buffered self and the disenchanted world of secularism: we deny the possibility of Life (and of spirits) in our disenchantment, and therefore leave subjectivity isolated from the world in a massive buffering of the self.

Henry's account of barbarism, therefore, gives us an account of how secularism impacts our entire ability to experience the world, including in "art, ethics, or religion"[26] but also in "cultures of food, shelter, work, erotic relations or relations to the dead."[27] A few especially important effects for our understanding of religion that Henry outlines are, first, the implicit assumptions about what knowledge looks like: in barbarism, knowledge is tied inherently to objectivity, understood as radically distinguished from subjectivity. This account of knowledge reaches a kind of cultural zenith in scientific practice, where individual researchers are called to diminish their subjectivity as much as possible, treating knowledge instead primarily in terms of data, information, statistics and demographics, but neglecting how things actually impact real, living people.

Some of the effects of this barbaristic spirit may be diminishing since Henry first published *Barbarism* in 1987, as evidenced by the fact that there are now some methodological approaches in the social sciences that are working to pay more attention to the lives of real living people. However, the vast majority of these methodologies—including, it appears, in the study of religion—still seem to account only for the real, living nature of people as the *object* of scientific inquiry, largely neglecting the real, living nature of the people carrying out scientific inquiry. And in the rare cases when the living nature of researchers is acknowledged, it is often accounted for by identifying and acknowledging biases in the researchers that are usually then characterized as "skewing" their analysis, thereby implicitly leaving the "disinterested spectator" as the ideal researcher. That is to say, although many movements in twentieth-century Western thought have outlined the impossibility of such a "disinterested" approach (perhaps none more effectively in the social sciences than those inspired by Foucault), we have generally been slow to affirm in its place an "interested" approach. Personal biases are still largely viewed within the lens of suspicion[28] ("special interests"); even when they are not, there is little attempt to offer a methodology that thinks through the subjectivity of researchers and includes it as part of the inquiry.

This problem is then further exacerbated by the increasing barbarism of the university as the major site of scientific inquiry. Today, universities in the West are overwhelmingly secular in their religious orientation. Yet the forgetting of Life endemic to barbarism means that universities (or subjectivities working within the university ecosystem) have largely forgotten their own religious orientation as secular. As a result, universities (and, increasingly, the researchers working in university environments) have ceased to see their practices and outcomes as the result of religious functioning taking place within one particular religious tradition (namely, the secular). This is nowhere more noticeable than in the predominance of "philosophy of religion" courses at Western universities that deal almost exclusively with secular-Christian concerns and questions, such as the reasonableness of belief in a transcendent God, or how a transcendent being's knowledge of our actions impacts our free will.

While decolonial and other forms of critique have been working to decentre those approaches, with varying levels of success, there is one area where the secular religious assumptions of the university seem to exert an undue influence on the contemporary study of religion that we should note for our purposes in this chapter: the assumption that religion is a thing (or set of things) that can be analyzed and studied. The sense that religion might also function transcendentally in how we experience (including in how we experience our practices of knowledge-formation) seems, to me, to be largely missing from the contemporary study of religion.

One manifestation of this secular assumption is in the largely implicit presumption of religious neutrality. In studying religion, we do not presume the truth or falsity of any particular religion but study it more or less "objectively": religion is the object, the "what" that we study; it is never (and should not be) the "how" of our studying. In critiquing this I do not mean that we should go back to identifying religions as, for example, either "true" or "false," "genuine" or "pagan," and so on based on how well they meet the demands placed upon religion by the researcher's particular religious tradition. Quite the opposite: I want us to continue to move beyond that colonial approach, even in those cases where secularism is the religious tradition from which researchers operate.[29] This means, I think, acknowledging that when we study religion, we do so always from within particular traditions (including at least one particular religious tradition), and that doing so impacts how we study religion. This impact is not exclusively cognitive, although it would certainly influence what we believe. Its impact would also be felt in what we do and do not find compelling in the way of evidence, in what affective force certain phenomena exercise on us, pulling us to study them rather than something else, and a myriad of other ways. In that sense, the lens of suspicion through which we view personal biases has to be lifted: we all think, speak, engage phenomena, and so on from particular traditions that shape our experiencing in profound ways. This cannot be avoided—and so it must be addressed.

My point is simply that our study of religion is itself an activity carried out within (a) particular religious tradition(s). It is, therefore, a practice (perhaps even a ritual) that is shaped in part by religious effects, even if we do not yet want to characterize it fully as a "religious practice" (a point we will return to next chapter). As such, the outcomes of our study of religion are phenomena shaped in part by religious effects that we may or may not therefore wish to characterize as religious phenomena. These phenomena, in turn, become part of the (religious) tradition that we are immersed in, shaping its future development in certain ways. Scholars of religion are, therefore, always implicated in the "object" they are studying. We never merely "observe" or "study" religion—we are always generating religious phenomena from within religious traditions.

Something similar to this has been noted by various critics of the "transcendent" definition of religion. Fitzgerald, for example, notes the Christian (in his words: "theological") nature of many uses of the term religion.[30] This, he shows, leads those researchers starting from within that tradition (that is, those using that definition of religion) to change the course of other "religious" traditions precisely by trying to have them account for this foreign understanding of religion.[31] In that sense, their study of Buddhism (for example) is not neutral, but ends up changing the nature of Buddhism and other similar non-Western religions. All this seems to confirm the non-neutrality of our religious engagements: we never merely study religion, but we are always altering religious traditions in and by our study of them. Yet, for all that, Fitzgerald's own understanding of religion, as that which "ought to dissolve without remainder into ideology or culture understood as institutionalized values and symbolic systems,"[32] is never itself acknowledged to be the product of a particular (religious) tradition that also has effects on that tradition in and through his uses of it. Some kind of "religious neutrality" seems to be functioning as an implicit assumption, precisely so that he can level his critique of the non-neutrality and impact of the "theological" understanding of religion.

I do not here wish simply to capitulate to the colonial understandings or uses of religion. Quite the contrary: acknowledging the non-neutrality of our own thinking about religion—acknowledging, that is, that we always think of religion from within some religious tradition or other—allows us to consider explicitly both some cautions and some responsibilities in relations to religious traditions. The cautions arise from the fact that we need to be attuned to how our immersion within a particular tradition might be impacting our work. Seeking to define religion by looking at what we already consider religion and trying to abstract from that what it is that makes things "religious" involves a kind of circularity that can, at best, give us an account of what one particular religious tradition means by "religion." To use that as a standard or measure of anything other than the assumptions of that tradition would be to take one tradition for the (correct) tradition, and all other traditions as "primitive" ("they only think that because they don't know what we know") or "pagan" ("they think that because they are actively working at purposes I consider evil"). Although this might seem obvious to any contemporary scholar of religion, it is not: think, for example, of the many scholars who reject out of hand any account of religion that could find religious significance in things like a mall, sporting event, or Christmas cake. This rejection, as mentioned previously, often happens under the rubric of "well, if everything is religious then nothing is." But this is just to repeat the (secularist) assumption that religion should denote a thing (or set of things) that can be isolated and set apart from other parts of our experiential life.[33]

Both claims—that religion should denote things (or sets of things) and that religion should be isolatable from other parts of our experiential life—can be and are denied by adherents of other religious traditions. Daosim, for example, would consider the way of the Dao to be something that impacts all of life. So, too, would certain Hindu engagements with *brahman*. Neither the Dao nor *brahman* are best understood as things or even as isolatable concepts or doctrines. There is to them not only a fluidity, but a living component that strikes many of their adherents as entailing precisely that all of life *is* religious, that is, that life is infused with *brahman* or follows the Dao. For some scholars, this inability to distinguish life from some non-religious component within it is sufficient reason to reject Daoism or Hinduism as "religions." My point here is not that those scholars are *wrong* to say that, but that they are *secular*: they are operating from a certain set of religious assumptions that lead them to produce certain accounts of the nature of religion that must be understood as marked inherently by those secular religious assumptions. So, too, are the hypothetical

Daoists and Hindus in our example. Everyone talking about religion is utilizing religious(ly inflected) phenomena (such as concepts and doctrines) generated within religious traditions (like Daoism or secularism) according to religious(ly inflected) rituals (like rituals of knowledge production). To forget this fact is to lapse into some type of colonialist project, where the standards of my tradition are taken as the standards of humanity itself and therefore normatively applied to others.

The use of brackets around the (ly inflected) in the previous paragraph gives us one further caution: that something is inflected or impacted by a religious tradition is not yet sufficient to characterize that thing as a "religious" phenomenon. That a person's experience of the mall, for example, is affected by their immersion in a religious tradition is not yet sufficient to claim that the mall is therefore a religious site or that a person's experience of it is a "religious experience." This is because practices, phenomena, and subjectivity are never located within only one type of tradition. Traditions operate intersectionally, as discussed earlier, and therefore phenomena (religious or not) are always the product of multiple types of traditions. I keep emphasizing this point precisely because I want to be clear that religion—when understood as a phenomenon or set of phenomena—need not be isolated from some other distinct set of phenomena called the "non-religious" in order to be understood as religious. Both of those assumptions—that religion should be understood primarily in terms of phenomena that can be the object or content of our experience and that religion so construed must be easily separable from other, non-religious phenomena—are rooted in the particular religious sub-tradition we call secularism.

What I am suggesting instead is that religion could also be understood in ways that do not align with those secularist assumptions, and that doing so is not religiously problematic simply because it does not fit with the assumptions of one religious tradition (i.e., secularism). Overall in this book, I am trying to argue that religion could be understood transcendentally, as how we experience rather than simply as the contents of what we experience. And what is beginning to emerge in this chapter, and what will be the focus of much of that next chapter, is that thinking religion in this transcendental way might show us that religion (or at least religious effects) might be a facet or dimension of all of our experiencing and hence of our experiences of all phenomena. Qua transcendental mode of sensing the world, for example, religiosity engages us with the world in a distinct way that must be accounted for, even as this distinct engagement is itself always engaged with other modes of sensing the world, and hence is not easily separable from them in our understanding of any particular phenomenon. Similarly, religious traditions have quasi-transcendental effects that have a real impact on how subjectivity is able to experience the world, even as they yield their quasi-transcendental effects always only alongside other types of traditions. To think that this intertwining of religious with other types of effects means either that what we are talking about is not religious or that there is no such thing as "religion" is to give in to secularist assumptions about the nature of religion (as being about things and as being separable from some non-religious component of life). I want to be clear that I am not saying people should not do that. That is something people are free to do—I only want to make clear that this is not something people *need* to do in order to be taken seriously as religious thinkers.

Engaging Religious Traditions Responsibly

Before we move on to examine in greater detail this question of how (and why) we might want to distinguish "religious phenomena" from "phenomena that are religiously inflected," we must first examine our responsibilities as religious thinkers. I have argued in this chapter that anyone thinking about or studying religion necessarily does so with religious(ly inflected) phenomena developed within religious traditions and is therefore operating from within a religious tradition. This, I said, leads to certain cautions and to certain responsibilities. I have laid out the cautions, but what are the responsibilities?

If, indeed, we are all operating within religious traditions, drawing on and producing religious(ly inflected) phenomena that will shape the future of the religious traditions we operate within, then it seems that we are all shapers of those religious traditions. Our work—as scholars and as practitioners—is never merely descriptive but is always transformative (even if only infinitesimally so[34]), and this precisely because the distinction between scholars and practitioners is ill-drawn at best, and downright false at worst. Insofar as I utilize phenomena from a particular religious tradition, I in some way enter into that tradition and so "practice" it, even if my use of those phenomena is based largely on assumptions or modes of experiencing shaped by other traditions and hence may be different than how others inhabiting the tradition may "practice" that tradition.

We have already seen an example of this alteration or transformation of a tradition by the work of scholars earlier, in relation to Fitzgerald's critique that Western scholars of religion have "Westernized" other religions simply by using the terms of those traditions in their scholarship on other religions. It is also true, as other scholars have pointed out, that Western scholars' and practitioners' fascination with Eastern religions has in some ways also "Easternized" the Western religions.[35] We could also point to the ways that secular scholars have changed the nature of Christianity, simply by the way they have developed and used Christian terminology. Indeed, the very creation of secularism as a religious sub-tradition within Christianity already alters the Christian tradition both additively (i.e., by adding more to the tradition than previously existed) and expressively (i.e., by altering the relations between the other relata within that tradition).[36]

Hence, work at the intersection of two or more religious traditions alters things within each of those traditions and potentially adds new sub-traditions, whose relations to the preceding traditions is, we have said, traceable even if it is difficult to do so. These alterations are likely minute, even infinitesimal; most practitioners of the tradition may never know or feel the impact of the change. They are alterations nonetheless. As such, those thinking about religion in relation to particular religious traditions (which, if my arguments earlier in this chapter are correct, is all people thinking about religion), have a responsibility to the religious traditions (and their adherents) that they engage with. Whatever the depth of our commitment or engagement with that tradition, we are making changes to it, changes that may impact others in those traditions, some of whom may have that tradition as a core part of their identity. Acknowledging that we are working within religious traditions, therefore, does not just impact our understanding, as scholars. It also calls us to be responsible to adherents of those traditions whose lives we are impacting with our work: what will we do to help ensure the alterations we make will be beneficial rather than detrimental?

The history of colonialism provides us ample examples of ways to make detrimental alterations to a tradition, from forced assimilation—an approach famously captured in the phrase "kill the Indian, save the man"[37]—to commodification (think, for example, of the deep irony of Che Guevara merchandise being for sale on Amazon). A key element of these detrimental alterations is that the "other" tradition is always seen only (or at least predominantly) in terms of what it can offer me or "my" tradition. If it has nothing "positive" to offer, it can be eradicated, so as to bring more people into my "superior" tradition. If it does have something to offer, then I can simply take from it what I need to further the needs and desires of my own tradition without seeing myself as joining that tradition and engaging with it from within (I doubt anyone selling Che swag thinks themselves a socialist). Either way, the focus remains on treating the other tradition I am encountering as something distinct from me and my original tradition, and something that makes no real call for change or alteration on me or on my tradition. Rather, I am interested only in how I can *use* that other tradition for my (or my tradition's) benefit. This seems a detrimental way to encounter, and therefore alter, another tradition.

If we can see that in the case of colonialism, I think we, as scholars of religion, are sometimes less willing to see it in the case of secularism. The very distance demanded by secularist study seems to reinforce the need to keep a distinction between the researcher's own (secular) tradition and the other religious tradition(s) that the researcher is studying. It becomes quite easy, in these circumstances, to see the other tradition simply for what it can offer me (publications; the chance to build a career) or my tradition (an increase in knowledge; further proof of the value of interiorizing religion). The solution here, it seems to me, is not to stop talking across traditions (I fail to see how that is a step forward), but rather to realize and recognize the necessity of a certain kind of moving into another tradition in order to talk about it. The nature of this "certain kind of moving into another tradition" may vary, depending on one's own tradition: it seems plausible that a committed secularist, for example, will want to keep themselves more removed from the tradition they are studying than others might. But there must be some recognition that I must enter into this other tradition in order to talk about it well.

And I would argue that this entering-into another tradition should not be construed simply in terms of utilizing some of its phenomena (doctrines, concepts, rituals, etc.). That seems to remain in the detrimental and colonialist approaches we characterized above. Rather, this entering-into must be phenomenological: I must acknowledge how my own subjectivity is being shaped by this tradition in a quasi-transcendental way. And once I realize that my own subjective capabilities are being altered, I can acknowledge that so, too, are the subjective capabilities of others within that tradition. We are being shaped, together, by this tradition and the alterations I am making to it by engaging it from or with another tradition. And we must then ask ourselves, not simply how we or our primary tradition somehow get something worthwhile out of the encounter with this other tradition, but also how this other tradition gets something worthwhile and beneficial out of our entering into and engaging with it.

Note that I did not ask this in terms of what we will do to avoid altering the tradition. Nor did I ask it in terms of what we will do to minimize the alterations we make to the tradition. The first option, I think, is not possible: in using phenomena and engaging a tradition, we necessarily alter it, however infinitesimally. The concept or doctrine we are interacting with now becomes "just a concept," something that could be used without conviction or with a different religious motivation or a differing set of assumptions. All of these create new possibilities that adherents of that tradition must engage with or ignore (which is a form of engagement: ignoring is itself an activity we undertake) or accept or fight against. Asad outlines clearly, for example, the changes made to the Christian tradition by its encounters with other traditions, as we noted earlier this chapter. Secularism, we saw, is one effect of those encounters, one that Taylor has shown to have had a profound impact on how people experience the world.

The second option—minimizing the alterations we make—is a potential approach one could take to this responsibility, but I am not sure it is the best one. If alteration is necessary, then it is not clear to me that our concern about those alterations should be primarily quantitative (how much am I changing things?) rather than qualitative or normative (should my alterations be beneficial or detrimental?). Thinking that our normative duty as scholars is to minimize alterations seems to hold only if we maintain some kind of secularist assumption about "distance" or "disinterest," that is, that we should be striving to have as little impact as possible. But is having a very minimal (although negative) impact really better than having a somewhat larger (although positive) impact? It is not obvious to me that it is. Alvin Plantinga, for example, argues that the task of philosophers working within the Christian religious tradition is to inhabit that tradition purposively, and to allow their philosophizing to address the issues and problems facing that tradition, to work for that tradition and not merely for themselves or for the sake of academic philosophy.[38] And Elaine Coburn argues that Indigenous research, rather than being neutral or seeking to have minimal impact, ought to understand itself as a form of resistance to colonial domination, changing in particular ways the experience of both Indigenous and colonizing traditions.[39]

There are dangers in thinking our scholarly responsibility in terms of benefits/detriments. A primary one is that we might put ourselves in the position of judging what is beneficial/harmful. That, too, seems a colonialist assumption: that I, as the Western scholar, must be in the best position to decide what is good or bad for any given tradition. I wonder, rather, whether those who are more deeply immersed in the tradition should have a greater say in what is harmful or beneficial than those who are less deeply engrained or immersed.[40] Someone for whom a particular concept or tradition is a new interest or a passing fancy seems less able to judge the relative health of their engagement with the tradition than someone for whom the tradition is central to their way of life or for whom the concept is a long-time companion.

Perhaps this means that someone should not talk about a particular tradition or concept without talking with people who self-identify as adherents of that tradition. Or perhaps that suggestion goes too far and is practically unrealistic. I'm not sure. My purpose here is not to lay out or definitively answer what an ethics of religious study should be. I simply want to recognize that the transcendental phenomenological approach I am offering here seems to suggest that engaging a tradition is a way of altering it,[41] and therefore some responsibility seems to open up to us, as religious thinkers, such that when we do invariably alter those traditions, we do so in ways that are more beneficial than harmful, whenever we can.

The positive spin to this is that it puts to bed the myth that religious scholarship, even in academic circles, is "useless." If the analysis in this chapter is correct, the world *is* changed by academic scholarship. We do make an impact—although often, perhaps, an infinitesimally small one, and not always a positive one, as our invocations of colonialism have made clear. And for those consciously and purposefully working within a tradition that they claim some adherence to, as Plantinga suggests scholars do, it is likely that the impact can be significant.[42] Which means, as mentioned above, that we have a responsibility to talk with those who live and practice within the traditions we engage with, and perhaps with those who self-identify strongly with the tradition. That is, it may not be enough to talk with other scholars of Buddhism if I want to write about Buddhism—I may also have to engage with practicing, self-identified Buddhists. I may have to enter into relationships with them, speak with them, and grapple with how my work may be impacting them. For if I work always within the traditions I engage, then I seem to have a responsibility to be a good co-member of that tradition, whatever that means and however we would determine that.

4

What Makes a Phenomenon Religious?

We saw in the last chapter that religiosity gives rise to religious traditions that have quasi-transcendental effects on subjectivity. In this sense, the religious mode of sensing the world produces both a distinct way of sensing the world and alterations in how we inhabit other modes of sensing the world. This is because traditions (*Stiftungen*, in the phenomenological sense) work intersectionally, shaping how subjects experience and engage the world via all the various modes of sensing. Phenomena, therefore, are always entangled with many of these traditions—including religious traditions.

If all phenomena are entangled with, and therefore at least partially expressive of, religious traditions, there is a temptation to consider all phenomena as "religious phenomena" insofar as they are phenomena that have a religious component to them. Doing so may prove problematic for the study of religion, as several scholars have suggested[1]—although, as we explored in the last chapter, this concern may be more rooted in the assumptions of a particular religious tradition (a secularized Christianity) than a problem for religion or religious studies as a whole. If we avoid thinking of religion as some thing (or set of things) distinct from other (sets of) things, we may find the claim that all phenomena are religious phenomena to be less problematic. Nevertheless, these assumptions likely color most of our commonsense assumptions about religion, at least in the West, because many scholars of religion in the West are also likely to be rooted in the religious tradition of secularized Christianity. So, at least in the secularized West, and possibly in other places, the claim that all phenomena are religious phenomena seems to be misleading, if not downright incorrect.

But what do we even mean by characterizing something as a "religious phenomenon?" In the context of the transcendental phenomenological approach to religion being outlined in this book, we can see that a phenomenon is religious if it evidences religious effects. But this, too, can be ambiguous: are religious effects a property of the thing or phenomenon in question or are they something in how experiencers experience the thing or phenomenon? Is it acts of subjectivity that give rise to these effects or something about the phenomena we encounter that do so? We could rephrase this question, in the language we are developing in this book, as a question about whether religiosity or religious phenomena are primarily responsible for religious traditions and their impacts on subjectivity. We will see that the material-spiritual nature of experience shows this question to be poorly formulated insofar as it sets up a false dichotomy. It is not one or the other, because both acts of subjectivity and phenomena are thoroughly enmeshed in material-spiritual circumstances that give rise to and influence each other: there is something in phenomena that cause people to engage with them in certain ways, and there is something in subjectivity that causes phenomena to appear or "give themselves"[2] the way that they do. In that sense, phenomena are a site that gives rise to quasi-transcendental effects on subjectivity, precisely because phenomena are themselves the products of subjective activities within particular traditions.

So if we consider as "religious phenomena" all those phenomena that give rise to quasi-transcendental religious effects, then it does indeed seem that all phenomena are religious phenomena. For if phenomena are always entangled with subjectivity and with various traditions, and if religious traditions are one type of tradition that is always entangled with the others (as established in the last chapter), then it seems that all phenomena are, in some way, touched by quasi-transcendental religious effects and are at least possible sites of religious experience, that is, for experiences of religiosity and experiences that are touched by religious traditions. While this may be true from a transcendental perspective—that is, while it may be true that religiosity in some way colors our experiencing of the world and of all phenomena—it seems nevertheless problematic or misleading from the perspective of the empirical study of religion. Misleading, because the phrase is ambiguous: do we mean that all phenomena can occasion a distinct type of experience that we can call "religious experience," or do we mean that there is a way in which religiosity and religious traditions play a role in all of our experiencing? Either way, the viability of the empirical study of religion seems to be troubled: if we mean the former, it seems difficult to figure out what unique things should be the object of our empirical study of religion, since all things are "religious phenomena." If, however, we mean the latter, then religion seems to be merely a matter of how we experience, something that is therefore understood via transcendental inquiries, rather than empirical ones, again calling into question what we would be doing in an *empirical* study of religion.

We will return to questions of religious experience in the next chapter. For now, let us stay with the issue of religious phenomena. For even if there is a religious element to all phenomena, we will see that there are reasons that we may still wish to distinguish certain phenomena as more purposefully or dominantly "religious," whereas others may be more purposefully or dominantly touched by some other mode of sensing. For this reason, we will see that, although all phenomena may have a religious dimension to them, this need not mean we consider all phenomena equally religious. As such, there may still be value, from an empirical perspective, in studying certain phenomena more than others in trying to understand religion. The point of considering also the transcendental questions concerning religion is not to replace the empirical study of religion with transcendental studies of the religious, but to let both of them shape a broader conception of religion and its various effects in our lives, as we will see in Chapter six.

The Provenance of Quasi-Transcendental Effects

We begin, then, by investigating where quasi-transcendental effects come from. If, as we said in the last chapter, there are religious effects on how people experience the world in a variety of sensings, what is the cause of those effects? Do religious effects arise primarily or exclusively in the subject, or are they found in the world?

This question, perhaps, echoes the famous debates on whether or not religion exists as a thing in the world.[3] I have already made clear that I do not think religion is best understood as a "thing" or a noun, but as a mode of experiencing the world. Whether religious effects are really *there* in the world as we experience it or whether they are simply the result of subjective activities remains significant to explore for our understanding of religion. At stake is whether the "material stakes" of religion (rituals, objects, etc.) are somehow essential to the religious effects that I am claiming alter subjectivity: does it matter whether a person prays in a church, meditates in an ashram, sits beneath a bodhi tree, or offers fruit on the family altar? Or is it simply subjective states that are at play in what I am calling religious effects, states that could be brought about under any number of circumstances? Are the empirical objects of religion in any way essential to the role and practice of religion as I am describing it in this book, or are they entirely accidental to religion and its effects?

Unfortunately, the question's formulation is conceptually unclear, in light of the transcendental phenomenological method we are using in this book. For the heart of that method, and the heart, therefore, of the approach to religion we are pursuing in this book, is the material-spiritual nature of experience. All experience, qua experience, is inherently material-spiritual in the sense outlined in chapter one: a relation that intertwines subjectivity, history, culture, and materiality in an inseparable bond. This means that the question of whether religious effects arise from subjectivity or from "the world" is poorly formulated, insofar as it creates a false dichotomy by excluding a third option: that those two things are intertwined in their shared emergence from material-spirituality, which itself is therefore the ultimate provenance of religious effects. Subjectivity names a particular mode of engaging the world, but it is always the world that subjectivity engages. An act of subjectivity is, therefore, always and inherently itself a material-spiritual act that occurs in the world. Believing, for example, is a material practice, as much as is reciting a liturgy, kneeling in prayer, or taking a pilgrimage. All of them involve subjective activity, not just in "the world" in general, but within a particular lifeworld that is marked by particular historical and cultural specificities.

Indeed, the question itself—is religion a matter of subjectivity *or* of things in the world?—can perhaps only be formulated under particular historical and social conditions, those we described in the last chapter as belonging to the religious tradition of secularized Christianity.[4] This is because some of the most important historical and cultural specificities shaping subjective activity in the world are the unique intersections of various types of traditions (*Stiftungen*) and sub-traditions, which themselves are among the very quasi-transcendental effects we are here considering. Those effects are both subjective (in that they affect how subjectivity operates: the painter sees differently than the geologist; the twenty-first-century Malian Christian loves differently than the fourteenth-century Norman one; the secular scholar "religions" [i.e., does or practices religion] differently than the Buddhist or Indigenous practitioner) and worldly. That worldliness is not simply the fact that subjectivity always comes to us in some tradition or other. It is also because those traditions themselves are shaped by their interaction with other traditions, interactions that happen in the lives of people in and through various phenomena, even as those phenomena exist in and through various traditions: the tradition of rattan chair-making is carried out and exists in both the activities of people making chairs and in the chairs that are made, even as the chairs themselves exist, not as "chairs" (in an abstract sense), but as rattan chairs, bearing the mark and style of a particular tradition or sub-tradition. Similarly, Impressionist painting, as a tradition, exists largely in and through the paintings that concretize it, just as those paintings exist in their actual, concrete form because of the "style" given them by the painters working within that particular tradition. A tradition is always expressed and embodied in and through phenomena in the world, and phenomena are always inherently expressive of the traditions that give rise to them. In that sense, a tradition (in the quasi-transcendental sense of *Stiftung*) just *is* the quasi-transcendental effects that phenomena have on subjectivity, effects that also shape the very material being of the phenomena.

Religious traditions therefore also find their existence in their material expressions, even as those material expressions find the particularities of their existence in the style of the religious tradition they express. So, the doctrines/concepts, buildings, rites, and tools of a particular religious tradition are how that tradition exists. This is the fact taken for granted by "comparative religion," which seeks to explain the various religious traditions precisely by explaining the various phenomena associated with each one: what its adherents believe, what types of practices they do with what regularity, what types of objects they use in their worship and in their day-to-day lives, what types of spaces they inhabit for what types of practices, and so on. But the reverse is also true: we explain the various phenomena precisely by explaining their association with the religious tradition of which they are a part. A church looks the way it does because it is inherently marked by the style of a particular sub-tradition of Christianity, just as a mosque expresses a particular Islamic tradition, a temple a particular Buddhist tradition, a shrine a particular Shinto tradition, or a synagogue a particular Jewish tradition. So, too, concepts and doctrines look the way they do because they are inherently marked by the style of particular (sub-)traditions, where those sub-traditions are shaped also by their intersections with other types of tradition: the Trinity is a uniquely Christian doctrine of God, but its Nicene formulation would not have been possible without the intersection with (at least) Greek philosophical thought and the Greek language. Its translation into Latin changed the understanding and was a partial cause of the split between the Roman Catholic sub-tradition of Christianity and the Orthodox sub-tradition of Christianity via the filioque controversy.

This is to say, then, that phenomena bear the style of the various traditions they are expressed within. Phenomena are how those traditions exist in concrete form. Phenomena are how those traditions live and continue through time. They are also, therefore, how those traditions are able to effect and impact subjectivity. Subjectivity is given a particular style within religious traditions by the phenomena that subjective experiencers encounter there: the concepts they are taught to believe, the practices they learn to perform, the objects they engage with. But, again, the reverse is also true: religious traditions are formed by the modes of subjectivity they encounter. Christianity as a tradition is altered, and new sub-traditions are formed, by the subjective activities of believing, desiring, worshipping, and more (as we saw in our discussion of secularism as a development of the Christian tradition in the last chapter). As those activities are altered by their contact with other traditions, not only are experiencers and their modes of subjectivity changed (i.e., individual people come to see differently, to believe differently, etc.), but so, too, are the traditions they inhabit changed (i.e., Christianity comes to have different beliefs, or to include different types of objects in its ritual practices). This, in part, is why analyses of religion that remain solely focused on beliefs and cognitive claims find it difficult to account for radical changes within a tradition. The difference between Sunni and Shiite Islam is not merely about beliefs regarding succession (although that is certainly an important part of the difference); rather, the differences encompass a whole range of social, political, linguistic, and historical factors that are almost impossible to pull apart nearly 1,400 years later. It is not simply a matter of *what* they believe, but also of *how* those differences in belief arose: why were some people motivated to believe in the caliphate, whereas others were motivated to believe only in direct familial succession? The differences in belief were not simply logical or rational; they were caused by the activities of subjectivities that had been altered in different ways by various different (social, economic, linguistic, etc.) traditions. The same could be said about differences that may seem, at first glance, to be more doctrinal, conceptual, or "theological": the Protestant Reformation was at least as much about politics, church governance, and economic mobility as it was about beliefs in the sufficiency of grace or Scripture. These were not simply four separate factors in the Reformation, but an intersectional nexus that gave rise to the Reformation precisely in how it shaped and altered all of those things.

To say this is not to deride the religious commitment of any of the people involved, nor to downplay the significance of the religious as one type of tradition influencing the phenomena involved. It is simply to acknowledge that religious commitments are performed subjectively (i.e., by experiencers exercising subjectivity), and as such are influenced by the various forces and traditions that shape subjectivity. To claim that religious traditions are only one of those forces is not to devalue the religious—it is to acknowledge it precisely as one force and one tradition (alongside others) that exercises quasi-transcendental effects on subjectivity, and therefore a force and a tradition that has real effects in and on the world. And therefore a force that, like the others, deserves to be analyzed both on its own terms and in relation to the others.

Religious traditions therefore change the world, both through how they change subjectivity and through their production of various phenomena. Those are not two distinct operations, even if we can distinguish them logically and phenomenologically. That is, part of the way that religious traditions change subjectivity is through the phenomena they produce, and part of the phenomena they produce are people who can access subjectivity in particular ways. Phenomena are, therefore, both the product of traditions and the means by which traditions have concrete existence. This is to say (to hearken back to the book's introduction) that the distinction between phenomena and traditions is a *phenomenological* distinction, not an ontological one: phenomena are not different things than traditions, but different ways of looking at our experience, our experiencing, and their various effects. The distinction between phenomena, traditions, and religiosity is a way for us to account for different kinds of effects in and on our experiencing. Both the effects and the causes remain fundamentally material-spiritual, and therefore deeply intertwined with subjectivity, materiality, culture, history, and more.

The Religious Dimension of all Phenomena

Given our preceding arguments, then, we are now better positioned to understand our earlier claim that the "religious" marks a dimension of experiencing (it is part of *how* we experience) more than a distinct realm of objects to be experienced (i.e., a distinct *what* that we experience). My suggestion in this chapter (and in this book more broadly) is that we think of the empirical, material objects of religion primarily as phenomena that are in some significant way tied up with religious effects (transcendental and quasi-transcendental).

To begin to see what it means to think of material things as phenomena rather than as objects, let us remind ourselves of the difference between them. A phenomenon, we said earlier, is always entangled in history, in culture, in subjectivity. To think of religious artifacts such as doctrines, concepts, rituals, buildings, and so on as phenomena rather than as objects is to acknowledge their embeddedness in, and the impact of, material-spirituality. It is to acknowledge that such things are not simply physically extended things (objects), but material-spiritually embedded phenomena whose material existence is always already tied up with history, with culture, with traditions, and with subjective activity.

To speak of religious effects, then, is to speak of the types of effects at work in our experiencing of phenomena. This is not to say that religiousness is simply a function of how particular subjects interpret the phenomena or is simply the product of individual whims; as we saw in the preceding section, phenomena are inherently caught up in and influenced by religious traditions that mark their very concrete, material existence. These effects are, therefore, inscribed into the materiality of phenomena, a materiality that is not simply physical extension, but also historical and cultural situatedness. That is to say, phenomena are what they are, at least in part, because of the religious effects upon them. Think, for example, of the cross, a major symbol of the Christian tradition. Prior to the crucifixion of Jesus of Nazareth, the cross was a symbol of Roman imperial domination and political power and/or a symbol of weakness, suffering, and death. In either case, it would have been no more imaginable to wear a gold cross around one's neck than it is now imaginable that someone would wear an electric chair or a guillotine around one's neck. As such, there would have been much fewer crosses in existence had the cross not become wrapped up in significant ways with religious effects, and the nature of those crosses would have been very different: simple, effective tools of execution, but not stylized, made of soft metals, jewels, or other ornate materials, and not worn as personal identity markers. Even now, the symbolism and the appearance of crosses varies across several distinct sub-traditions of Christianity: Celtic, Latin, Maltese, Basque, and Novgorodsky are but a few of the different aesthetic styles of crosses tied to particular regions or areas, each with their own history and tradition (including, via the Maltese cross and the historical connection between Malta and the Order of St. John, the connection to health care as evidenced in the Red Cross). Symbolically, the weight or power of the cross has significantly different meanings across white and black traditions of Christianity in North America, leading to very different emphases, not just in their theology, but in how they inhabit political traditions, social traditions, and more, to use an example highlighted by James Cone.[5]

This way in which phenomena are necessarily caught up in, and marked by, religious effects enables us to refer to a religious dimension to phenomena. Because all phenomena are at least possibly marked by such religious effects, all phenomena can at least possibly be considered as having this religious dimension. This follows from our earlier analyses: our experience is marked by the interaction between all the different modes of sensing the world to which we have access; that interaction occurs, in part, as the intersection of various types of traditions that play a role in and for our experience of particular phenomena. In that sense, our experience of phenomena occurs *as* the intersection of various traditions of experiencing, one of which is a religious tradition of experiencing.

Therefore, one main category of religious effects is the way that religious traditions act upon phenomena. These religious traditions can have an impact on phenomena even when an individual does not themselves have subjective access to the religious mode of sensing the world. By "subjective access" I mean that a person is able to access a particular mode of sensing via their own subjectivity. This is not the only way to participate in a particular mode of sensing. For example, a person who is blind from birth does not access visibility via their own subjectivity (i.e., they do not see), and in that sense they do not participate in visibility as a subject. However, they are still able to be seen by others who can access visibility in their subjectivity, and in that sense the blind person participates in visibility as an "object," so to speak: although they cannot see, they can be seen, and therefore they still participate in visibility.

There seem to be people who do not have subjective access in this way to religiosity, people who are unable to "religion" in the verbal sense. Although it may seem like the experiences of such people would not have a religious component to them, there are a few ways in which their experiences might still have a religious component. The first, as just mentioned, is that others may experience them as an "object" of religiosity somehow (as a "gift from God," for example, or the object of charity [in Christianity] or of *sadaqah* [in Islam]). A second way, which pertains more directly to our current conversation about religious traditions and their effects on phenomena, is if the experience has itself been marked by religious traditions in ways that those who cannot participate subjectively in religiosity may not be able to fully experience subjectively, although they may be able to acknowledge: although a person who is not subjectively able to access religiosity may experience a church simply as a beautiful building like a museum or a castle, the church itself is shaped, in its material existence, by its immersion in the Christian tradition, as we said earlier. Their inability to subjectively experience the religious dimension does not undermine its presence there, any more than a blind person's inability to see undermines the presence of color or of different aesthetic styles. In that sense, the religious component of a phenomenon is not wholly dependent on the subjective capabilities of the individual.

But a church is an obviously religious example. Let us test the impact of religious traditions on a phenomenon in which the religious dimension of the experience seems to be entirely lacking. The turn indicator on a car, for example, does not seem to be an example of a particularly religious way of sensing the world (an example of love or of *maya*, for example). Its development does not, as far as I know, emerge from any type of inherently religious tradition (unlike a church). It seems to serve no religious function at all, at least not inherently so. Although it remains possible that someone could experience the turn indicator religiously (as a prompt to rhythmic yogic breathing, perhaps, or as a supernatural sign for something), it is likely that, most of the time, it is not experienced as a religious phenomenon. And yet, even here there remains a significant connection to a religious tradition. Because the radical disjunction between religion(s) and a "non-religious" sphere is itself the product of a particular religious tradition (that of secularized Christianity, as discussed in the last chapter), the fact that no purposeful religious attention was paid to the creation, production, or use of the turn indicator *might* itself be suggestive that its emergence in the West during the time of secularism *could* be, in some way, influenced by a religious tradition. Similarly, that people *could* interpret it as having religious significance or could utilize it for religious motivations (as a way to "love our neighbor," perhaps) might be suggestive of at least a *possible* latent religiosity at work in the phenomenon of the turn indicator.

It is therefore possible, logically speaking, and perhaps even likely, phenomenologically speaking, that every phenomenon has a religious dimension to it. It is also likely the case that some religious traditions will find such a claim easier to agree with than others: religious traditions with a strong sense of the cosmos as the creation of a good God, for example, might find it easier to agree that every phenomenon is, in some way, marked by the religious. In non-theistic traditions, certain forms of Buddhism and Daoism also, it seems to me, could easily skew in that direction, to say nothing of Indigenous and Celtic spiritualities. Indeed, the notion that all things could have a religious component to them has support in various historical forms of religion (for example, the "mystical" traditions of, at least, Christianity, Kabbalahic Judaism, and Sufi Islam would all have some proponents who have made claims to this effect), and in contemporary philosophy of religion.[6] So suggesting that all phenomena have a religious dimension to them is not prima facie implausible—except, perhaps, for those operating within certain religious traditions (including secularism). In which case, if the belief "not all phenomena have a religious dimension to them" is something that is more likely to be believed within certain religious traditions (like secularized Christianity) than others, then perhaps our convictions about the religious nature of phenomena tell us something about the religious tradition(s) shaping the subjectivity of the person evaluating the claim and, through that evaluation, something about the nature of the phenomena themselves. For even our beliefs about whether all phenomena have a religious component to them seem to be marked by a religious tradition, and so are themselves, in some important way, religious phenomena.[7]

Although this may seem like semantics or simply playing around with language, it is not. I am attempting to illustrate the various ways that religious traditions could impact a particular phenomenon, thereby rendering it religious in the sense of having religious effects or being marked, in some important way, by the religious. And one of those ways, we are seeing here, is the way we are able to evaluate, engage with, or form beliefs about phenomena, including how easily we are able to see a religious dimension to the phenomena. This, then, is an example of what was discussed last chapter: our thinking about and engaging with religion is never divorced from our own immersion in particular religious traditions. For we can see that many people in the world would be more comfortable with the claim that "all phenomena have a religious dimension" than are people immersed in the secular tradition, insofar as many people in the world inhabit religious traditions that claim to impact a much wider variety of phenomena than those that secularists would consider "religious."

Hence, a religious tradition can impact or mark a phenomenon in a variety of ways, from its physical make-up to its historical provenance to how it calls to particular people to take it up. Given this, it becomes much more plausible, even for secular people, to acknowledge a religious dimension to (potentially all) phenomena. To speak of a religious dimension to phenomena, therefore, is not to invoke any kind of supernatural force at play sacralizing what is, on its own, a neutral or mundane reality. Indeed, nothing like the (secular-Christian) category of supernatural, sacred, or mundane need exist for us to say that there are religious effects on a wide variety of phenomena. Rather, many (perhaps all) phenomena bear, in some significant way, the traces of the religious way of sensing the world (as concretized in the style of particular religious traditions) that is operative in the subjectivities engaging with and in the phenomena.

Distinguishing "Religious" Phenomena

We have seen, then, that the claim that all phenomena have a religious dimension to them might have some widespread appeal. But to say that every phenomenon is potentially marked by religious effects does not mean that it cannot also be marked by other effects arising from other types of sensings and traditions. That there is a religious dimension to our experience of a phenomenon does not mean that there is not also a linguistic dimension, an auditory dimension, a social dimension, and so on. In chapter two, for example, we talked about the fact that many concert-goers describe a religious dimension to that experience.[8] I'm sure those same people would also say the experience was social (as they went with friends or loved ones), auditory (as they listened to the music), visual (as they saw things), and so on. This is a concrete reminder that one does not experience the religious as opposed to other modes of experience—they come to us together, as different (and therefore differentiatable) facets of the same experience.

Therefore, we can make the move from "all phenomena have a religious dimension" to "all phenomena are religious" only with some caution. For to say "all phenomena are religious" is potentially misleading, if we slip back into certain (secular) understandings of religion. The first such assumption is that religion is exclusively about things. As we just saw, religion is also about how we engage with or experience phenomena and is not just about the things we experience. Hence, to call a phenomenon "religious" is to say something about our experiencing of it. The second secular assumption to be avoided is that religion must be separate or distinct from other things. In this latter case, the claim "all phenomenon are religious" is potentially misleading because it might cause us to miss the equally accurate claim that "every phenomenon is also social, visible, economic, and so on." The religious dimension of a phenomenon is not an eidetic nature that comes at the exclusion of other possible natures, but rather one of a multitude of dimensions or factors shaping our experiencing of phenomena.

The religious, as an adjective describing a phenomenon, therefore describes our experience of a phenomenon in at least one of two ways: first, the phenomenon is able to induce religious (alongside other) effects upon subjectivity; and/or second, the phenomenon's existence is itself marked in some (non-exclusive) way by religiosity or religious traditions. In the first case, we describe one way that a phenomenon is able to impact or effect subjectivity. In the second, we are more interested in how a phenomenon has been impacted or effected by religiosity or religious traditions. In both cases, the experience of the phenomenon is, in some important way, religious(ly inflected), even if the nature of that inflection is different in the two cases.

To begin with the first case, a phenomenon can have religious effects on subjectivity in at least three different ways: empirically, quasi-transcendentally, and in the mode of transcendental sensing. Empirically, it can enable people to have an experience in which religiosity is a major or dominant sensing, and in so doing it imparts a religious tincture to the experience of a particular phenomenon. Just as a visible phenomenon is one that enables people to have a visual experience (e.g., is something that people can see), so a religious phenomenon would enable people to have a religious experience, as understood in the context of our earlier analyses. That is, a "religious experience" here is not necessarily a mystical experience of being overwhelmed by something excessive and transcendent. It is simply an experience in which religiosity is deployed as a viable mode of sensing in the experience, thereby giving a religious quality (alongside other qualities) to the experience. There is a great deal of variety in terms of what concrete experiences could be sensed in that way, and even a great deal of variety in how that mode of sensing itself is understood or experienced. For as we discussed in Chapter two, religiosity may be experienced by some as a feeling of close connection with all that is; by others as loving (in the sense of *caritas*) the world or feeling loved by the world; by still others as detachment due to the illusory nature of what I perceive; and so on. In that sense, feeling closely connected to all that is would be a religious experience—but so, too, might be loving my neighbor by bringing them food after the death of a loved one, or seeking to lessen my attachment to my career or my possessions. As long as religiosity (in whatever style that takes in a given religious tradition) is one of the modes of sensing at work in the experience, the experience can be characterized as, at least in part, a religious experience, just as going to a concert, for example, can be characterized as (also) a visual experience, insofar as what I see at the concert is part of the experience.

This talk of tradition brings us to the quasi-transcendental level of experiencing. On that level, religious effects are ones that shape the religious tradition that people inhabit and which is partially constitutive of how they experience the world. Just as seeing the world in front of him motivated Monet to paint in his Impressionist style, thereby altering the tradition of painting in a significant way, so too do particular religious phenomena sometimes alter a religious tradition in a significant way: Luther's ninety-five theses and the invention of the printing press, for example, which radically altered the tradition of Western Christianity, or the arrival of Buddhist missionaries at the court of Emperor Ming of the Han dynasty, which radically altered the tradition of Buddhism. Not all quasi-transcendental effects are so momentous, however. Most of the time, the quasi-transcendental effects of any one phenomenon are quite small, almost infinitesimal: Monet's first short brushstrokes, or the first time he failed to wait for the paint of a stroke to dry before applying another stroke were not world- or even art-momentous events. He likely did not even realize he had inaugurated something "new." He was, probably, just playing around. In doing so, it made a change in the tradition of painting, a change that would, many, many similar small changes later, produce a new sub-tradition. Similarly, seeing a dead body for the first time, or encountering a person who is sick may not be phenomena that change the religious world, but they can impact how one hears and engages with one's religious tradition nonetheless: one's finitude becomes more real, motivating one to consider afresh our relation to our ancestors or to those who will come after us; or one encounters a concrete need and the tradition's urging to care for the needy becomes less a doctrine to be believed and instead becomes a normative injunction to be followed. These quasi-transcendental alterations can be individual (I come to inhabit the tradition differently) or communal (multiple people in the tradition come to inhabit the tradition differently), and most often are both in one order or the other: either an individual's relation to the tradition is changed, which causes ripple effects to others; or the communal approach is changed, which causes ripple effects for individuals. Either way, the tradition (as the style by which people experience the world) is altered, which has effects on the subjectivities shaped by that tradition, including how people experience religiosity, as a mode of sensing the world. If empirical effects trace what mode of sensing is at play in our experience of a phenomenon, quasi-transcendental effects begin to trace the effects on the style(s) by which we experience, a style that acts in and upon individual subjects, but is never strictly individual.

At the level of transcendental modes of experiencing, religious effects are ones that shape how one is able to sense the world religiously. Looking at paintings, creating one's own paintings, and noticing distinctions in shades of color and the impact of light on color are all visual activities engaging with visual phenomena (paintings, colors, lighting, etc.) that shape how a painter inhabits visibility. So too, then, could engaging with particular religious phenomena (understanding a doctrine, attending worship rites, meditating, or engaging with others in one's religious tradition) shape how a person is able to, for example, love the world in concrete ways, see oneself as essentially one with the world, or come to better follow the Dao.

These three ways that phenomena can impact subjectivity are not exclusive. In most cases, our experience of a phenomenon will have effects on all three of the levels outlined above: in feeling compelled to help my neighbor that I encounter as in need, I am simultaneously: (1) drawing on religiosity as a mode of sensing (I feel connected with my neighbor in a way that motivates me to help them); (2)

deepening the ethical and social implications tied up with my religious tradition (love of neighbor becomes not just an idea to be believed, but a motivating call on my life and practice); and (3) shaping the very way I experience religiosity (as love, in a Christian mode, or as submission to *sadaqah*, in an Islamic mode). The effects that one phenomenon has on my subjectivity can be traced on all three of the levels outlined above, and the effects are slightly different in each case: one is simply a matter of which sensing is at work; another impacts the tradition that I and others inhabit; and the third shapes how I use the relevant mode of sensing, now and into the future. The three are deeply connected but can be phenomenologically distinguished.

Nevertheless, all of these types of effects are ways that phenomena can affect subjectivity. But there can be a religious dimension to phenomena also based on how phenomena are marked or affected by religiosity or religious traditions. Here we indicate not how the phenomenon can affect subjectivity, but how subjectivity has affected the phenomenon, which exists, partially, in and through religiosity and its effects in the world. Some examples of this type are obvious: mosques would not exist in the form they have if not for the religious tradition of Islam and the religious mode of sensing that gave rise to it. Others are, perhaps, less obviously "religious," in that they are not formally used in religious rites, but are nevertheless still significantly shaped by a religious tradition: the presence and cultivation of sacred fig trees (Latin taxonomy: *Ficus religiosa*) across southeast Asia (and even into Hawaii, California, and Brazil), for example, or the wandering of cows in the streets in some parts of India that would be penned (or slaughtered) if they lived in Texas. Still other phenomena seem to have lost almost all of their explicit connection to religion, although a historical connection remains: the first hospitals in the Western world were begun out of a desire to love the sick and wounded, in keeping with Christian charity.[9] Therefore, the hospital began as a religious phenomenon and it remains in some way essentially marked by the religiosity that brought it into being: it would not have existed in its current form had it not been for religiosity and its effects in the world.

The point, then, is that the religious nature of a phenomenon is not just based on how the phenomenon is taken up or "interpreted" by particular individual acts of subjectivity, nor on how it impacts or alters the subjectivities that encounter it in religious ways. The religious nature of a phenomenon can also be inscribed into the very material existence of things, whether that religious nature is noticed, dwelt on, engaged with, or not. And that religious nature might not be noticed precisely because that "nature" is better understood as a dimension of the phenomenon rather than as the essential "nature" of a substance. That is, a phenomenon's having a religious dimension need not mean that that religious dimension characterizes the whole of the phenomenon or even that it is the most significant dimension of the phenomenon. Just as we discussed previously the way that visibility (or tactility) is a crucial dimension of the phenomenon of reading a book but is not likely the main or dominant dimension (that would be linguisticality or meaning), so too a phenomenon could have religiosity as a dimension of itself, without it being the dominant dimension.

Take, for example, a university. It has a visual dimension (you can see its campus), a spatial dimension (its campus takes up space), a linguistic dimension (it engages in meaningful discourse), an economic dimension (it takes in revenue and pays out expenses), a social dimension (there are social mores on a university campus that are different than in other places: the dynamics between professors and students, for example, or the intellectual discussion of difficult texts or issues that may not be appropriate to discuss other places), and more. We might say that there is also a religious dimension, insofar as the university has (in the West at least) a religious history as an institution. Beyond that, almost all universities (again: at least in the West) currently operate by assumptions that we saw in the last chapter are broadly secularist, and therefore in keeping with a development of the secularized Christian tradition. Most of us would agree, I think, that in most instances the religious dimension is not the primary dimension of the university: it is neither the dimension that most closely captures why universities exist (which would likely be for either pedagogical or research-related reasons) nor the dimension that is most closely felt by those engaging with the university (which would hopefully be linguistic and/or theoretical—the search for meaning—although likely would be, in the current environment of higher education, primarily economic—an investment in the future). But that the religious dimension is not primary is not to say that the religious has no impact on the university at all. There is at least a historical connection at many universities, and perhaps even a shaping of research questions and assumptions along secular lines. While the university is not, in most instances, primarily a "religious" institution, it has a religious dimension.

We see another example in the American Constitution. There is clearly a religious dimension to the American Constitution: it utilizes language deeply steeped in the Christian religious tradition and draws on concepts that some political philosophers have claimed are deeply rooted in the (Protestant) Christian tradition.[10] In that sense, we can see that it is marked by the Christian religious tradition, and therefore bears the mark of a religious tradition in itself.

As such, the American Constitution can be considered a phenomenon that has a religious dimension. But it is not primarily a religious phenomenon, in the sense that its religious effects pale in comparison to its social and political effects. Hence, most people engaging with the U.S. Constitution would not pay attention to its religious dimensions, because they are (likely) not overly relevant for their concerns: that the notion of "blessings" in the preamble seems drawn from a Christian background does not overly influence how the House of Representative should be run or who is susceptible to a charge of treason, at least not from the perspective of law makers or the judiciary.

The point, then, is that our conclusion that all phenomena are (or at least may be) religious is not a reduction of everything to religion, as understood in a secular-Christian paradigm. It is not a denial of social, political, economic, or any other dimensions to the phenomena, but the claim that, alongside those other dimensions, there is also a religious dimension. We can therefore consider a "religious" phenomenon to be one that, in some significant way, has religious effects as part of its concrete existence, that is, as part of the concrete ways it is entangled with subjectivity, history, culture, and materiality, even if those religious effects are not the primary thing one would normally note about that phenomenon. Naming it as a religious phenomenon does not set it apart from history, culture, and so on, but rather highlights one of the types of effects it has and that it expresses in history, culture, and so on. We name it a religious phenomenon, then, not to distinguish it from other types of phenomena—it is religion and therefore *not* language or economics—but to understand that phenomenon better by appreciating one type of effect it can have, one kind of way it is entangled in the world alongside other ways. Failing to acknowledge this religious dimension of the phenomenon's existence would, in these cases, be to fail to notice one of the ways that phenomenon is engaged with the world and so would be to understand that phenomenon a little more narrowly than it could otherwise be understood (a point we will return to in Chapter six).

This also means that the failure to notice a phenomenon's religious dimension is not proof that something is not a religious phenomenon. A phenomenon need not exercise transcendental effects in order to be a religious phenomenon, or, at least, we need not be paying attention to or aware of those transcendental effects in order for something to be a religious phenomenon. Empirical effects are sufficient to make something a religious phenomenon. So, too, are transcendental or quasi-transcendental effects sufficient to make something a religious phenomenon, in this sense, even if it did not have or obviously exercise empirical effects. That is, even if we are paying attention to other modalities of the phenomenon, that phenomenon might still occasion religious effects. A mall, for example, may strike us empirically as being primarily a social and economic phenomenon: it is primarily a place where people gather and engage in particular customs and rituals, which are driven primarily by economic concerns (people go there to spend money, and malls exist primarily to make money). But that does not mean that it might not also exercise religious effects, as James K.A. Smith has suggested.[11]

Should we then call the mall a "religious phenomenon"? The appropriateness of doing so depends, it seems to me, on the context in which I name it as such, and what, precisely, I mean in naming it so.[12] For me, as a transcendental phenomenologist, I am interested primarily in the transcendental effects of religion. As a scholar of religion, that is what I am interested in, and that is what I'm studying. So, for me, I would certainly consider the mall to be a "religious phenomenon," at least to the extent that I am considering the way that malls have altered the development of the Christian tradition (the "strip mall church" being, in this case, not simply an accidental example, but a concrete manifestation of various elements that can be found in a more widespread consumerized Christianity: a focus on individual happiness; the devaluing of submission as a posture for worship; the focus on being "seeker friendly" as a tool of evangelism, etc.). To the extent that I am interested in how going to the mall has altered the ways that people inhabit their religious traditions and their religiosity, I must pay attention to the religious effects of the mall. And insofar as I am considering the mall as something that both bears and occasions religious effects, I would consider the mall a religious phenomenon, that is, a phenomenon that has and generates religious effects.

A sociologist of religion, however, might see things differently. They may be more interested in studying worship rites, doctrinal beliefs, or meditative practices, and to the extent that they do not see those operating at a mall, they would not consider the mall to be a religious phenomenon. The mall is, perhaps, not the best site to study the type of (empirical) effects they are looking for. I would, however, caution against the claim that the mall is not, therefore, a religious phenomenon. It would, in this instance, perhaps be more accurate to say that "this phenomenon is not relevant for the religious purposes I am currently studying." In this way, we would signal that "religion" is not an essential type that accrues to some phenomena but not others. Rather, the religious names a dimension of experiencing that accrues to phenomena in light of their entanglements with religiosity and religious traditions, and can do so to various degrees. It is not exclusive—something can be religious *and* social *and* linguistic—but it does name a unique dimension of a phenomenon, and so is something worth taking account of, at least for certain ends.

The ends to which we are putting a phenomenon, therefore, impact how easily we see it as religious. But so too, as we said earlier, do the traditions out of which we are operating in our engagement with the phenomenon. Certain traditions seem to make it easier than others to see a wider (or narrower) scope of what counts as religious. This is certainly the case with religious traditions as we said: a secularized-Christian religious tradition might make it more difficult to see everything as having a religious dimension, in part because it seeks to separate religion from other elements of our experiencing, and in part because it thinks of religion primarily in terms of (separable) content rather than in terms of a dimension of our experiencing. This makes clear that our religious traditions influence how we inhabit religiosity (as argued in the last chapter), but also influence how we understand, articulate, and interact with distinct phenomena (as argued earlier this chapter). Our engagements with religious phenomena are therefore never religiously "neutral" either: we always engage in ways that are influenced by our prior engagements with religion, and in ways that have effects on our future engagements with religion. This is the case because phenomena are always expressive of their own immersion in religious (and other) traditions. In that sense, understanding objects as (religious) phenomena helps us see the ways in which they impact our experiencing and the ways in which they have been impacted *by* our experiencing. The *how* of our experiencing influences even the concrete *whats* that we experience. The religious is a dimension of that *how* and therefore exercises a role in our experience of various types of phenomena, even those that (some) scholars of religion might not consider to be "religious phenomena."

5

Religious Experience and Materiality

If all phenomena (potentially) have a religious dimension to them, then our experience of any phenomenon also (potentially) has a religious dimension. As such, all experience could be religious, insofar as there is a religious dimension to it. This is in stark contrast to a notion of religious experience that reserves the term for some particular experiences that can be easily differentiated from other (non-religious, profane, mundane, etc.) experiences. The latter, of course, was the view of religious experience propounded by the "phenomenologists of religion" in the early days of the discipline of religious studies. That that approach implicitly smuggled in various Christian presuppositions is now a well-established thesis in the field.[1] That at least some of those assumptions remain in the secularized version of Christianity that is the dominant religious tradition shaping the field currently was argued in Chapter three. What I want to explore in this chapter is how we should understand the nature of religious experience, in light of the analyses of previous chapters. Specifically, I want to clarify what is meant by the term "religious experience," how it picks out something distinct from "experience" in general, and how this "religious experience" manifests itself in the lives of actual, living, concrete people.

In short, I want to understand how thinking religion transcendentally rather than transcendently impacts our understanding of religious experience. Three distinct approaches to the question of religious experience deserve our interest in this regard. First, a materialist approach that is prevalent among those religious studies scholars who are critical of "religion" as a meaningful concept. This approach to religion will help us both understand the terms of the contemporary discussion and will suggest a latent reliance on transcendence in its understanding of religion that need to be overcome. The second approach is one that we will call a "sacramental" approach. It understands religious experience in terms of the sacralization of materiality by a seemingly transcendent power. Here, religious experience begins to move away from direct experiences of transcendence, even if some reliance on transcendence seems to remain as part of the account. The third approach, which we will call an event-al approach, sees religious experience as uncovering a religious impulse at the heart of experience without (it seems) appeal to transcendence at all—although we will see that this is not entirely accurate. Each of these three approaches brings to the fore something important for a transcendental account of religious experience, but all three maintain vestiges, in different ways, of the transcendent approach and so cannot provide a robust and coherent transcendental understanding of religious experience. I will end the chapter by offering a more genuinely transcendental account of religious experience that I think will prove helpful for the empirical study of religion.

Religious Experience and Materiality

The sacramental and the event-al approaches to the question of religious experience emerge from philosophical phenomenology, and as such are not usually cast in terms of "religious experience" per se. They are often framed as an account of the relationship between religion and materiality, attempts at a "religious materialism." The reasons for this framing are complex, and include a general suspicion of the category of experience in post-structuralist discourses and the wariness about subjectivity in most Continental philosophies after 1968. This suspicion and wariness do not mean that questions of experience have been abandoned. Rather, they are radically recast in a different ultra-transcendental context: instead of seeing subjectivity as the ultra-transcendental and *a priori* cause of experience, subjectivity and experience are both understood as emerging from a broader background or context. Once subjectivity is understood as being generated from a broader context, the category of experience is freed from solipsistic assumptions: if subjects arise in particular historical and material circumstances, then their experiences are, in some way, a product of those (shared) circumstances and hence not so easily cast as solipsistic. Through these moves, experience is philosophically and phenomenologically re-inscribed into materiality, alongside subjectivity.

The question of religious experience, therefore, is recast as a question of religious materialism. It is no longer a question of how religion appears to an individual subject but of how we understand the religious to be at work in material conditions. This is a dominant question in the philosophical phenomenology of religion in the last few decades. The question of religious materialism has also moved to the forefront of the empirical study of religion with the so-called "Material Turn in Religion" in recent years, but often at the expense of the category of experience. With this "turn," the empirical study of religion shifted its focus away from beliefs (including the related tropes of language and linguistic formulations) and subjective experiences and oriented itself instead toward the material practices and objects of religion. Religion is thought to be found in material things—such as the phenomena we discussed in the last chapter—rather than in subjective experience.

But this turn to material things comes at the expense of subjective experience only if we assume that materiality and subjectivity are mutually exclusive and at odds with each other. This assumption followed from the traditional understanding in the secular-Christian, post-Cartesian West that distinguishes the material from some immaterial realm (often called the "spiritual" or "subjective"). Traditionally, this understanding posited that religion primarily concerns the latter. So, although religion may show up in certain material forms or conditions, those material forms were generally thought to be religiously interesting only for the spiritual dimensions they exhibited: the bread and wine of the Christian Eucharist, for example, become religiously interesting only in their (physical, symbolic, or conceptual) transubstantiation into the body and blood of Christ.[2] On this account of the religious-material relationship, there is little impetus for a turn to the material study of religion, for the material is largely that which is not religiously interesting.

This traditional account of the religious-material relation is no longer dominant in religious studies, at least not explicitly, but some contemporary movements in the study of religion seem to maintain this assumption, albeit implicitly. When religion is understood, not just as the *product* of material production (be that symbolic, cultural, via power relations or technologies, etc.) but as reduced to that material production with no remainder, when religion "dissolves [...] without remainder into ideology or culture understood as institutionalized values and symbolic systems,"[3] then we seem to be right back in that traditional secular-Christian dichotomy between spirituality and materiality. If there is nothing "spiritual" that religion adds to culture and symbolic systems more broadly, then it seems that religion can simply be abandoned, done away with as an unhelpful concept. In tying religion necessarily to "transcendence" (as Fitzgerald, for example, does, albeit in a critical way), we seem to necessitate that religion be supernatural (which is, implicitly, to say: immaterial) if it is to exist as a meaningful category. The material turn in religious studies, then, can be cast precisely as a throwing off of the shackles, so to speak, of religious superstition, in a move toward the eventual emancipation of serious scholarly inquiry from the category of "religion" at all. If religion is material, then it is *just* material, and we no longer need to talk meaningfully about religion.

To be clear, Fitzgerald's criticisms are, on the surface, more complex than that. Yet his denial of religion as a sub-category of culture seems to boil down precisely to a critique of super-naturalism. He rejects Jenson's claim that religion has to do with anything super-human,[4] and therefore argues that there is no need to talk about religion. Rather than rejecting supernatural religion, this embraces it as a definition and then posits that the definition results in an empty set: religion *is* those things that pertain to the supernatural, but there is simply nothing (cross-culturally speaking at least) that satisfies that definition. What *does* satisfy that definition are merely things that follow from Christian (or Abrahamic) presuppositions that we can therefore call theological rather than religious.

What is telling is that Fitzgerald seems to reject religion as a cross-cultural category precisely insofar as it "cannot be separated out as a genuinely distinct areas [sic] of research separated from the economic, political, and more broadly ritual aspects."[5] That is, because what he is describing is necessarily economic, political, cultural—because it is *material*—it cannot be distinctly religious. Fitzgerald is here illustrative of a particular moment in the development of religious understanding, perhaps a necessary one. The transcendent and supernatural element of definitions of religion deserved criticism, but to therefore abandon religion as a meaningful category simply because we find reason to critique the notion of transcendence is to concede the definition of religion as transcendence rather than to challenge it.

The Sacramental Approach to Religious Experience

To truly challenge the supernatural understandings of religion, alternative definitions of religion would need to be offered, alternative accounts of how religion could interact with materiality, or could perhaps even be material. The question of a genuinely religious materialism is thereby opened up as a crucial question for the philosophy of religion, and with it, new possibilities emerge for religious experience as a material phenomenon or, as we will see, as a phenomenality of material phenomena.

Several new models for understanding the relationship between religion and materiality have emerged in the scientific study of religion in the nearly 30 years since Fitzgerald published his important article, largely focused on thinking religion as a material phenomenon.[6] Our interest in this chapter, in light of the transcendental method adopted in this book, is primarily with those approaches that seek to think religious experience along the lines of phenomenality, i.e., those approaches to thinking religion as *how* we experience rather than simply as *what* we experience. In that vein, philosophical phenomenology of religion has offered two broad alternative definitions of religion and religious experience. The first characterizes religion and religious experience in fundamentally "liturgical" or "sacramental" terms. Here, the idea is that material is never simply "just" material but is always imbued with an immaterial or invisible element. This invisible element—in some sense a transcendent element, but not in the secular-Christian notion of transcendence, as we will see shortly—"sacralizes" materiality, rendering it religiously significant because of this participation in or with the invisible.[7] Jean-Luc Marion is probably the most significant contemporary figure to hold this position. For Marion, there are distinct moments of experience (which he deems "saturated phenomena"[8]) in which we encounter something that overwhelms our categories of experience, leaving us awestruck. In these moments, what we encounter "exceeds" our normal ability to make sense of it,[9] exceeds our finite horizons, and "bedazzles" us.[10] For him, an encounter with the Christian God is the paradigmatic example of such a saturated phenomenon, but not the only one: we can also be similarly struck by a work of art or a glass of wine.

Marion's analyses are phenomenologically astute and have done much to shape our understanding of phenomenology and phenomenological methodology. They also seem consistent with a certain type of experience that many people in various religious traditions have. What we have here, at least initially, is a kind of equation of religious experience with mystical experience: religious experience is a distinct encounter with a transcendence (understood here as excessive) that somehow makes itself at least partially intuitable in our experience. This partial intuition seems to be a crucial part of such an experience: in the experience, we have an experience of something, but that experience simultaneously makes us aware that what we are experiencing far exceeds what we seem to be experiencing. There is a sense of vastness or mystery that we are made aware of in this type of experience, made aware of precisely because we encounter it as in some way escaping our encounter: we experience it as not fully experienceable, but experienceable enough to leave a mark on our psyche.

This does not yet yield us an account of religious experiencing. Even if one grants the reality of such "saturated phenomena," and, further, even if one grants the existence of an excessive transcendence that could effectuate them, even then one is left to wonder about the experiential impacts of such encounters. After all, these encounters seem to be not only rare but also bedazzling and stupefying. If they leave my horizons shattered, then it is not clear how they are to have any impact upon my other, non-saturated experiences. And if they do not have such an impact, we seem left with an account of religious experience that cannot account for regular, everyday experiences, nor for any real sense of religious experiencing, that is, of the religious as *how* we experience. For if such experiences are possible, they do not seem regular or common: even if many people claim to have such experiences, they do not have them very often.[11] So "religious experience" seems to remain confined to particular experiences, with little impact on the rest of our experiences or how we live.

Some people have traditionally attempted to solve this problem by suggesting that those experiences give us something (some knowledge or some feeling) that provides a kind of "big picture" that gives meaning to the rest of our experience. In some cases, those experiences leave behind a textual trace that can be studied, learned from, and used to construct systems and institutions for living that would be consistent with the transcendence that gives (religious) context to our material existence. The Islamic account of the origin of the Quran in Mohammed's trance-like experience of the angel Gabriel would be a paradigmatic example here. Such an account is ambiguous on whether the trace left behind is itself a religious dimension of our experiencing or a distinct kind of religious experience.

Marion's suggestion, on the other hand, seems to be that this encounter (especially when it is with God) leaves us not only able but perhaps almost compelled to engage the world in a distinct way. In keeping with his Catholic tradition, Marion characterizes this new way of engaging the world as "love." In this sense, the primary revelation we receive from the transcendent via a "saturated" or "excessive" experience is not the revelation of a particular (cognitive, epistemological) content, but the reception of a new way of being in or engaging with the world.[12] This new way of being—love, for Marion—stays with us, long after the saturated phenomenon has passed out of our direct experience. As such, religious experience is no longer confined exclusively to the direct experience of a "saturated phenomenon." A new way is opened up to allow for more regular and banal religious experiences to emerge, via a new mode of religious experiencing.

This idea that a mode of religious experiencing is made possible by some encounter with the transcendent seems characteristic of the "sacramental" approach to religious experience and to religious materiality. It is not necessary that there be a primary overwhelming experience—Richard Kearney prefers to speak of "epiphanies of the everyday" and "micro-eschatology,"[13] rather than overwhelming experiences of saturated phenomena. These epiphanies are more regular, everyday encounters that open us to the mystery and abundance inherent in things. As such, he more strongly emphasizes the sacramental nature of phenomena themselves, rather than leaning on subjectivity acquiring new ways of accessing things. This sacrality[14] is something that we experience, though, and not simply something we posit, think about, or hope for. We feel it, we see it, we touch it—in part because of the traditions we are a part of and the hermeneutical horizons they provide us.[15] Given its embeddedness in things and in our hermeneutical horizons, there is a less radical sense of transcendence in Kearney than there is in Marion.

However it achieves this status as sacramental—whether through an overwhelming and excessive experience or through small, banal experiences—materiality itself is understood as sacramentally charged on this sacramental understanding. This sacramental charge provides a kind of religious force to materiality, and so moves beyond the traditional secular-Christian divide between materiality, on the one hand, and spirituality, on the other. Here, we see a materiality that comes infused with a kind of religious charge, and this therefore constitutes a species of what we earlier referred to as a religious materialism. Material itself is now understood as inherently religious—albeit because of its connection to some kind of transcendent force that seems to give it that charge.

Understanding materiality in this religious way opens two possibilities that are relevant for our conversation about religious experience. First, because materiality itself is sacramentally charged and therefore religiously infused, it becomes possible to have more regular and more banal religious experiences: rather than "religious experience" being reserved for rare and overwhelming experiences of transcendence, the way is now cleared for people to have religious experiences of banal, everyday things. We see examples of this especially strongly in Kearney, who likes to talk about finding God in "the pots and pans,"[16] or in a cry in the street.[17] Hence, the set of things that can become possible objects of a religious experience is now greatly expanded—virtually any material thing can, potentially, become part of, or be the occasion for, a religious experience.

Second, this expanding of the scope of what can be the occasion for a religious experience follows from the invocation of a potentially religious mode of experiencing. We see this in the role that love plays in Marion, and the role that "epiphanic transformations of little things into holy things in our most everyday experiences"[18] plays in Kearney. It is not, therefore, simply that more things can become the source of religious experience in the overwhelming or mystical sense of that term. Rather, there is a new way of experiencing religiously, one that emerges in our regular, everyday experience and which adds a new, religious dimension to how we experience the world in general.

This new way of experiencing religiously seems to mirror the notion of a religious dimension to our experiencing discussed in the last chapter. But there is one crucial difference: in the sacramental account it seems to require some appeal to transcendence in order for it to count as a "religious" way of experiencing. This is not the same relation to transcendence as is found in the understanding of religious experience adopted by the phenomenologists of religion: the content of the religious experience is not transcendent, on this sacramental view. But it still seems to require transcendence, insofar as it requires some relation to transcendence in order to sacralize materiality and/or transform our ability to experience religiously.

The Event-al Approach to Religious Experience

Sacramentalism's appeal (implicit or explicit) to transcendence is not shared by the other predominant approach to religious experiencing in the philosophical phenomenology of religion that I wish to discuss in this chapter. Where the sacramental approach seeks to account for how the transcendent (thought of as excessive, invisible, etc.) appears in and alters our experiencing of material conditions, the event-al[19] approach presumes a wholly immanent, non-transcendent frame. It then strives to account for how religion makes an impact in such an immanent world. It usually does this by appealing to religion as a kind of "force" or "energy,"[20] drawing on Deleuzian, Nietzschean, and Derridean inspirations. In that sense, religion is about insistence (a push, a prompt, a nudge in particular directions) more than it is about existence (of a deity, for example, or any other transcendent super-being).[21]

The most prominent contemporary religious thinker of this approach is John D. Caputo. His claim is that religion is an event in a dual sense: first, religion is a happening, an unfolding, a living-through of something (rather than the thing or substance that happens or is experienced); and second, religion is the significance or meaning in what happens. Qua event, then, religion reveals that what really matters is not simply the *what* that occurs in the empirical world, but *how* that pushes things in a particular direction: towards justice (or its opposite), toward the poor, the widow and the orphan (or their opposite),[22] and so on. The other trappings of religion—doctrines, concepts, buildings, rituals—are there simply as the way we encounter this religious impulse.[23] Of course, those trappings also end up shaping the force that they purport to express: the religious force pushes us in different directions in post-Vatican II Catholicism, in white evangelicalism, and in Meister Eckhart, to cite a few of Caputo's favourite interlocutors. Still, there is a sense that the material is somehow secondary to the force of religion, and as a result some critics have accused Caputo of being allergic to the particularities and determinacy of actual, concrete, historical religious communities and phenomena.[24]

However, this critique is misplaced (although not entirely unfounded). Caputo does not seek to oppose the force of religion (which he sometimes call "religiosity") with concrete religious traditions, but rather to emphasize that the two are not the same thing, phenomenologically speaking: we can distinguish, in our experience of religion, between the force or impetus that religion puts on how we experience the world and the different traditions by which it may exercise that force,[25] a distinction that mirrors the distinction outlined here between religiosity, as a transcendental mode of sensing the world, and the quasi-transcendental effects of religious traditions. To say that no religious tradition wholly captures the force of religiosity is not the same as saying that religiosity can never be expressed in a particular religious tradition. In that sense it should be noted that Caputo's work is almost exclusively done in the context of the Christian religious tradition: he is (generally) analysing religiosity and the religious force using Christian tropes and how they have been deployed in the context of Christian institutions and histories. His is not just a mere phenomenology of Christianity, though, insofar as he points to the fact that this religious dimension could be analysed differently in other traditions, according to other tropes, and so on.[26] In that sense, there is work being undertaken toward a broader phenomenology of religion in this event-al approach, even if it is not usually exercised in ways that would be amenable to empirical scholars of religion.

We will return to this distinction between a phenomenology of religion and religious phenomenology next chapter. Here, the point is to analyse the notion of religious experiencing at work in this event-al approach, as an alternative to the traditional secular-Christian account of religious experience as something pertaining to distinct, concrete experiences of transcendent and/or immaterial contents or objects. In that regard, the deconstructive component of Caputo's project is also illustrative: religion is cast as exercising a certain force that is inevitably expressed in particular institutions, concepts, practices—in short: phenomena—but that can never be entirely reduced to those phenomena.[27] As such, phenomena must constantly be deconstructed precisely in service to the "mystical" force (to use Derrida's terminology) that animates them, a force that is often subjectively experienced as surprising or unexpected,[28] as a certain mysteriousness or inexplicability. For religious phenomena, this force is religiosity. It is not God, conceived as a transcendent super-being. Rather, "God" is one phenomenon that arose in some religious traditions (especially the "Abrahamic" ones) as a response to this mysterious and inexplicable force of religiosity, one attempt to name the unnameable or the always-re-nameable.[29] Because this impulse cannot be fully contained in the names given to it, there is a need to be constantly deconstructing those names (like "God," in Abrahamic traditions) in order to not lose our focus on, and the energizing force of, that original force or impetus. In other words, on this score, the name "God" should be understood as a name given to the force at work grounding these particular traditions, and not to some immaterial super-being. The religious is therefore not some transcendent being we have to work our way up to; for the event-al approach, the religious is a dimension of the very depths of our experiencing, the ground we stand on rather than the heights we reach for.[30] If there is mystery, unknowability, and so on, it exists in the heart of our experiencing, not in some transcendent realm.

This force of religiosity is lost or covered over in phenomena in part because phenomena are immersed in the world. This loss can be construed, from a transcendent perspective, as a kind of "fall" into finitude and materiality (à la Plotinus).[31] Or this can be construed simply as the inevitable result of counter-veiling forces: because institutions and phenomena are not just the result of the religious impetus, but also of political, social, racial, economic, and other impetuses, there are forces other than the religious force also at work in those phenomena. Given that there is nothing that transcends this play of forces to guide it (on an event-al approach), it is almost inevitable that the forces end up working as counter-forces, pushing each other off-course and letting phenomena lose their way.

Religious experience, then, on the event-al account, is about focusing on the religious impulse at the heart of various phenomena and trying to let that impulse emerge more clearly and more strongly in religious institutions, phenomena, and lives. It is not simply about particular, concrete experiences, but constitutes an entire way of being in the world that in turn shapes an entire way of life.[32] Religious experiencing is an acknowledgment that our lived experience is premised on events that radically precede our experiencing. It therefore constitutes a praxis that is not opposed to reason but is the ground of and for reason: a religious experiencing that is not about what we experience, but an opening onto a new force or dimension at work within our experiencing, which therefore alters how we live.

Remnants of Transcendence

In these approaches, then, we see a move beyond thinking religious experience simply as discrete, mystical encounters with a transcendent force. Even where such an encounter is posited (in Marion's version of the sacramental approach, for example), the encounter is not the totality of our religious experience, but a kind of precursor to it. Religious experience, understood as religious experienc*ing*, is about how we engage the world in a distinct way: there is a religious dimension to our experiencing, but this dimension is not primarily characterized by discrete experiences of concrete phenomena, but by a new depth or dimension that is awakened or discovered in our other experiences. Religiosity is found as a dimension of phenomena, and not somehow beyond them. As such, religious experience does not refer primarily to an experience of transcendence, in the secular-Christian sense. Rather, it refers to a way of experiencing the material world differently.

While both the sacramental and the event-al accounts move religious experience beyond discrete experiences of transcendence, neither account entirely leaves transcendence behind as a necessary part of religious experiencing. In Marion's version of the sacramental approach especially, some encounter with transcendence seems to be a necessary precursor for religious experiencing: revelation (his name for our ability to experience the world religiously) comes from elsewhere, as his recent book title suggests.[33] It must be noted that the transcendence at work here is distinctly not transcendence in the secular-Christian sense: although that which is transcendent (God, for example) cannot be reduced to the horizontal conditions by which we experience the world, it nevertheless gives itself in and within those conditions. The givenness is not exhausted in our experience of it—the givenness always exceeds our ability to make sense of it—but it *is* given and experienced in the world. Further, the transcendent is most definitely *not* a being that could be "located" elsewhere (logically or ontologically),[34] somehow beyond the world and therefore not causally efficacious within the world. Whatever the transcendent is, on the sacramental approach, it is *not* wholly transcendent in the secular-Christian sense, but is rather understood as excessive and supra-natural (rather than supernatural): it structures the natural from within, even as it also exceeds the natural, and as such is eminently efficacious within the world.

However, even if it is not the same notion of transcendence as the one operative in the secular-Christian tradition, there still seems to be some notion of transcendence presumed in the sacramental approach. Granted, Kearney's version of sacramentality seems to require less transcendence than Marion's, so perhaps the transcendence is not, strictly speaking, necessary to the approach. Yet it is difficult to read the sacramental approach other than as a claim that something beyond the material—something transcendent, excessive, invisible— baptizes and sacramentalizes the material, making it somehow religiously or spiritually interesting, thereby seeming to at least implicitly affirm some notion of transcendence as necessary for materiality to be experienced religiously.

The notion of transcendence does not seem to be at work so strongly in the event-al approach. However, vestiges of it remain: it seems to be precisely the secular-Christian notion of transcendence that is rejected in the explicitly "immanent" reflections on the event. In that sense, the metaphysics of the event may continue to presume the metaphysical model of secular-Christian transcendence, simply positing transcendence as an empty set, as we earlier saw with Fitzgerald. Where the event-al approach to religious experiencing differs radically from Fitzgerald, though, is in its insistence that religion not be equated with that transcendence. Hence, religiously speaking, transcendence is not simply maintained and neutralized—it is done away with as having any kind of essential or definitional connection to religion. Unfortunately, at times the event-al approach seems to go to the other extreme: qua event, there may be no room for transcendence of any kind, thereby problematizing the viability of an event-al approach for religions where some notion of transcendence is required or at least must be possible.

At stake for us in these discussions is not so much the fate of transcendence, but rather our understanding of the possibilities for religious experience. The sacramental approach (especially on Kearney's version) gives us an account of materiality that is itself religiously significant. As such, all experience is at least possibly religious, in that it is possible for all phenomena to be experienced religiously. This is consistent with our analyses in the last chapter—although the precise way that materiality gets this religious character may seem to require a notion of transcendence in order to render the material religiously significant. If materiality is made religiously significant because of its relation to the transcendent, this could prove problematic for those traditions that would deny that such transcendence exists and is possible. At stake in that denial here would be, then, not simply the existence of a transcendent entity, but the denial of the very possibility of genuinely religious experience itself: is religious experience ever justified as religious experience, or is such language ever only the product of a false attribution?

The event-al approach, on the contrary, does not seem to require such transcendence; indeed, it seems premised, in many ways, on the denial of such transcendence. Religious experience is made possible here by the work of a force or energy within the world that exercises a religious impulse, generating religiously insistent phenomena that people engage with and can be shaped by. Where does such a force come from? This question is, perhaps, thoroughly theological rather than phenomenological, and its answer, too, may be theological: Jean Grondin claims that the event-al approach is "a replacement theology of sorts" for a secular age in which "we cannot speak of Gods or spirits."[35] It must be acknowledged, in this light, that Caputo's work emphasizing the event (which we drew on so heavily in our analyses) is done in a thoroughly theological register, although explicitly not a confessional one.

Can a non-theological account of the force of religiosity be supplied, one that does not require (implicitly or explicitly) a notion of transcendence that many people would find religiously problematic? This would seem necessary for the project of offering a method for the study of religion that could be used across a variety of religious traditions and which would presume as little as possible the tenets of one tradition over the others.

A Transcendental Phenomenological Account of Religious Experience

In this book, I am arguing that it is indeed possible to provide an account of religious experiencing that is not premised on transcendence. That account begins with the method of the (phenomenological) approach to the problem. Phenomenologically speaking, the question of transcendence can be bracketed altogether: phenomenology is simply not interested in ontological origin stories. Of course, that lack of interest may just repeat the transcendence assumed in the secular-Christian tradition that dominates the contemporary study of religion if researchers using this method are not careful. Hence, the careful deployment of the phenomenological method, via the epochē, can help us, methodologically at least, to leave the question of transcendence in abeyance, as much as possible[36]: we will neither affirm nor deny transcendence, because its existence (or lack of existence) is not crucial to our claims.

What will assist us in meticulously avoiding transcendent speculations, then, is (perhaps ironically) our interest in transcendentals. We bracket the question of the ontological status of the phenomena we experience by focusing on our experiencing of them. The account of religious experiencing we offer in this chapter should hold, whether someone believes in transcendence or not. This is important for a general phenomenology of religion insofar as some religious traditions do believe in, and want to be able to account for, transcendence and its impact on experience, whereas others explicitly deny it or simply have no categories for it. An account of religious experiencing that denies the possibility of transcendence (as some formulations of the event-al approach do) would therefore be rejected by traditions that seek to affirm it, whereas other religious traditions would resist an understanding of religious experience that required transcendence. A broadly applicable phenomenology of religion would need an account in which transcendence is possible but not required.

I think the notion of material-spirituality outlined in chapter one can provide the basis of such an account. The claim there was that experience is necessarily material-spiritual, because materiality and spirituality are inherently intertwined. Spirit, in that context, has largely cultural and human connotations: it is about meaningfulness and subjectivity, culture and history. It is an impetus that drives further development and a meaningfulness embedded in phenomena, and as such is thoroughly intertwined with the material and vice versa. The metaphysical provenance or ontological origins of material-spirituality was not discussed, precisely because I am interested in how it works (now that it's here), not where it came from. If one wanted to posit a transcendent origin for it (in the will of Allah or the Spirit of God, for example) one could—as long as one was then willing to acknowledge that, qua material-spiritual, it works in phenomenologically describable ways. That is, how material-spirituality operates in our experiencing would not change depending on our theological or metaphysical assumptions of where it came from. In that sense, transcendence is neither presumed nor denied. It remains possible, but it is not overly relevant to our study of religious experiencing, which is about a particular dimension of phenomena that we are able to experience and that shapes various modes of our experiencing (empirically, transcendentally, and quasi-transcendentally) and thus shapes a wide variety of our experiences.

Religious experiencing, then, is not to be found in concrete experiences of transcendent realities. Rather, religious experiencing is that experiencing that results from our engagement with the religious mode of sensing the world, much the same way visual experience arises from our engagements with visibility. In that sense, religious experiencing is premised on religiosity, not on (material-) spirituality. To say that material-spirituality could have a transcendent origin is not somehow to smuggle religion into materiality via a backdoor, because the spiritual is not (yet) religious. It can take on a religious tone or dimension, insofar as religiosity is one mode of expressing and of engaging material-spirituality, alongside others (visibility, sociality, tactility, linguisticality, etc.). As such, it is religiosity that makes experience "religious," in a meaningful sense. And it *is* a meaningful sense precisely because the term "religious" does therefore seem to pick out something distinct (and thus worth naming and studying): what it picks out is not primarily distinct *things* but a distinct *way* of engaging the world. Just as touch and visibility name distinct ways of engaging the world but not necessarily distinct things (most things that I can touch I can also see, without that contradicting the distinction between visibility and tactility), so, too, do religiosity, sociality, and ethicality name distinct ways of engaging the world that can be simultaneously found in the same phenomena without thereby contradicting the distinction between them as modes of experiencing. That a particular phenomenon has religious but also linguistic, social, ethical, and so on dimensions does not mean that the category "religious" can be dismissed as having no explanatory power, precisely because the religious gives us another way of understanding the phenomenon, another way the phenomenon gives itself to us, a distinct dimension to our experiencing of the phenomenon.

In that sense, this religious mode of engaging the world is something that we can acknowledge as present in our material-spiritual situation: as we argued in chapter two, people do seem to have this mode of experiencing the world, even if its details vary widely between different traditions and communities. Again, the origin of this mode of sensing is not our concern. It could be attributed to transcendent origins (a type of *semen religiosis*, perhaps, or even the result of revelation, à la Marion), although it need not be. It could also just be a thing we do because of how our brains are wired or because of how our societies have developed over time. Neither understanding is either assumed or precluded in our analyses of how religiosity functions.

By engaging us with the world in a uniquely religious way, religiosity opens up a new, religious dimension to our experiences. But this is not merely subjective or individualistic. This religious dimension is communally shared among members of the same religious (sub-)tradition and impacts both how subjectivity functions and the nature of the phenomena produced within that tradition. That is, religiosity gives a religious dimension both to subjectivity and to the phenomena that are generated in their entanglements with us and our experiences. The influence of this dimension on a particular phenomenon can be greater or lesser, given either the nature of the phenomenon or our modes of engaging with it (as we discussed in the last chapter): some phenomena may strike us as more religious than others. But even when the religious dimension is lesser, it is not absent. Even when it is denied, it might still be operative (as our discussions of barbarism and secularism suggested in chapters three and four), because religiosity does not require subjective awareness or cognitive assent in order to be efficacious. Religiosity is not based on the influence of particular beliefs or practices or individual voluntary acts. It is a dimension that is at work structuring (potentially all of) our subjective activities through the impact of the religious traditions that effect our subjectivity and the entanglement of religiosity with other modes of sensing (as discussed in Chapter three).

What this means is that religious experience is not simply concrete experiences we have of objects or phenomena that are primarily explained in terms of some kind of religious essence that they possess. Rather, religious experience is primarily a force or factor at work in all our experiencing, something that gives experience a unique flavour or energy that pushes our subjectivity in certain directions—although the precise way it pushes us will, no doubt, depend on the phenomena we are encountering and how we have been shaped to use our religiosity by the religious traditions we inhabit. A secular economist and a Christian phenomenologist may experience the mall quite differently, and part of that difference is attributable to the differing religious traditions they inhabit and how that has shaped their modes of experiencing. As such, there is a religious dimension to their experiencing of the mall, whether or not either of them considers going to the mall to be a "religious experience" (in the traditional narrow sense).

There are elements of both the sacramental and the event-al approaches in this description of religious experiencing. As in the sacramental approach, this account of material-spirituality gives materiality a kind of religious charge that we are able to access, even if we do not always access it (or at least, if we do not always focus on that element of it or become aware of it). This religious charge enables us to engage the world differently than we would if the world was not religiously charged in this way, and this different mode of engagement has impacts on a variety of experiences and on a variety of ways of experiencing. As in the event-al approach, one of the effects of religiosity is that the religious charge is at work in a variety of the phenomena we both produce and encounter.

Even if we do not always see it or acknowledge it, the religious charge is at work as a force or impetus, pushing not only how we engage with those phenomena (i.e., inviting us to take them up religiously, in addition to other ways they might be taken up) but also how we ourselves are shaped by them (given the quasi-transcendental and transcendental religious effects outlined in the previous chapter). That is to say, the religious charge shapes both particular experiences of particular phenomena and shapes our experiencing of (potentially all) phenomena in general.

These effects always come to us embedded in the particular traditions we inhabit, though none of those traditions is itself equivalent to religiosity—it is simply how we experience religiosity in this tradition or that tradition. In Marion's Catholic-Christian tradition, then, this religiosity comes embedded as love. This leads us not only to love particular phenomena in unique, distinctively religious ways (like the Eucharist, in one of Marion's famous examples); it also leads us to be loving in our experience of other phenomena and in how we experience in other modes of experiencing. Other transcendental modes of sensing the world—such as sociality, linguisticality, and ethicality—are impacted by the religious mode of loving: those inculcated in the Catholic-Christian tradition would come to see socialization as including a type of loving ("love your neighbours"), language use as including a type of loving (e.g., speaking or telling the truth "in love"), ethics as including a type of loving (e.g., loving the poor, the widow, and the orphan), and so on. Here we see how religiosity—which always comes to us embedded in a particular religious tradition—impacts both our experience of particular phenomena and our subjective ways of experiencing more generally.

The transcendental view of religious experience outlined draws on a variety of previous research in phenomenology, philosophy of religion, and the empirical study of religion to provide an account of religious experiencing that can better explain religion as it functions in our experience. Specifically, I think this model better accounts: (a) for how religion need not be opposed to other cultural forms (like politics, economics, language, etc.), but works with them to shape our experience; and (b) how religion can, therefore, be a dimension of our experiencing and not simply be confined to particular experiences. In that regard, the religious is not a content that is separable from other parts of our life but is a mode of living that shows up in everything we do. This need not mean that "all of life is religion" in the sense that all the phenomena we encounter are best engaged predominantly by religiosity, or that all of the phenomena we encounter are best understood by thinking of them primarily in terms of religious traditions. It simply means that there is a religious dimension to everything we do, and accounting for that dimension would then give us a more robust understanding of the phenomenon in question. In part, this might help explain the very situation that Fitzgerald (among others) complains about in which "such diverse institutions as totems, the principle of hierarchy, Christmas cakes, witchcraft, Unconditioned Reality, the Rights of Man, the National Essence, Marxism and Freudianism, the Tea Ceremony, Nature, Ethics, and so on"[37] are seen as religious, without giving in to what he (and others) find problematic with that, namely, the expansion of the category of religion to so many things that it is no longer helpful as a category for making distinctions in scholarly inquiry. For the transcendental account of religious experiencing enables us to see a crucial distinction: the religious way of experiencing things is different from the linguistic way of experiencing things, or the visible way of experiencing things, or the social way of experiencing things. But that difference does not manifest itself primarily in different experiences (this one religious, that one linguistic), but in a different way of experiencing: the same phenomena will have a religious component to our experiencing of it, as well as a linguistic, a visible, a social, and so on way of experiencing it.

The religious dimension of our experiencing, therefore, enables us to see something religious in all the diverse phenomena mentioned by Fitzgerald (and many more besides). Yet we need not treat them all as equally religious, in that not all of them are experienced or should be examined *predominantly* through the lens of religious traditions and religious effects. Because the religious is just one dimension of our experiencing of phenomena alongside others, several phenomena will be more dominantly marked by other types of traditions and other modes of sensing. Just as we might find it odd to consider a concert *primarily* a visual phenomenon while acknowledging that it has a visual component, so, too, are we now able to say things like Marxism or Christmas cakes may have a religious dimension to them without that meaning that they are best thought primarily as a religion or in religious terms.

Beyond these definitional concerns, though, I think this account of religious experiencing will also help us better understand actual, material practices in their religious dimension by allowing us to see that religious effects are not confined to worship rituals, theological or metaphysical concepts, or specifically prescribed actions. Many religious practitioners from a variety of religious traditions would claim that their "religion" (even if they wouldn't use that term) affects their lives in a multitude of ways: it causes them to treat other living creatures better (or sometimes worse), or to be more concerned with the environment, or gives them feelings of hope or guilt, or inspires them to persevere in difficult situations, or just changes what they do in regular, everyday ways. Most traditional, secular-Christian accounts of religious experience are unable to adequately account for these effects, insofar as they have a quite narrow category of what can be considered a "religious experience." Things that are not "religious" in that sense cannot be the object of a "religious experience." And because religion is only concerned with transcendent realities, mundane, everyday experiences cannot be or have a "religious" component to them, even if the person in question would acknowledge a kind of religious dimension to the situation.

Take, for example, a Muslim businessman selling a product to a client for a previously agreed-upon price even when the market suggests he could now get more for it than was originally agreed on. This is not an experience that most religious studies scholars would characterize as "religious," in that it is an experience that is not best understood as an example of a thing called "religion." However, the person's being Muslim seems to be an important dimension of that experience, insofar as his commitment to Islam and to Allah is part of what motivates his desire to keep his word on the previously agreed-upon price. As such, failing to acknowledge the role that Islam plays in this situation would be to miss something important about the experience. That is plausible enough, regardless of one's intuitions on religion, it seems to me. Yet, if it is plausible that a person's religious tradition is an important dimension of properly understanding an experience, why would we not consider that to be a "religious experience"? Why should we restrict the category of religious experience only to certain overwhelming experiences of religion, and not use it for all experiences in which the religious play an important role? Secularism provides some reasons for doing that, via its assumptions about a disenchanted world and a buffered self. But that is only one religious tradition, and it is not clear why its (religious) assumptions should get to structure the entire category and understanding of religious experience *in toto*. And if we do want to be able to consider any experience in which the religious dimension plays an important, meaning-giving role as a religious experience, then we need an understanding of religious experience that can account for how the religious is one dimension of the experience, but not the only one, or even necessarily the dominant one.

If all phenomena are (potentially) religious phenomena, as we argued in the last chapter, then it seems equally true that all experiences are (potentially) religious experiences. This is not to reduce everything to a kind of mysticism, but to acknowledge that there are more types of religious experience than just mystical ones.[38] Religious effects on our experiencing are wide-ranging, and we therefore need a more complex and nuanced account of religious experience.

One thing that will have to be accounted for in such a nuanced account is the fact that religious experience is not just empirical, but also transcendental: we do not just have experiences of phenomena we take to be religious; we also experience phenomena religiously. There can be religious components to how one eats breakfast or goes to work or drives a car or deals with pets or any of the many other activities we do or phenomena we engage with on any given day. A sufficiently robust and comprehensive account of religious experience must be able to account also for those, and not simply for those experiences of which "religion" is the object.

6

Thinking Religion Cross-Culturally

Last chapter, we tried to articulate an account of religious experience that did not retain the elements of transcendence that characterized the secular-Christian account and rendered it problematic for cross-tradition conversations about religion. This should make the account I am developing in this book less problematic for cross-cultural and comparative studies of religion.

At stake in the critiques of transcendence-based accounts was not simply their transcendence, but how that implicated them also in colonialist approaches to cross-cultural conversations. Having this assumption of transcendence as a necessary condition of religion caused religious scholars to apply that category to other religious traditions, even those where transcendence was not natively operative. In that sense, the transcendence-assumption caused religious scholars to misunderstand those religious traditions by trying to interpret them through a lens of transcendence.[1] Another colonialist problem also arose from this transcendence-assumption: not only did the category of transcendence cause Western scholars of religion to misunderstand those other traditions, but, given the power differentials in place in our current globalized context, that misunderstanding actually caused those traditions to change such that they become more consistent with the transcendence assumption. In this sense, the problem is not simply that Western scholarship misunderstood or misrepresented other religious traditions, it is that it actually started to change or alter them in (presumably) negative ways.[2]

Having sought to eliminate the transcendence-assumption from the transcendental account being developed in this book, the hope is that it can avoid these colonialist problems and so offer a way of having cross-cultural conversations about religion that do not assume the merits of one tradition or use one tradition as the normative standard against which others are measured. Given our analyses in Chapter three, we can say clearly that this account will *not* do so by offering a religiously neutral take on religion, one that would—by dint of its religious neutrality—be automatically and obviously reconcilable with all religious traditions. That is neither possible (as we demonstrated in Chapter three) nor desirable, for it is, perhaps, the height of colonialist thinking to assume that one's own account is the implicit Truth behind everyone else's account. To pretend that transcendental phenomenology could somehow give us an account of religion that was universally viable because it was not located within any particular tradition would be to repeat the mistakes of early phenomenologists of religion and simply re-entrench the assumptions of this account as universal criteria. That is something that I will do my utmost to avoid. Instead, I will seek a basis for cross-cultural (or what we might call cross-tradition) conversations about religion by emphasizing categories of experiencing that may be accessed, albeit potentially in very different ways, by other traditions also. In this sense, the conversation between traditions will not be rooted in similarity or in simple difference, but in the relations that give rise to both similarity and difference.

For this purpose, simply swapping transcendence out for the transcendental will not be sufficient to provide a better basis for cross-cultural conversations about religion. Indeed, what we have established so far may seem actually to undermine the very possibility of cross-cultural conversations about religion. Chapter three argued that all discourse about religion always takes place within some particular religious tradition or other. This is true for two reasons: first, any discourse on religion necessarily involves the use of religious phenomena (doctrines, concepts, ideas, rituals, etc.) that have themselves been shaped by, and are expressive of, a particular religious tradition. Second, given the account of quasi-transcendental effects on the function of subjectivity explored in Chapters three, four, and five, it is also the case that religion is never merely the object of scholarly inquiry but is also part of how that scholarship is experienced and carried out. In that sense, it is not only that we must employ religious phenomena from within a religious tradition to talk about religion, but also that we ourselves have been shaped, in our religious experience (in the broad sense outlined in the last chapter), by a religious tradition or the intersection of various religious traditions. Shaped by (at least one) religious tradition, our way of talking about religion is itself influenced by particular religious traditions. For both reasons, one's own approach to religion is itself the product of religious tradition(s). As such, all of our engagement *with* religious traditions always also happens *from* a religious tradition. When engaging with religious traditions (one's own or another's), therefore, we can never assume a transcendent or "God's eye view."

This fact seems to undermine the very possibility of the cross-cultural study of religion: if there is no neutral vantage point from which to view and talk about other religious traditions, how can we ever talk meaningfully or knowledgeably about them? If we only speak from our own religious tradition, it's not clear that we ever get to understand another tradition itself, on its own terms. As such, the cross-cultural study of religion would threaten to misinterpret or misunderstand those other traditions necessarily, interpreting them through lenses that are not their own. If, on the other hand, a scholar tries to enter into those other traditions in order to understand them "from within," this very act threatens to alter or change those traditions by its very participation in them (as discussed at the end of Chapter three). Hence, the cross-cultural study of religion seems inevitably doomed. At best, it seems, all it could be is a chance for people to talk about their own religious tradition and discuss its merits and drawbacks with people of other religious traditions.

Perhaps there is another way to discuss religion across different traditions, however, one that neither presumes we can get outside of our tradition to a "neutral" religious place, nor one that presumes we must simply champion and apologize for our own religious tradition as the "best" one. My wager in this chapter is that transcendental phenomenology (which is precisely what was missing from the early phenomenologists of religion) can open us to one such other way of talking about religion. In that sense, it is not merely the rejection of transcendence that is important for the cross-cultural study of religion. It is also the embracing of the transcendental as a method. For the transcendental approach enables us to articulate and account for the distinction (and the connection) between methodological categories and expressions and articulations of those categories. This distinction was first introduced at the end of Chapter two, where we highlighted the need to distinguish between religiosity (as a category) and distinct attempts to articulate the nature of that category. It was possible, we said then, that an articulation (including the articulation offered in that chapter) could be incorrect without that meaning the category of religiosity itself was incorrect or non-existent. This distinction between categories and articulations can be mapped more broadly on to our distinction between transcendental modes of sensing the world (and, specifically, the category of religiosity) and the particular articulations of that category found in the various religious (sub-)traditions and in the various religious phenomena. As long as we can keep this distinction open, we are able to talk about our tradition and its phenomena as a way of expressing religiosity, while leaving open the possibility for other articulations of religiosity and even the role of other categories.

Yet this approach threatens to leave us in a sophomoric relativism if we cannot account, somehow, for a way of talking between different traditions, a way of thinking philosophically and rigorously about the relationship between categories, their articulations, and the things we engage with in our everyday experience. The language of transcendental phenomenology we have been using in this book provides us a way to do just that. Beginning by understanding the things we engage with every day as phenomena (rather than as distinct things), we have seen how our empirical experiences are always caught up in traditions and modes of sensing. Hence, studying empirical phenomena gives us a way to better understand religious traditions and religiosity, and vice versa. As such, we will come to see the value of providing a transcendental phenomenological account, first of religious phenomena, and then of particular religious traditions. A phenomenology of a religious tradition takes seriously the transcendental and quasi-transcendental effects phenomena can have on our religious experiencing and so provides not only a deeper understanding of the tradition and the phenomena within it (as argued in Chapters three and four, respectively), but also helps us understand a way of accounting for the relationship between religiosity and the particular expressions of it as found in a particular tradition and its phenomena. Doing a transcendental phenomenology of a particular religious tradition therefore offers us something different, philosophically speaking, from an empirical account of a religious tradition or a phenomenological account of a particular phenomenon.

The philosophical (as opposed to simply the empirical) value of such a phenomenology becomes clear when we try to offer a transcendental phenomenology of religion. This latter would attempt to account for the relevant methodological and phenomenological categories at play in our religious experiencing. These categories are lived and experienced through their particular expressions, and they are philosophically elucidated primarily through distinct articulations. But because transcendental phenomenology is able to account, methodologically, for the relationship between the (transcendental) categories, the (quasi-transcendental) articulations, and concrete phenomena, it is able to try to account for the ways that any one tradition's articulations open it onto the broader category without precisely capturing or reducing that category to the articulation. In that way, it opens up the possibility of a cross-cultural conversation about religion, not simply at the empirical level, but also at the transcendental (and quasi-transcendental and perhaps even ultra-transcendental) levels. This is done, not by abandoning one's own tradition nor by naively assuming my tradition is the (universal) category, but by enabling us to conceive one way by which my tradition gives me access to something that other traditions may also access in quite different ways.

Insofar as the category is not merely performed but is expressed (and therefore continually generated) alongside its articulations,[3] what we are seeking is not a category that is what it is apart from its articulations, and into which each articulation must, somehow, give us a glimpse. That would be a transcendent understanding of the categories as something distinct from or other than the world of our experiencing. Instead, if the category (here, of religiosity) is itself shaped by its articulations, then exploring and examining the different articulations gives us insight into the ongoing generation of the category itself. What connects the different articulations is not a similarity of content or of performance, but a certain way of accessing the world that can be similar even across its differences. We see this already in terms of language, in which both Mandarin and English give us insights into how language works, even though each offers very different semantic and syntactic environments and so different accounts of how language works. Ricoeur highlights this structural similarity between religion and language, pointing out that while we do not speak language as such but always a particular language, we do not remain trapped in that particular language: we are able to learn other languages, translate between languages (if not perfectly), and so on. Similarly, he says, we do not do religion as such, but only a particular religion—although we are nevertheless able to enter into other religions, to "translate" between them, and so on.[4]

This approach means that we do not need to look for similarities (in content) in order to find ways of talking meaningfully about "religion" in a cross-cultural way, thereby decreasing the likelihood of colonialist abuses. Instead, we can learn from analyses of other religious phenomena and other religious traditions about the different ways that certain experiential categories express themselves and are articulated. This approach to cross-cultural religious analysis therefore takes as primary the categories of experience (religiosity, traditions, etc.) in their expression(s) and articulation(s). This gives us insight both into those categories themselves as well as their articulations in our own traditions and the phenomena we encounter. In this way, we can acknowledge not only a difference in focus for the study of religious phenomena, religious traditions, and religiosity, but also an ability to learn from these different tasks in service of a deeper and broader understanding of the role that religion plays in our experiences and in our experiencing.

Phenomenology of Religious Phenomenon

Let us begin our account of this approach to the cross-cultural study of religion by talking about how we phenomenologically analyse and make sense of empirical phenomena. Such work needs to account rigorously for how a phenomenon is experienced. There has historically been an assumption that because the phenomenological method begins with first-person analyses, it is necessarily condemned to solipsism, only able to offer accounts of a particular person's experience of something. But this assumption ignores the transcendental dimensions of experiencing that operate in every individual's experience. That is, it ignores the fact that every individual's experience is necessarily marked by the various traditions they participate in, the socially embedded meaningfulness of the phenomena they encounter, and the production of their own subjectivity within (quasi-)transcendental categories that are inevitably shaped by concrete historical and social conditions. There are, therefore, social and political forces that are a necessary part of "individual" experience, and individual experience is, therefore, always social and political.[5] Robustly and rigorously accounting for how a phenomenon is experienced, therefore, requires accounting both for the individual nature of an experience and the social and political dimensions of that experience.

When I speak of "robust" and "rigorous" phenomenology, I mean a phenomenology that (robustly) tries to cover the full breadth of a phenomenon and one that (rigorously) tries to describe as accurately as possible the phenomenon in question. These two ways of evaluating a phenomenology of a particular phenomenon need not always go together. One could do a rigorously detailed account of only some facets of a particular phenomenon without trying to account for all of it: for example, a rigorous analysis of the embodied affects of yogic practices might purposefully have to bracket its ability to talk also about the historical constitution of those practices, their linguistic dimension, or the social dynamics at play in those practices (especially to fit into a standard article-length presentation). Similarly, one could provide a robustly detailed account of a phenomenon that would accurately try to lay out all the different dimensions at play in a phenomenon without, therefore, being able to explain each one in pain-staking detail: one may wish to show how liturgical practice, for example, includes transcendental and quasi-transcendental elements alongside some of its empirical effects, and would therefore limit the description of the empirical effects to allow time to account also for the transcendental and quasi-transcendental effects.[6] Ideally, such choices would be made explicitly and methodologically, and indicators could be given of where one could expand the analysis to provide a more robust or more rigorous approach. But it is highly unlikely that any one analysis of a phenomenon can be both truly rigorous and truly robust, given the interconnection of all the various traditions, modes of sensing, empirical interactions, and so on that go on in each of our experiences.

For example, to robustly understand the Christian liturgical practice of the Eucharist, we must account for the religious phenomena that make it up (the bread, the wine, the words ritually spoken or recited alongside it, the theological claims that accompany and justify it, etc.). We must also account for the Catholic religious traditions in which the Eucharist is expressed, and how that differentiates it (materially as well as theologically) from the Protestant "Lord's Supper." Next, we would have to account for the transcendental effects it has on how people experience the world (e.g., the more material account of divine presence imparting a direct salvific effect in Catholic traditions vis-à-vis the more symbolic account of the Eucharist as an urge to greater personal piety in most Protestant traditions). Doing a robust "phenomenology of the Eucharist" requires looking at all those elements (and more). One could, however, at least in principle, perform a rigorous phenomenology of the Eucharist that entirely ignores the transcendental realm, as long as one lays out clearly what one is attempting to describe (e.g., the empirical effects of liturgy on one's affections, one's relation to the divine, or one's sense of communal involvement), and how one wants to describe it, and then performs those functions well. A phenomenology of lay Catholic experiences of taking the Eucharist, for example, could ignore the experiences of those from other religious traditions and still provide a rigorous account of how lay Catholics experience the Eucharist.

However, in practice, the relationship between the different levels of transcendental analysis complicates this picture. That is, because the transcendental is defined as the processes shaping *how* we experience particular phenomena, transcendentality necessarily affects the empirical: the devout Catholic not only interacts with highly different material phenomena than the pious Protestant does (wafers versus bread; wine versus grape juice; a shared ritual goblet versus individual, one-use disposable plastic cups; etc.), but is also likely to be more worried about missing the Eucharist for several weeks in a row than her Protestant neighbor. These empirical differences (different foods to eat, higher levels of anxiety) are the result of the differing quasi-transcendental contexts (Catholic versus Protestant) and the transcendental effects that growing up in those contexts have on an individual's self-understanding of religiosity and its role in their lives. However, these transcendental effects are themselves also generated within and by particular (empirical or quasi-transcendental) situations: because of differing implicit understandings of the relationship between God/divinity and materiality (which the average lay person is likely unable even to articulate clearly) arising in part from the different ways they have experienced the Eucharist/Lord's Supper, the Catholic and the Protestant may live with extremely different accounts of how to be devout/pious, what they need to do to be "saved," the spiritual significance of church participation vis-à-vis individual "devotions," the necessity of regularly taking the Eucharist/Lord's Supper, and so on. In this way, the transcendental processes are necessarily impacted also by the empirical (and quasi-transcendental) context of their generation. This means that even a phenomenology of religious phenomena should, in principle, account for transcendental and quasi-transcendental effects, and so should be purposeful, explicit, and methodological in its decision to exclude discussion of those effects from particular analyses.

A few things follow from this for a phenomenology of religious phenomena. First, a robust and rigorous phenomenology of a religious phenomenon requires analyses of all the modes and dimensions of experiencing. In turn, this entails that phenomenological insights must be gained from various fields and disciplines, including psychology, sociology, health sciences, architecture, religious studies, philosophy, and more, for a truly robust and rigorous phenomenology of a religious phenomenon. Simply "doing phenomenology" in a philosophical way is not enough to understand religious phenomena phenomenologically. Nor is a strictly sociological or strictly material analysis enough to understand a religious phenomenon robustly. Insights are needed from those who study religious phenomena empirically and from those who study phenomenology transcendentally in order to produce a rigorous and robust phenomenology of a religious phenomenon.

Second, because religious traditions function quasi-transcendentally, they impact our analyses on all the levels, including the empirical. Not merely the phenomena we consider, but also the scholars performing the analysis, are inexorably shaped by the traditions they inhabit and express. As such, a rigorous and robust phenomenology of a particular phenomenon should include research carried out by people within various traditions, to provide a broader, more robust and more rigorous understanding of the phenomenon in question. If a painter does not see a mountain the same way a geologist does, but both see the mountain, then a robust and rigorous phenomenology of the mountain would have to account for both what the painter sees and what the geologist sees. And the same would hold true for a phenomenology of a religious phenomenon: it would have to account for the differing styles by which a phenomenon is experienced by people of various different traditions. This means a robust and rigorous phenomenology of a religious phenomenon should include people working in (at least) different religious, linguistic, and professional (e.g., academic or clergy or lay person) traditions, and probably more traditions besides.

Third, there is reason to believe that at least some phenomenological analyses of the empirical effects of religious phenomena would benefit from a better understanding of the various levels (transcendental, quasi-transcendental, etc.) that help to constitute or produce those empirical effects. In this regard, although it is not necessary for everyone engaged in the broader project of a "phenomenology of a religious phenomenon" to be familiar with the work and results of transcendental phenomenology (which tends to take place in philosophical phenomenology), it would be beneficial for the field of religious studies if at least some people working in the more empirical elements of the field were to be familiar with the transcendental elements of the field, and vice versa.[7]

It should be clear from these three points that no one person can conduct all of the work on all the levels required for a robust and rigorous phenomenology of any religious phenomenon. The phenomenology of religious phenomena seems to require interdisciplinary research teams that can engage meaningfully with the work of religious studies, sociology, ritual studies, psychology, health studies, architecture, and others. But it should also include those who can engage meaningfully in transcendental phenomenology, just as transcendental phenomenology must include those who can engage meaningfully with the work of various empirical inquiries and disciplines.

Phenomenology of a Religious Tradition

Although the phenomenology of religious phenomena already includes accounting, in some way, for the quasi-transcendental effects of religious traditions, it does not yet take those religious traditions as themselves the object of philosophical (and phenomenological) inquiry. A phenomenology of the Catholic lay person's experience of taking the Eucharist is not a phenomenology of Catholicism, although it may certainly be an important source and reference for someone working on a phenomenology of Catholicism.

To offer a philosophy or phenomenology of a particular religious tradition would be to elucidate, phenomenologically, how that tradition functions as a religious tradition in a quasi-transcendental sense. This would include explaining how religiosity functions in a unique way in that tradition. It would also include how religiosity interacts with other transcendental modes of sensing the world in unique ways in that tradition, that is, how religiosity (in its unique function in that tradition) shapes how adherents of that tradition see differently, touch differently, appreciate beauty differently, use language (or symbolic representation) differently, have different social forms, and so on. In trying to elucidate the "style" of that particular tradition, a phenomenology of a religious tradition would need to draw heavily on empirical evidence and information in establishing its claims, because the "style" of a particular religious tradition is not simply a case of logical consistency (e.g., between its doctrines and its practices) but is how that tradition is uniquely expressed in the various phenomena generated by that tradition, and in the way that subjectivity operates in that tradition. In that sense, providing an account of how subjectivity functions within a particular tradition could be part of a phenomenology of a religious tradition, but it would not be the whole of it. At stake is not just the self-understanding of the religious tradition, but the unique style it imparts to life, to living beings, to phenomena—to the world. This is not simply a question of philosophical consistency or logical coherence. It is also a matter of what happens, by whom, in what ways in the world.

Articulating this style is not the same as arguing for its truth or accuracy. A phenomenology of a religious tradition need not be an apologetics for that tradition, nor an implicit justification of it. It is, rather, the attempt to notice and then accurately describe the difference that tradition makes in *how* the world is experienced, that is, how participating in that tradition impacts how one then interacts with the world. While it should be informed by empirical scholarship, it is not simply a matter of tracing out what distinct concrete phenomena are produced by a particular tradition. Although the difference a tradition makes in how the world is experienced would be expressed in phenomena, it would express itself also across all the various levels of analysis we have been discussing in this book: empirically, it would show itself in certain demographic differences (white evangelical Christians are X% more likely to perform Y action[8]), in the aesthetic style it gives to certain objects, the ethical style of living it calls for, the cognitive claims it makes more or less plausible, and so on. Quasi-transcendentally, it would show itself in the types of experiences and experiencing it opens up and makes possible, the types of experiences and experiencing it closes down or makes less likely, and the types of subjectivity it encourages and generates (i.e., what phenomena will or will not show up for them, how one engages with them, and so on). Transcendentally, it would show itself in the form of religiosity it yields (e.g., loving, detaching, submitting [e.g., to the will of Allah], or following the Dao) and the alterations it gives to other transcendental modes of sensing (e.g., seeing in loving ways, speaking in loving ways, etc.). A phenomenology of a religious tradition seeks to account for all these facets as it describes the unique style by which a particular tradition experiences the world.

Providing such a description can be normative (in a qualified sense) without being apologetic or triumphalistic. That is, in articulating the style of a particular religious tradition, it also, implicitly or explicitly, seems to provide the normative standards at work in that tradition: it is good to love your neighbor, or it is bad to become over-attached to things. But by restricting itself precisely and only to this or that tradition, those norms are never compared in a universalistic sense either to other traditions or to some purported Reality. Rather, they offer a kind of "grounded normativity,"[9] one necessarily aware of its rootedness in particular traditions, places, and historical circumstances.[10] A phenomenology of a religious traditions says "this is what this tradition thinks is better or worse on this modality or in this register" without ever trying to justify those positions for other traditions or even for itself: it will say "in Christianity, it is good to love your neighbor" without suggesting that all people everywhere should love their neighbors or without needing to establish some logical or theological justification of this normative standard within the confines of the Christian tradition. This is not, of course, to say that such a description is ever religiously (or ethically) neutral: it remains rooted in one particular tradition and adopts the normative standards of that tradition even in its description of itself. It does so always and only as a description of this tradition's expression of broader phenomenological categories, and as such remains aware (at least theoretically) of its limited nature: it is an analysis of the style of a particular *Stiftung*, and as such requires no justification other than the rigor and robustness of its descriptions. The question is not "is this tradition correct?" so much as "how does this tradition affect experiencing?"

This kind of phenomenology of a religious tradition is therefore not reducible to a religious phenomenology: a phenomenology of Christianity is not the same as a Christian philosophy. The difference is not just methodological (i.e., phenomenology versus other modes of philosophizing). The difference is also in how it understands the relationship between the tradition and the philosophizing being carried out. A Christian philosophy is inherently ambiguous: it could refer to a philosophy of Christian phenomena (analyses of Christian doctrines or claims, descriptions of Christian objects or building, etc.); it could refer to philosophy done based on the desires or needs of Christian people (e.g., recognizing Christianity lacks a sufficient understanding of the arts and therefore working to provide a better philosophy of the arts in relation to other parts of life); it could refer to the philosophical or logical coherence of Christian claims, or of Christian claims with prescribed Christian rituals, social mores, or ethical prescriptions; or many other things besides.[11] None of those is, inherently, a phenomenology or a philosophy of

Christianity itself. In that sense, religious philosophies or phenomenologies may be helpful toward a phenomenology of a religious tradition, but they are not the same thing.

Michel Henry seems to give us an example of a phenomenology of a religious tradition in his *I am the Truth: Toward a Philosophy of Christianity*. There, Henry is clear that what he is after is not an evaluation of Christian truth claims,[12] but the very style of subjectivity that Christianity imposes or provides for those living within it. Henry characterizes this style as "auto-affection," and endeavors to show that it opens an entirely new way of being in the world, one that, precisely, does not privilege our being in *the world*, but which privileges instead our being, our *living*, itself.[13] As such, Christianity—as a *Stiftung*, a tradition in the quasi-transcendental sense—gives an entirely new style to life, one that has implications for theological claims,[14] ethics,[15] language,[16] and more. This is not simply the tracing out of philosophical implications of Christian doctrines, concepts, or claims. It is the description of the style of living that is offered in the religious tradition called "Christianity."

The problem with Henry's phenomenology of Christianity is that his description of the style of Christianity is so heavily indebted to Henry's idiosyncratic reading of transcendental phenomenology that it seems to draw on very few empirical observations and so is not compelling (or even understandable) to the majority of people who would self-identify as Christian. By failing to build his analyses on empirical results or trace his analyses back to empirical outcomes—that is, by failing to adequately account for Christianity as it is actually practiced by those who self-identify as Christian—Henry's phenomenology of Christianity ends up being not a very robust account of Christianity: much is missing from Henry's analyses, including any sociological, anthropological, or other empirical evidence that could substantiate or ground his claims. There are some methodological reasons for this, mainly pertaining to the sharp distinction he draws between the truth of the world (which shows up in appearance) and the truth of Life/auto-affection/Christ(ianity) (which, precisely speaking, does not "appear" to us, but is our affectivity itself). While I am largely sympathetic to the (ultra-) transcendental phenomenological claims being made by Henry, his phenomenology of Christianity does not seem to be drawn from anything other than Henry's philosophy and his reading of certain texts in the Christian scriptures. As a philosophy, perhaps that is sufficient. But as a phenomenology, it is sorely lacking. And as an account of Christianity, it is perhaps downright erroneous, as many have criticized Henry for losing the thread of Christianity in his desire to make it fit his own phenomenology of Life.[17]

Hence, although *I am the Truth* seems to offer an example of a phenomenology of a religious tradition, it does so more as a proof of concept than as a solid example.

However, the accuracy of Henry's account of Christianity is not our concern here. Indeed, that one can criticize the account that Henry offers of a phenomenology of Christianity does not obviate the possibility of offering a phenomenology of Christianity or of any particular religious tradition. Quite the opposite: it shows us that such a phenomenology is not only possible but perhaps is even necessarily multiple. That other Christians debate the accuracy of his account of Christianity as a *Stiftung* may mean that Henry simply gets his description wrong. But it could also mean that he has defined the object of his inquiry too broadly. Perhaps "Christianity" is too broad a tradition to be accurately described, and instead he should have offered it as a phenomenology of anti-barbaristic (or anti-secular) Christianity in late twentieth-century France or some similar sub-tradition. If no one resonates with his description, then, indeed, he seems to have gotten something wrong. But if not everyone resonates with his description, perhaps that is a sign that "Christianity" as a phenomenological tradition is itself multiple, and that one analysis of the style of one sub-tradition of Christianity may not be sufficient to account for the style of Christianity itself (if there is such a thing).

All these kinds of questions can be opened up precisely by recognizing that Henry is offering an account of Christianity as a quasi-transcendental tradition and not of Christianity as a simply empirical tradition nor of Christianity as a collection of theological doctrines.[18] In that regard, *I am the Truth* can perhaps be seen as a kind of parallel to *Barbarism*, the latter of which offers a kind of phenomenology of Barbarism/secularism as a religious tradition. *Barbarism* offers much more in the way of concrete phenomena and examples (scientific thinking, television, labour markets, the university, etc.), and so offers another example of a phenomenology of a religious tradition.

A Phenomenology of Religion

This brings us, then, to a transcendental phenomenology of religion, as opposed merely to a phenomenology of religious phenomena or a phenomenology of a religious tradition. At stake here are the very categories we are using phenomenologically when we experience "religion," including religiosity, religious traditions, and religious phenomena.

As we just said with Henry's phenomenology of a religious tradition, that we can critique the nature of a particular articulation of the category need not imply either that the category does not exist or that the category cannot be talked about meaningfully, even if the category is always experienced in a particular tradition and never, so to speak, "in-itself."[19] To provide a phenomenology of the category of religiosity, then, seems to require or build on the analyses of phenomenologies of particular religious traditions and of particular religious phenomena. Without recourse to those as points of our analyses, we will perhaps inevitably treat our own religious tradition's account of religiosity as religiosity itself. This conflation of our articulation with the category threatens not only to misrepresent the category but also threatens to make other religious traditions feel pressured to show how they could fit with our account of religiosity (now masquerading as religiosity itself) if they want to be considered religious. That is to say, hearkening back to the beginning of this chapter, that this threatens to employ the category of religiosity (and perhaps also of religion) in colonial ways.

The solution, as we were starting to see with the Henry example in the last section, is not to avoid the particularities of concrete religious traditions or religious phenomena, but to lean into them as articulations or expressions of a broader category. In attempting to do away with the articulations or expressions, we end up with nothing substantial to talk about: talking about a transcendental category without recourse to quasi-transcendental structures is to talk, concretely speaking, about no-thing, as the category only ever comes to us via the mode of being of *Stiftung*, of some tradition or other.[20] That is to say, religiosity does not exist in the world. It operates within experiencing, but only as loving (in the Christian tradition) or as detachment (in some Buddhist traditions) or in some other concretized form in some tradition or other. The category only exists, concretely, in its quasi-transcendental and empirical expressions, that is, in and through traditions and the ways that people embedded in those traditions sense and interact with various phenomena in the world.

This is not to say that religiosity is not "real" or present in our religious experience. It is just to say that the type of reality it has—as transcendental structure—is not the same type of reality that empirical phenomena have. Visibility does not show up except in visual phenomena (i.e., concrete acts of seeing something), which are inevitably shaped by visual traditions (i.e., the styles in and by which we see). Linguisticality does not show up except in linguistic phenomena (i.e., concrete acts of meaning something), which are inevitably shaped by linguistic traditions (we mean something in English or Swahili). So, too, religiosity does not show up except in religious phenomena (i.e., concrete acts of religioning something), which are inevitably shaped by religious traditions (in which that "religioning" is taken as "loving" something or "submitting" to the will of Allah or as "detaching" from something, etc.).

Talk about religiosity, then, must always be connected to talk about religious traditions and religious phenomena, and this precisely because religiosity is a transcendental structure of experiencing. Given the material-spiritual nature of experience, transcendental structures are not transcendent structures. They remain fully rooted in our material-spiritual situation. In that sense, they do not simply appear in traditions, but they are themselves formed and shaped by their expressions in phenomena and traditions. What visibility is and how visibility works is shaped and altered by the various uses of visibility by the painter, the geologist, the optometrist, and the people wearing bifocals. Is seeing primarily about appreciating colors, shading and the interplay of light and dark? Or is seeing primarily about becoming aware of what is "just there" in front of us? Primarily or essentially, seeing is the giving of the world in a way that is able to do both of those things, and other things besides. What visibility is, therefore, is a shifting target that must account for how visibility works. And religiosity would work the same way: religiosity is the giving of the world in a way that is able to do a variety of things: loving, submitting, detaching, and so on.

However, this does not mean that I have to take all forms of religiosity as examples of "loving" or "submitting" or what have you. Quite the opposite: I must come to see "loving," "submitting," "detaching," and others as expressions of religiosity. What makes them examples of religiosity (qua expressions) is not some similarity that either they all share (in an essentialist understanding of religion) or that various of them share in various ways (in a family resemblance understanding of religion). No, what makes them examples of religiosity is that they are concrete expressions of a particular way of engaging the world. In that sense, religiosity is not an abstraction that we arrive at beginning from our shared religious experiences, but a way of experiencing that is able to encompass a wide variety of kinds of (religious) experiences. The point is not to fit a variety of experiences or ways of experiencing into one box labeled "religion," but rather to see whether the category of religiosity gives us a helpful way to account for what is happening in a variety of experiences: we engage with the world and various phenomena within it via a uniquely "religious" element of our experiencing. I am not claiming that loving, submitting, detaching, and so on *must be* examples of religiosity because they are doing the same thing (or even similar things). I am suggesting, rather, that thinking of them as examples of religiosity *might* open up new ways of understanding those experiences for which loving, submitting, detaching, and so on are important constitutive elements.

This is not simply a matter of limiting scholarly hubris. It is a matter of how we would be able to evaluate religiosity or have meaningful conversations about it. If the only way to talk about religiosity is through its expressions, that means that a phenomenology of religiosity cannot be carried out apart from the insights and findings of phenomenologies of various religious traditions and phenomenologies of various religious phenomena. The latter are not just examples to illustrate religiosity, they are the means by which we come to see, understand, and articulate religiosity as a category of our experiencing. Trying to abstract from those concrete articulations is to seek a universal or "neutral" explanation that, although theoretically amenable to everyone, is actually likely amenable only to those from a particular tradition. There is nothing wrong with that—but we should acknowledge that it remains rooted in a particular tradition and not pretend it is itself somehow tradition-less. In that sense, the earlier definition of religiosity as an experience of connectivity was a strategic decision: assuming the majority of readers of this book would be empirical scholars of religion who are therefore immersed in the secular-Christian religious tradition, describing religiosity in the widest possible terms was an attempt to get people who might otherwise be unlikely to countenance the possibility of religiosity as a category to be more open to the possibility. The hope is that, once they are open to the possibility, they would come to appreciate differing articulations of the category or different expressions of it.

The attempt to articulate religiosity in terms of connectivity, then, is a way to try to articulate an account of religiosity from within a particular religious tradition that, I expect, will be a familiar tradition for a majority of readers of this book. It does not define the "essence" of religiosity of which all other forms of religiosity are variations. Rather, it articulates something about how those in the secular-Christian tradition experience the world, in the hopes that others will find something resonant with that articulation. And that resonance is, hopefully, not exclusively for those in the secular-Christian tradition. By pointing at other times to loving, submitting, detaching, and other potential forms of religiosity, I hope also to get people to see some resonances between what makes a lot of sense to them (given whichever tradition they are native to) and what makes some sense to them but potentially a lot of sense to others (from a different tradition). In talking about and experiencing these resonances (or lack thereof, for we can also have interesting conversations about the differences between traditions not simply the similarities), we come to expand our own understanding of religiosity's possibilities and its capacity as a category of experiencing. In seeing new (to us) expressions of religiosity, we not only learn about other traditions, we also learn more about religiosity, and what it can do. This, in turn, recontextualizes our own experiences of religiosity within a broader framework: this is one way a person can "religion" the world, but there are others. Perhaps this helps us come to appreciate some of those other expressions of religiosity and to adapt versions of them in our own lives, even as we can imagine the geologist, after touring the mountain for two weeks with the painter, starting to notice a few of the intricacies of light and dark and maybe even lose himself, occasionally, in the visual appeal of the mountain. Perhaps it helps us to inhabit our own mode of religiosity a bit differently, even as we can imagine the painter starting to recognize the beauty of granite formations and the play of colors in the levels of sedimentation. Perhaps it simply helps us recognize the arbitrariness of our own religiosity and come to appreciate it in and for its non-necessity, even as we imagine the painter and the geologist each being a bit happier with their own styles of visibility, now that they recognize not everyone sees the way they do.

Whatever effects it has on how we inhabit our own religiosity, a phenomenology of religiosity, necessarily arising from concrete analyses of religious traditions and religious phenomena, seems to give us a way to talk about a broader unifying term that could hold together the various phenomena being studied under the rubric of "religious studies." As such, it serves the role of a phenomenology (or even a philosophy) of religion, in the broader sense, but now understood with the proviso that religion is probably better understood as "the religious": a modification of experience rather than a distinct kind of thing.[21] Such a transcendental phenomenology of religiosity or of the religious seeks to understand the category itself, and as such is a different type of inquiry than a phenomenology of a religious tradition or a phenomenology of religious phenomena. These are three different approaches to the phenomenological study of religion. Each serves a necessary and important role, and each seems to build on the insights of the others in order to do its own job best.

That said, the distinction between these approaches might be more descriptive or meta-philosophical than actual. That is to say, it is likely that any phenomenology of religion will have elements of all three kinds of phenomenologizing: a phenomenology of the Eucharist (as our example from earlier this chapter) that was aware of and accounting for its empirical, quasi-transcendental and transcendental effects would, by virtue of that, also seem to include some elements of a phenomenology of religious traditions and a phenomenology of religiosity. This is not necessary—one could, perhaps, keep the boundaries sharply distinct—but it is likely, given the interconnected nature of the various levels of experience. If we think of the three types of phenomenologizing as three distinct tasks, we might find that any one project or analysis could be in service of more than one of those tasks, and that a robust and rigorous phenomenological analysis of religion would require all three tasks to be fulfilled.

Cross-Cultural Religious Studies

We see, then, that it is possible to have meaningful cross-cultural and cross-tradition conversations about religious phenomena, religious traditions, and religiosity. If we treat these things explicitly in a transcendental phenomenological way (e.g., as phenomena rather than objects; as quasi-transcendental traditions rather than simply empirical traditions; as a mode of sensing the world rather than a distinct set of things in the world), we can also have meaningful cross-cultural and cross-tradition conversations about the very categories of religion. We can explore how the categories of religion interact with each other and mutually express each other in our own tradition and seek to compare that to how other people describe them interacting and expressing each other in their traditions. We can, therefore, find reasons to talk across traditions about the religious as a meaningful category of our experiencing. We can do this without trying to evaluate other traditions according to the assumptions of our own tradition, that is, without assuming other traditions must be like mine in order to be significantly religious.

These categories and their interconnection also give us a way to acknowledge different legitimate uses of religious categories that mean empirical scholars of religion can do their thing even if philosophers of religion cannot decide, precisely, on what "religion" is. Various types of religious scholars (sociologists, philosophers, phenomenologists, linguists, etc.) can pursue different approaches while still learning from each other in ways that can significantly impact our own work and analyses. There is, here, a set of tools for the study of religion that can have broad applicability and be mutually helpful. Those will be elucidated more clearly in the conclusion. Here, I simply want to show a way of pursuing the cross-cultural study of religion that would let us talk with other cultural traditions in non-colonizing ways. Rooted in material-spirituality, focusing on experience and experiencing opens us on to a transcendental method for the study of religion that avoids the trap of transcendence, precisely by accounting for how even our categories of experiencing are themselves rooted in material-spiritual experience.

Conclusion: Material-Spiritual Religion

In this book we have been trying to think religion through the lens of experience. Not, to be clear, through the lens specifically of "religious experience," in line with the early phenomenologists of religion, but rather through the lens of experience in general. We have tried to account for the broad structure of experience, and then asked how religion might fit into that structure. In doing so, we have elucidated both a transcendental account of religion as a dimension of our experiencing and, implicitly at least, some elements of a transcendental method for thinking about religion. It might behoove us to make both of those points a bit more explicit as we conclude, to clearly lay out what we have accomplished in the book.

Material-Spiritual Religion

To begin, let us examine the account of religion laid out in this book. Rooted in the material-spiritual nature of experience, religion was revealed to be an entanglement of subjectivity, history, culture, and materiality. That means that religion is made up both of phenomena and of subjective modes of engaging the world. Those two facets of religion are phenomenologically distinguishable, even if they are experienced as a unity: it is religious phenomena that affect and produce particular communal styles of religious experiencing, even as those styles, and the religious mode of engaging the world they express, are also significant factors affecting and producing phenomena. Part of understanding religious phenomena, then, is accounting for how they affect subjectivity, and part of understanding the religious modes of subjective engagement with the world is accounting for the phenomena they produce and affect.

Unfortunately (at least for a simple understanding of religion), experience is such that subjective modes of engaging the world are not only individually entangled with history, culture, and materiality, but they are also entangled with each other. That is to say, the religious mode of sensing the world (religiosity) is not only affected by questions of culture, history, and material engagement; it is also affected by other modes of sensing the world, such as linguisticality, visibility, tactility, sociality, aestheticality, and so on, each of which is itself also affected by questions of culture, history, and material engagement. This means that religious effects are found not only in phenomena that are clearly and obviously marked by those religious effects—phenomena that are primarily the result of acts in which religiosity is the dominant mode of sensing—but also potentially in phenomena that are primarily the result of acts in which another mode of sensing the world is dominant but whose expression has been affected, in some way, by that mode's interaction with religiosity. In other words, it's not just obviously "religious" phenomena that are both affected by, and therefore in turn affect, religious effects. Even phenomena that seem primarily tactile or economic or social could be impacted and marked in significant ways by religious effects. Think, for example, of how the sale of candy is impacted by "religious" holidays such as Easter, Christmas, and Halloween, or the ways in which social justice movements have often been marked by religious motivations (both pro- and anti-).

What this all means is that religion is much broader in its scope than a merely empirical analysis of religious experience or religious phenomena might reveal. More things must count as religious, and perhaps also as religion, than much of the contemporary understanding of religion allows for. This includes enabling us to account for the religious dimension of certain results that empirical analyses of religion have revealed—such as the fact that white evangelical Christians are significantly more likely than other Republicans to believe there's a deep state working against President Trump and significantly less likely than both non-white evangelical Christians and white non-evangelicals to believe in human rights for groups other than their own.[1] On their surface, there is nothing inherently "religious" about these kinds of beliefs. Hence, there is a tendency to view these kinds of results as demographic curiosities but not religiously significant in their own right: that a certain kind of Christian thinks these things needs explaining, but the explanation is rarely sought in the realm of religion itself. However, given that their religion clearly plays a role in these beliefs, attitudes, and resulting actions (because they are significantly and statistically different from those who do not share that religion), it seems fair to see those beliefs, attitudes, and resulting actions as phenomena that have a religious dimension. If that's true, then those beliefs, attitudes, and resulting actions seem to become part of their religion, at least as far as thinking about and analyzing that religion goes, even though the nature of those beliefs, attitudes, and actions would not have traditionally been considered to be "religious" in nature.

Now, perhaps the word "religion" is being asked to do too much at this point, to carry too much semantic weight. If people would rather say that those beliefs, attitudes, and resulting actions are part of the religious *tradition* (rather than simply the religion) of white evangelicalism, you will get no argument from me. But then we must acknowledge that a religious tradition is not simply a collection of doctrines, rituals, and practices that its adherents ascribe to. Rather, a religious tradition, when understood quasi-transcendentally as *Stiftung*, marks the ways that its adherents experience the world differently because of their alignment with a particular religious tradition. In that sense, our material-spiritual account of religion not only adds more types of phenomena to what must be accounted for in a religious tradition, it also pushes us to include elements of phenomenality (e.g., communal styles of subjectivity) and not just phenomena as part of what must be accounted for in a religious tradition, precisely because those elements of phenomenality, of *how* we experience, are also altered by their participation in this religious tradition rather than that one.

Saying this is not an attempt to de-materialize religion (by adding a subjective component) but rather of expanding its materiality (by including subjectivity as a material[-spiritual] element of a religious tradition). A religion's materiality includes those things that we may traditionally have wanted to consider immaterial, such as beliefs, doctrines, and the types of subjects it produces. This is significant, because it reminds us that believing, too, is an action that takes place in the world, carried out in particular material-spiritual circumstances and performed by people engaging the world via subjectivity. It also reminds us that subjectivity is not given *a priori*, but develops within particular material-spiritual conditions and therefore functions somewhat differently than the subjectivity being drawn on by people in other religious traditions (or other ethical, social, economic, etc., traditions). In that sense, religion is—or, if you prefer, religious traditions are—material(-spiritual) all the way down.

What are the implications of this claim? For one, the nature of a particular religious tradition will be determined, not only by its religious engagements (i.e., religiosity), but also by the intersection of those religious engagements with social, linguistic, economic, aesthetic, tactile, and so on engagements. In our earlier example, we discussed *white* evangelicalism in part because it is notably distinct from non-white evangelicalisms in a variety of ways, many of which would not be considered "religious" in other accounts of religion. While their beliefs or doctrines about God, about the church, about sin, salvation, and so on might be almost entirely the same, and many of the religious rites and rituals would be quite similar (prayer, communion, songs of worship, etc.), the way that they engage the world (especially the social world) seems markedly different. There is a significant difference here that must be accounted for. One might be tempted, in a case like this, to consider evangelicalism the shared religious tradition, and then mark out the other differences as being political, or social, or socioeconomic differences that alter behavior, but not the religious tradition itself. However, the problem is that those differences, over time, end up marking out differences in how the religious tradition is lived out. These differences tend not to be doctrinal, but rather in how those doctrines are enacted and enlivened for the life of the community: white evangelicals put comparatively more focus on the first person of the Trinity, black evangelicals tend to put comparatively more focus on the third person of the Trinity. Both read the Bible, but they take very different messages out of it.[2] They both sing worship songs, but they sing different songs and sing them differently. To use the language of this book, the *style* with which they express their shared Christian religion is vastly different, both in terms of what we would traditionally consider religious activities and in terms of what we would have traditionally considered to be non-religious activities (such as political engagement, labour practices, etc.). I do not want to deny the political or socioeconomic dimension to many of those differences—I simply do not want to ignore the religious dimension of those differences either. While we can distinguish—at least phenomenologically and theoretically—the religious, the socioeconomic, the political, and so on as different dimensions of an experience of a phenomenon, the fact is that those dimensions are always intertwined and intersected in various ways in our experience of any phenomenon. Those intertwinings are not accidental to the development of different religious (sub-)traditions but are essential to it. Religious traditions are determined by more than simply the religious dimension, as any good historian will tell you.

Similarly, religious phenomena are also determined by more than simply the religious dimension. Even those phenomena for which religiosity is the primary mode of sensing or engaging the world are inevitably and irrevocably shaped also by other modes of sensing, and the various styles and traditions by which we experience them. We see this quite easily in religious objects, which serve a religious function but also clearly and obviously bear the marks of different aesthetic styles and traditions (Gothic versus Romanesque cathedrals, Arabian versus Mughal mosques, lingam-yoni versus Dhara linga). We see this also in doctrines and concepts, which serve a religious function while clearly and obviously bearing the marks of different linguistic and philosophical styles and traditions: the Christian doctrine of the Trinity, to use an earlier cited example, could probably not have been formulated, in its commonly accepted Nicene formulation, in a language other than post-Platonic Greek. Doctrines and concepts, too, are material phenomena determined by more than simply the religious dimension.

For these reasons, religious traditions are always constituted within cultures and express those cultures in a multiplicity of ways. Yet, something significant would be lost if we did not mark them also as "religious" traditions, as opposed to simply "aesthetic," "linguistic," "economic," and so on traditions. That religious phenomena also have aesthetic, linguistic, economic, and so on dimensions to them, in addition to the religious dimension, does not negate the distinctiveness of that religious dimension. Nor does the fact that religious traditions often have a panoply of sub-traditions negate that there is something important about the style of that overall tradition. For it is not the similarities that are primary and significant, nor the differences; both similarities and differences help us better understand phenomena, traditions, and modes of engaging the world. Similarly, that religious traditions are constituted within, and significantly marked by, other cultural traditions does not mean that religious traditions are simply cultural traditions. There is a uniqueness to the religious modality that bears noticing, if we are to properly understand religion and the role it plays in our experiences (and experiencing) of the world.

In that sense, to acknowledge the deeply cultural nature of religious traditions is not to deny them a religious significance. It is, rather, to note that the distinctly religious significance is not about being pulled out of culture or the world. It is, instead, about how one inhabits and engages with culture and the world. Saying this operates as a denial of the necessity of transcendence for an understanding of religion but is not necessarily a denial of the possibility of transcendence: although religion is necessarily material-spiritual, it could (but it need not) refer to things purported to exceed the material-spiritual. Transcendence is possible, but not necessary and not absolute. Whatever may be transcendent, if we are to have (religious) experience of it, qua experience it must be material-spiritually constituted: Allah must dictate the Quran in a particular language and to a particular person if it is to be revelatory to actual, real people; the spirit of God must be at work in particular ways in particular moments of history if it is to inspire actual, real people; *brahman* must appear in particular, concrete forms if it is to be expressed in actual, real things in the world. Acknowledging the experiential component of this does not deny the possibility of the non-experienced, it merely roots our understanding of it in experience as we experience it. In doing so, this material-spiritual approach to religion acknowledges that religion is a human (or at least subjective[3]) endeavor, but one that cannot be restricted exclusively to subjective actions. The impacts and effects of religious expressions resonate throughout the world (and perhaps beyond, although we cannot experience that directly), seeming to give a religious inflection to all phenomena in the world and to all subjective activity. Everything that we experience is (at least potentially) affected by the religious. That is not a denial of the significance or uniqueness of religion, but precisely a way to try to mark and acknowledge it.

Experience and Religious Effects

How, then, can we mark and acknowledge the uniquely religious dimension of the world and our experiencing of it? Different religious traditions will answer that question quite differently, and none of us can ever answer that question without being situated in at least one religious tradition, as we showed in Chapter three. However, that does not mean we cannot talk seriously and meaningfully about this question across different religious traditions, as we showed in Chapter six. Some distinctions that we have made throughout the book might be helpful in furthering those conversations. It is those that I would like to highlight and further explicate now, to help us consider more carefully and methodically how we think and talk about religion.

The first important methodological distinction for the study of religion is the distinction between that which is experienced and our experiencing of it. An experience is the concrete moment we have in which we sense or engage the world in a variety of ways. This experience, as we have been noting in this book, necessarily has both a content (*what* is experienced) and various modes of experiencing (*how* it is experienced). Let us take a simple example of sitting before a fireplace. The content of the experience is me sitting before a fireplace. That is what is experienced. My experiencing of the fireplace includes a variety of ways I engage with it: I feel its warmth; I see the flames burning; I smell burning wood; I recall childhood experiences of fireplaces, which fill me with warm and nostalgic feelings; the scene strikes me as beautiful.

Within the broadly Kantian framework that has characterized Western knowledge for the last few centuries, this distinction between experienced and experiencing within experience was mainly viewed additively: experienced + experiencing = experience. Although different theorists might do the math differently (some, such as the empiricists, claiming that experience was much more influenced by the experienced while others, such as idealists, claiming that experience was much more influenced by experiencing), most people agreed that experience was put together in this kind of additive fashion. Experience was a combination of otherwise distinct things: the experienced and experiencing, content and form.

This distinction has proven significant for the study of religion. Historically, the field of religious studies began with phenomenology, and therefore with religious experience in some sense. Experiences of the holy or of the numinous became the foundation of religion as an empirical practice that could be studied. As these religious experiences were understood to be constituted additively, one could ask whether it was the experienced or the experiencing component that made a particular experience "religious." Over time, the religious dimension of this experience came to be viewed almost exclusively as what was experienced in the experience, and not our experiencing of it. The result of that shift—from religious experiences to religion-as-experienced—has had a profound impact on the study, understanding, and perhaps even the practice of religion. For once religion was equated solely with what is experienced, religion became separable from both the lives of experiencers and from other things in the world as possible contents of experience. That is, religion was one type of content, and it was this content that would make an experience a "religious" experience rather than some other kind of experience. As such, religion was *not* a subjective process, but a (in theory discoverable) content that was somewhere to be experienced. Understood as such a content, it was distinct also from other types of content that would make an experience a different kind of experience: aesthetic content that would make for an aesthetic experience, or romantic content that would make for a romantic experience.

When people like Foucault came along and challenged the sharp distinction between experienced and experiencing by showing that subjects (and, by extension, subjective processes of experiencing) were themselves constituted in the same power relations that constituted the experienced world, two challenges were posed to religious studies: first, whether the category of experience was relevant to the study of religion at all; and second, whether religion could actually be distinguished as a distinct type of content. The first challenge went something like this: experience is a useful category insofar as it allows us to combine two distinct types of things: experienced content and experiencing subjects. If both of those things are equally constituted in relations of power, then their combination does not seem to require any recourse to experience at all. We can just as easily account for both of them in the language of power. Because power is the baseline that gives rise to and generates both what is experienced and how we experience it, accounting for power will be more illustrative than talking about experience. At best, the category of experience tells us nothing we cannot already get from examining power relations. At worst, it reinscribes particular power relations that are problematic insofar as they privilege some groups of people over others. There was, therefore, no meaningful reason to talk about experience in religious studies following the Foucaultian focus on power.

Of course this situation arose beyond religious studies as well. Across the humanities and social sciences, the category of experience lost explanatory power. This created another problem for the study of religion, one that is perhaps more pertinent to the study of religion than of other things: insofar as the subject matter of religious studies was religious experience, abandoning the category of experience threatened to leave religious studies with nothing to study. Initially, the content of what was experienced provided the subject matter for the continued study of religion beyond the category of experience. Once this content was itself subjected to the play of power relations, it became clear that the experienced things of religion—beliefs, rituals, objects, practices— were themselves constituted by a play of cultural, social, linguistic, and so on power relations that left people wondering what value remained to talking about "religion." If religion was a content that was generated by cultural, social, linguistic, and so on forces, why not just talk about those forces, and stop talking about religion? If religion was just a content in the world, it seemed it could be explained entirely without recourse to "religion" as something distinct from other forces. Therefore, religion either did not exist as a content in the world, or it existed only as referencing things outside the world, beyond the play of power relations. Insofar as there was significant skepticism about what, if anything, could exist beyond the play of power relations (because subjective processes were themselves now understood as contents that were generated in the world of power relations, any subjective access to that which is beyond the world would, itself, necessarily be something that takes place in the world, and as such be reducible to the various forces of power), there were few people left who could articulate what religion was, as a content to be experienced in the world.

The material-spiritual nature of religion, however, as revealed to us in transcendental phenomenology, is a fundamental rejection of the Kantian additive picture of experience. Instead, it suggests an expressive, generative picture, in which experience (as material-spirituality) is the background that generates the distinction between experienced and experiencing. In this scenario, experienced and experiencing are not ontologically distinct components that need some other category (like experience) to bring them together. Rather, experienced and experiencing are mutually generated in their expressive relationship to each other, a relationship we call experience.[4] This means, first, that the impact of the experienced on experiencing that is highlighted in the work of people like Foucault need not alter our fundamental understanding of experience, experienced content, or processes of experiencing. We should not be surprised that processes of experiencing are themselves constituted in experience, because those processes are, and must be, generated within the material-spiritual nature of experience. Second, this does not reduce experiencing to experienced content, precisely because the distinction between them is generated and sustained by the generative unfolding of experience: it is in reflecting on experience that we come to distinguish subjective processes from experienced content. This distinction is therefore a theoretical (and phenomenological) distinction: the two have different functions in the constitution of our experience, and so they can be distinguished—as a matter of method or abstraction—even though they are generated in mutually interconnected ways. The distinction between experienced content and processes of experiencing is not an absolute distinction, but a phenomenological one.

This, in turn, implies a third point: because they are both generated by experience, both experienced content and experiencing subjective processes will be marked by the nature of experience. Religious experience—which was, and perhaps still is, the starting point of religious studies—should therefore be expected to have effects on both experienced content and the processes of experiencing. Indeed, this is precisely what I have argued in this book: there is a religious dimension both to phenomena (as *what* we experience; see Chapter four) and to the transcendental and quasi-transcendental modes of our experiencing (as *how* we experience; see Chapters two and three). Trying to understand "religion" without also understanding its "religious" effects is to fundamentally misunderstand religious experience (as we demonstrated in Chapter five).

Understanding these religious effects means accounting for the fact that religiosity is, like other subjective processes, also generated in and out of the material-spiritual nature of experience. Just as experienced and experiencing are mutually generated in the expressive unfolding of experience, so, too, are the various modes of experiencing mutually generated in that expressive unfolding. In other words, religiosity is a unique mode of experiencing, but not one that can be absolutely separated from other modes of experiencing. Its uniqueness comes, not from picking out one type of experience vis-à-vis others, but from imparting a distinct way of engaging any (and perhaps every) phenomenon and content we experience. We marked this in this book by talking about religious traditions (themselves generated in particular historical and social circumstances) as the way that religiosity expresses itself in concrete situations. Religiosity always comes to us in particular religious styles, which are themselves also marked and affected by other modes of engaging the world and the styles and traditions expressing those other modes of engaging the world. As such, religious effects shape experience not by producing phenomena that are exclusively or exhaustively religious (i.e., religious instead of being something else), but rather by adding a religious dimension to the production of, and engagement with, phenomena in general. Some phenomena might be marked more by religious effects than others, as we discussed in Chapter four, but no phenomenon is exclusively or only marked by religious effects, and few (if any) phenomena are not affected at all by religious effects. Discovering that a phenomenon that we thought to be a religious one is also marked by linguistic, cultural, social, and so on, effects does not mean that its religious dimension can be ignored or reduced to those other dimensions. Rather, its religious dimension shapes how those other dimensions appear in the phenomenon, even as that religious dimension is itself shaped by the effects those other dimensions have had on it in its expression in the phenomenon.

All of this means, ultimately, that our investigations of religion must seek to account for all the ways that religion impacts the world that we experience. This cannot be done if we seek to understand religion solely as a thing in the world, distinct from subjective processes. Nor can it be done if we seek to understand religion solely in terms of subjective processes and discredit its expressions also as things in the world. Nor can it be done by seeking phenomena that are only or exclusively marked by religious effects. Rather, we must, as we said earlier, attempt to mark and acknowledge the uniquely religious dimension of the world *and* of our experiencing by seeing how they mutually reinforce and influence each other.

Disambiguating the Study of Religion

There is therefore no shortage of work to be done in the study of religion. In marking the various types of religious effects, we have to pay attention to at least three distinct types of effects religion has within experience. This corresponds to the three levels of phenomenological analysis that pertain to the study of religion: the transcendental modes of sensing, quasi-transcendental traditions, and empirical phenomena. There are unique religious effects on all three levels, although this need not mean the effects are entirely separated: one phenomenon is likely to induce effects on all three levels at the same time, and so the effects seem to mutually reinforce each other, as described in Chapter six. Nevertheless, the types of effects we are looking for affect everything from the object of inquiry to the methodology employed. As such, without overly separating the effects, it may be helpful to be clear which type of effect(s) we are talking about in a particular religious study.

To do that, I distinguished between three distinct tasks or approaches in the study of religion (see Chapter six). Elements of several of these tasks often happen in one particular study, and therefore sometimes the distinct nature of the tasks is confused. In an effort to disambiguate the study of religion, and using my own specialization of philosophy of religion as the primary example, I will encourage us to distinguish more sharply between a philosophy of a religious phenomenon, religious philosophy, and a philosophy of religion proper. Currently, all three of these tasks happen under the rubric of a "philosophy of religion," which is partially responsible for the existence of at least three distinct fields called "philosophy of religion" which often have very little to do with each other: critical philosophy of religion, Continental or phenomenological philosophy of religion, and analytic (or Anglo-American) philosophy of religion. I will accentuate the differences, in part to make clear the distinct tasks and how they require different approaches. I want to be clear here, again, that all three tasks are better achieved if and when they learn from the insights and approaches of the others.

The first task is the philosophy of a religious phenomenon. Here, we are trying to understand a particular phenomenon better. We discussed at length in the last chapter what this might look like for empirical studies of religion utilizing phenomenology, and I will only re-emphasize it briefly here: understanding a particular religious phenomenon robustly and rigorously requires accounting for all of the ways it is both religiously affected and has religious effects, on all three levels of analysis. So, a phenomenology of a religious phenomenon cannot simply look at empirical effects, even though it is interested in a particular empirical phenomenon. That phenomenon has all three types of religious effects (transcendental, quasi-transcendental, empirical), and all must be examined in a phenomenology of a religious phenomenon.

Philosophically speaking, the task is to better understand that particular phenomenon. It seems to me that the majority of Analytic philosophy of religion does this kind of work: trying to understand the coherence of particular religious beliefs (e.g., theistic beliefs) in light of various problems, logical or existential; justifying the rationality of particular beliefs, in light of particular evidences or data; or, in more recent years, highlighting the empirical effects of particular religious doctrines (e.g., the relation between substitutionary atonement theories in Christianity and instances of child abuse), or of particular religious communities (e.g., in literature on religious trauma). In all these cases, the goal, philosophically, is to provide a better understanding of some particular phenomenon.

That is a distinct philosophical goal from trying to understand the nature of religion itself. This is the task of a philosophy of religion, properly speaking, in the same way that a philosophy of science attempts to understand the nature of science and how it functions. Chapter six highlighted particular details of how to pursue this task in a phenomenological way, and so I need not repeat them here. My point here is simply that the task of elucidating the nature of religion is a different task, philosophically speaking, than the task of understanding a particular phenomenon. Critical philosophy of religion seems the sub-tradition of philosophy of religion that is most concerned with this particular task.

Finally, both of those tasks differ, philosophically, from the task of understanding a religious tradition. In Chapter six, I distinguished between a phenomenology of a religious tradition and a religious philosophy. Here, I think that distinction still holds, but I admit it becomes somewhat more muddled: how is a Christian philosophy (of the type propounded by Plantinga, for example) distinct from a philosophy of Christianity, or a Jewish philosophy (of the type propounded by Buber or Rosenzweig) distinct from a philosophy of Judaism? It seems to depend on what is meant by a religious philosophy. Levinas provides an interesting case study here. He is quite clearly bringing resources from the Jewish tradition to bear on philosophical issues in a way that could be called a Jewish philosophy (even if he himself might be uncomfortable with that terminology) without being a "philosophy of Judaism." The difference is in the end goal: is someone trying to offer a better understanding of Judaism, as a religious tradition? Or are they using insights from Judaism to answer questions in phenomenology or meta-ethics? In Levinas' case, it is more clearly the latter.[5] For someone like Plantinga, however, the answer may be more complex. There are times when he certainly seems to be taking insights from Christianity (e.g., the *sensus divinitatis*) and applying it to questions in epistemology (i.e., in the notion of religious commitment as a "properly basic belief"[6]). That seems to be a case of Christian philosophizing, but not a philosophy of Christianity. At other times, however, he is clear that philosophers should let their questions and concerns be guided by the questions of the Christian community.[7] Here, philosophical insights are being used to answer problems in Christianity in a way that is not simply a Christian philosophy (in the sense outlined above), but is also, perhaps, not yet a philosophy of Christianity. Instead, it is a mobilization of philosophical insights for Christian questions: if Levinas offers a Jewish philosophy, perhaps we should call this a philosophical Christianity. Is this, then, a philosophy of Christianity?

To be doing a robust philosophy of a religious tradition, the end goal has to be a better (philosophical) understanding of that religious tradition. This can easily slide into the philosophy of a religious phenomenon but must be kept distinct: investigating the coherence of theistic beliefs is not yet to offer a philosophy of theism, per se, but rather philosophical defences of certain theistic phenomena (in this case: beliefs). To be a philosophy of a religious tradition, the goal must be articulating something essential about the nature of a particular religious tradition qua that tradition. The best examples of this might be found in people attempting to do a philosophy of religion, but doing so in a way that only seems to apply to their own religious tradition: perhaps Otto, for example, offers a philosophy of Christianity in his attempts to offer a philosophy of religion. Similar questions could be raised about the "theological turn" in French phenomenology. Insofar as Marion, for example, attempts to offer a philosophy of revelation, but does so almost exclusively from the tradition of Catholicism, we could ask whether he instead offers a philosophy of Catholic revelation, rather than a philosophy of revelation per se. Emmanuel Falque would seem to be similarly situated: his philosophical insights into religion seem to hold only for Christianity, given the authorities he appeals to, the way he proceeds, and his own admitted rootedness in that tradition.

Given these examples, we may question the viability of a philosophy of religion. If we always speak from within a particular religious tradition, can we ever successfully carry out a philosophy of religion? Chapter six talked about how this could be done: one attempts to articulate the categories of religion in general but acknowledges that one does so from within a particular religious tradition and tries to suggest how that has influenced one's approach. As we said above, this would not prevent Marion, for example, from talking about revelation in terms of love, but suggests that he also should acknowledge that loving is a particular Catholic understanding of the mode that revelation takes, and that others might interpret religiosity differently. That, in turn, would help him acknowledge the broader category of religiosity (i.e., of a particularly religious mode of engaging the world) without having to deny that, in the Catholic tradition, that category is often taken up as love. Similarly for Otto, distinguishing more carefully between the details of his own tradition and a broader category might have helped him better distinguish experienced content and structures or categories of experiencing in his account of religious experience.

In differentiating a philosophy of religion from the philosophy of a religious tradition, then, the goal or the task is the crucial element. As long as a person is attempting to articulate something true for religion in general, they are doing a philosophy of religion; if they are attempting to articulate or say something about the nature of a particular religious tradition, they are doing the philosophy of a religious tradition. That is the dividing line between the distinct tasks of a philosophy of religion and a philosophy of a particular religious tradition.

Distinguishing these philosophical tasks is important because they often end up getting confused in ways that lead to problems. As mentioned in relation to Otto, confusing a philosophy of a religious tradition (which is probably what he offers us) with a philosophy of religion (which is what he was taken to be offering) led to colonial understandings of religion that interpreted everything through the lens of one religious tradition. Similar category mistakes happen also when philosophizing about particular theistic beliefs is substituted for a philosophy of religion. Here, the mistake is twofold: first, particular phenomena (in this case, certain beliefs about the nature of a theistic God) are conflated with a religious tradition (in this case, Abrahamic monotheism); second, that tradition (now reduced to cognitive beliefs about a supernatural deity) is conflated with religion itself. The result, for several decades, was an understanding of religion solely in terms of cognitive beliefs about supernatural beings. Both of those category mistakes had to be ameliorated for a broader understanding of religion to occur: not only did we need to realize that the Abrahamic religions of transcendence could be distinguished from religion in general, we also had to realize that cognitive belief claims did not sufficiently capture the whole of the Abrahamic religious tradition in general.

The problem, then, was not that particular religious phenomena were being investigated or that people were investigating religion from within the confines of a particular religious tradition. Both of those are good and necessary things to do, and to do otherwise is to misconstrue the task at hand. The problem, rather, was that their investigations were being confused with a philosophy of religion in general. Instead, the philosophy of a religious phenomenon and philosophy of a religious tradition must be understood as sub-moments or sub-tasks within the larger task of a philosophy of religion in general. This means not only keeping the tasks distinct (acknowledging that *my* philosophy of a religious phenomenon is not yet a philosophy *of religion*), but also acknowledging the connections between the tasks: that a philosophy of religion requires careful thinking about the philosophy of a particular religious tradition and the philosophy of particular religious phenomenon. An understanding of the phenomenon must inform our understanding of the religious tradition, and vice versa: we build up our understanding of the tradition by understanding the phenomena it expresses and gives rise to, even as we must understand those phenomena in the context of the religious tradition they express. Similarly, as we said above, our understanding of a philosophy of religion must be informed by our understanding of religious traditions, and vice versa: we only access the categories of religion in general from their expression in particular religious traditions and acknowledging those expressions as situated in a tradition that itself expresses a broader category helps us see the unique "style" at work in a particular religious tradition.

I have made this argument here in terms of philosophy, since that is the approach to religion that I know best, but I think it holds more broadly than that, as suggested already in Chapter six. That is, I think our understanding of religious phenomena in general (and not just our philosophical understanding of them) must be informed by our understanding of religious traditions in general, and vice versa: our understanding of a tradition must be influenced by our understanding of the phenomena it expresses and gives rise to, even as our understanding of those phenomena must occur in the context of the religious tradition they express. This is true, not just for philosophy, but for all attempts at religious understanding. This means we must be careful to remember that articulating an understanding of the phenomenon is a distinct (although related) task to articulating an understanding of the religious tradition and we must conduct our investigations into religion accordingly. We must purposefully and methodologically situate our understanding of phenomena in light of traditions, and vice versa, just as we must also situate our understanding of religious traditions in light of our understanding of religion (or religious categories) in general, and vice versa.

Distinguishing these as tasks need not entail distinguishing them as projects. That is, it is likely the case that an attempt to rigorously and robustly articulate an understanding of a particular religious phenomenon (like the Hajj or the Eucharist) will require also at least partial articulations of an understanding of the religious tradition they are taking place within and that, in turn, will require some recourse to broader religious categories (like religiosity or religious traditions). My point in distinguishing them as tasks is not to restrict who can carry out which tasks or require people only to do one of them. Rather, it is to make clear that investigations into religious phenomena seem to require three different but related tasks and failing to see that leads to confusions in our understanding of religion and our understanding of particular phenomena. This is, then, an encouragement to note the three distinct tasks, make clear which task one is pursuing when, and try to articulate, as best as possible, when it is necessary to draw on insights from the other tasks in order to complete the project of one's primary task. The result of this would be better investigations of religious phenomena, religious traditions, and religion precisely because they would be better able to account for their generation within the material-spiritual intertwining that is characteristic of experience, including religious experience. Realizing that the distinct levels of experiencing are intertwined and expressively related in our experience will allow us to better articulate those experiences by paying closer attention to the various intertwinings, rather than ignoring them or miscategorising them. Here again we see that acknowledging the material-spiritual nature of experience can help lead us to more robust understandings of religion and religious phenomena.

Recovering Experiencing in and for the Study of Religion

This understanding of religion and religious phenomena is more robust precisely because it accounts for the difference (and connection) between experienced and experiencing within experience. The main task of this book, then, has been to return an understanding of experiencing—of how we experience—to the study of religion. This understanding has been largely lacking from the contemporary study of religion. This lack manifested itself in at least two ways that we have discussed in this book: first, religion was understood solely in terms of being a content of experience, rather than also as a dimension of experiencing; and second, the religious element of our studying of religion has largely been ignored, leading people to think a religiously neutral method for the study of religion was both possible and desirable.

We have discussed the first of these points at great length already in this conclusion, and it probably does not need much more elaboration here: in studying religion and religious effects, we must also account for religious effects on quasi-transcendental traditions and on transcendental modes of sensing the world, in addition to religious effects on empirical phenomena. These (quasi-)transcendental effects are not simply additive but expressive: we do not merely add new effects, on the transcendental and quasi-transcendental levels, to the effects we already understand on the empirical level, but rather we must see that the (quasi-)transcendental effects shape our understanding of the empirical effects, and vice versa. All three types of effects must be understood in relation to the other types of effects, as explained in the last section.

The second avenue where the lack of experiencing was felt in religious studies might require further elaboration. By ignoring that our own investigations into religion and religious phenomena are themselves acts shaped by religiosity and religious traditions, scholars of religion made category mistakes: they took the religious phenomena, and perhaps even the style, of one tradition (secular-Christianity) and acted as if was indicative of religion as a whole. Specifically, we came to assume that the radical distinguishability of religious phenomena from other types of phenomena and of religious modes of engaging the world from all other modes of engaging the world were indicative or illustrative for religion as a whole. This had two significant consequences for the study of religion: first, we came to think that religious phenomena had to be entirely distinct from other types of phenomena, such that their being also immersed in cultural, linguistic, social, and so on contexts came to be seen, at least by some, as evidence that they were no longer distinctly "religious" phenomena. At the least, those other contexts were separable from the uniquely "religious" nature of the phenomena in such a way that their intertwining undercut that religious nature, until there was (for some) nothing uniquely "religious" left to the phenomena.

Second, we came to think that it was possible to think about religion in a way that was not itself shaped by some religious tradition or other. This claim is easily misunderstood, so I want to proceed carefully here. In saying this, I am not saying that all thinking about religion necessarily requires that people adopt an epistemic position on the existence or non-existence of super-natural entities. To interpret it that way is already to allow religion to be defined by the assumptions of the secular-Christian religious tradition. Rather, what I am saying is that, as argued in Chapter three, all thinking about religion happens within some religious tradition or other. This need not take the form of distinct epistemic claims or commitments, although it could. More generally, it is the acknowledgment that thinking, too, is an act of experience taking place within material-spiritual conditions. As such, it requires people to engage subjectively in particular ways with the world. Insofar as we are thinking about religion, religiosity must be one of the modes of engaging the world operative in that experience. It need not be the dominant one, but it does seem to need to be at stake: how can I think religion without in any way drawing on the products and expressions of the religious mode of engaging the world? It would be like talking about visibility without having ever been able to see and without talking about what other people have seen. Both what I'm thinking about, when I think about religion, and how I think about it will be touched, in some way, by religious effects. In that sense, they bear the mark of some religious tradition or other.

This, in turn, implies that thinking about religion could (and probably will) happen differently, depending on which religious tradition the thinker draws on, not just in the object of their religious inquiry but also in the subjective style by which they inquire or think. Insofar as secularism is itself a particular religious tradition (as argued in Chapters three and four), this means that secular approaches to thinking religion will give their own style to the study of religion. I am articulating that style here, at least in part, in terms of the separability of religion from other types of phenomena and from other types of experiencing. Methodologically, this manifested itself in the search for a religiously neutral approach to the study of religion, an approach that we now see is not "neutral" at all, but indicative of a particular religious tradition.

That this approach is indicative of a particular religious tradition does not, however, mean that it is bad or should be abandoned. After all, if all religious thinking takes place in some religious tradition or other, we can hardly criticize secular thinking about religion for taking place in a particular religious tradition— how else could it operate? Indeed, the secular approach to the study of religion has led to some great breakthroughs in the study of religion (in general), in part by helping us realize that the standards of one's own religious tradition need not be normatively binding on all other religious traditions: my religious tradition is not the "true religion" from which all other religious traditions are "false," "idolatrous," "pagan," and so on. By the same token, however, the separability of my religious tradition from other aspects of my life and thought also should not be applied as a normative standard for all other approaches to religion, including other scholarly approaches. To think scholarship must maintain this "secular distance" is, perhaps, to ask all scholars to function in accordance with the norms of the secular religious tradition. And that is colonial, not just theoretically but often politically and socially as well, insofar as secularism tends to be predominantly white, Western, and upper-middle class.

To avoid this type of colonialism, it must be possible to think religion seriously and scholarly from non-secular traditions as well. Here we have to avoid the possible conflations with religious philosophy that we talked about last section: to say that, for example, Islamic or Buddhist people can think about religion from within their own traditions is not simply to say that they can draw on Islamic or Buddhist insights to answer questions posed in and by the secular tradition. It also has to mean that they can approach the study of religion in ways that are entirely in keeping with their own tradition. Earlier, I have suggested this could take the form of articulating how particular categories of religion are expressed in a variety of different religious traditions, and I still think that option works. Now I want to acknowledge that this model threatens to make people's differing religious traditions mere fodder in the service of the conceptual problems and categories of my tradition. To avoid this, the categories that I have suggested have to be both changeable and disprovable: not only might I be wrong in my articulation of religiosity and religious traditions, but I must be open to the fact that I might be wrong about the broadness of the very categories of religiosity and religious traditions. Perhaps they work entirely differently than I have suggested because my own suggestions might maintain unthought assumptions of my own religious tradition.

I have been clear that the primary tradition I am drawing on in the formulation of the method of this study is transcendental phenomenology. That is not a religious tradition, per se, although it would be surprising if it did not bear the mark of Christianity, Judaism, and secularism in significant ways, given its historical provenance. Whether and to what extent those marks lead to problematic assumptions or outcomes for the study of religion remains to be seen. My hope is that the categories laid out here—religiosity, religious traditions, religious phenomena; experience, experienced, experiencing—and the tasks that follow from them provide the means not simply for formulating a method for the study of religion, but also for the criticism of that method. They need not offer a final vocabulary, in Rorty's sense,[8] merely a provisional one: something that is helpful now, but loose enough to be abandoned in the future if necessary. For my desire, in this book, has not been to offer the final account of religion or of the methodology of its study. It has simply been to remedy a particular lack I found in the contemporary study of religion—a lack that I, drawing on the language of experience, have labeled "experiencing." In asking us to pay attention to religion's impacts on how we experience the world in a variety of ways, I am seeking to remedy that lack. Doing so will, I think, give us a more robust and rigorous understanding of religion and its effects in our lives.

Glossary

Since many readers of this book may not be overly familiar with phenomenology, I have included a quick reference glossary here to help explain the meanings of key terms. My hope is that this will be easy to consult while reading the book, and will help readers keep track of what these key terms mean and are doing in the book (other glossary terms are **bolded** in definitions, to assist in cross-referencing).

Critical Philosophy of Religion: the type of philosophy of religion that takes place predominantly in religious studies, it is interested in trying to define what is meant by the term "religion" and its permutations (religious, religions, etc.). Exemplified by the work of figures such as Russel McCutcheon, Jonathan Z. Smith, Talal Asad, and Kevin Schilbrack, it draws heavily on insights gained from the empirical study of religion and tends to be critical of traditional attempts to equate religion with some kind of belief in **transcendent** realities. In this book, it functions as one of three distinct intersections of the study of religion, alongside **Phenomenology of Religion** and **Philosophical Phenomenology of Religion**.

Experience: an encountering of the world that always includes an individually lived-through or felt component (**experiencing**) and a shareable content (what is **experienced**). Both parts are necessary for experience: although there is a shareable content to a video recording, the camera does not experience insofar as it does not live through or feel its recording of that content. At the same time, the lived-through or felt component is always a living-through-of or a feeling-of something: without a shareable content, there is nothing to be experienced. This necessary intertwining of experiencing and experienced undermines both naïve empiricism (which privileges the experienced at the expense of experiencing) and naïve idealism (which privileges experiencing at the expense of the experienced). As a result, thinking experience becomes an important philosophical and methodological approach to thinking the relation between individuals and the world. But experience itself is neither a theoretical nor a philosophical construct: it is the most basic mode of engaging the world, at work in a wide variety of living things. Often tied to consciousness or to **subjectivity**, experience is a basic element of human existing, and of the mode of existing of several non-human animals as well.

Experienced: the contents of **experience** that are in principle shareable with other experiencers. In this book, it is often tied to the empirical "what" of our experience, and is distinguished from the **transcendental** how of our **experiencing**.

Experiencing: the living-through of our **experience**. **Philosophical Phenomenology** has revealed that the living-through of our experience has diverse and recognizable patterns or structures, including various **transcendental** ways of **sensing** the world (such as visibility, tactility, linguisticality, etc.), socially and culturally situated *Stiftungen*/**traditions**, and more. Therefore, experiencing is never a neutral revealing of what is "just-there," but is always shaping our experience in particular ways that must be accounted for if we want to understand phenomena.

Epochē: a methodological "bracketing" of certain questions or assumptions that allows us to examine a problem in a uniquely phenomenological way. Generally, it is the "natural attitude" that is "bracketed" in this manner, meaning the question of whether an **experience** of something corresponds to something beyond that experience is suspended (not denied but ignored) to allow us to better understand the importance of both the **experiencing** of that **phenomenon** and that phenomenon as **experienced**. Often (although not universally) understood as an element of the phenomenological method, it is generally credited with opening up the **transcendental** register that allows scholars to consider how experiencing shapes experience and thereby impacts both our theoretical understanding and our living in the world.

Material-Spirituality: the fundamental intertwining of **subjectivity**, history, culture, and materiality that is the **ultra-transcendental** background of experience as it is explained in this book. This is not simply a tying together of separately existing things—subjectivity + history + culture + materiality—but the recognition that all of those things are necessarily intertwined and mutually generative of each other, and can only be separated by theoretical acts of abstraction. This means that **spirituality** is always shaped by materiality, which itself is always shaped by subjectivity, history, and culture, and materiality is always, therefore, also shaped by spirituality, in the form of subjectively informed history and culture.

Phenomenon: a "thing" understood as always embedded in **material-spirituality**, which is to say, in **experience**. This entails that the objects of our experiences are always embedded (in culture, history, etc.), and that those modes of embeddedness are as much a part of the objects of our experience as are their material structures. In this book, this notion of phenomenon is contrasted with things-in-themselves, which are what they are apart from any relation to other things.

Phenomenology: an approach to understanding or thinking the world theoretically that focuses especially on the role of the first-person perspective. It is normally understood to begin as a distinct methodological approach with the work of Husserl, although Hegel also uses the term prominently in some of his writing. Its concern is to understand **experience** and the role it plays in both our understanding of the world and our living in it. It is used across a variety of different disciplines, including philosophy, health sciences, psychology, nursing, education, architecture, sociology, anthropology, and many more. In this book, our primary interest is in applications of phenomenology to the study of **religion**.

Phenomenology of Religion: work done in the empirical study of **religion**, first introduced by people like Eliade, Otto, and Van der Leeuw. It re-thought religion in terms of religious **experience**, and tried to establish the essential conditions that made an experience "religious." It tends to articulate the essential nature of religion based on *what* is experienced, and thereby largely misses (this book argues) the **transcendental** component of religious **experiencing**. In this book, it is contrasted with **philosophical phenomenology of religion** and **critical philosophy of religion** as three distinct intersections of the study of religion.

Philosophical Phenomenology: the application of phenomenological insights and methods to philosophical questions. It usually centres around accounts of **subjectivity**, and draws especially on the work of Husserl and his philosophical followers (Heidegger, Merleau-Ponty, Levinas, etc.). One key facet of philosophical uses of phenomenology is the distinction between the **transcendental** (as how we experience) and the empirical (as what we experience). This distinction opens **phenomenology** to rigorously pursue the relationship between subjectivity and objectivity, and hence to help us understand the role of things like culture, social mores, and individual biases in the scientific and theoretical study of the world. It deals with a wide range of subject matters, and is not restricted to the philosophy of religion.

Philosophical Phenomenology of Religion: as suggested, this a method of approaching the study of **religion** that focuses on **philosophical phenomenology**. It tends to employ phenomenological categories such as the reduction, the **epochē**, and **subjectivity** prominently in its analyses and includes figures such as Jean-Luc Marion, Emmanuel Levinas, Emmanuel Falque, and others in the so-called "theological turn" in phenomenology. In this book, it is contrasted with **critical philosophy of religion** and **phenomenology of religion** as three distinct intersections of the study of religion. This approach is more likely to consider **transcendental** matters than are the other two approaches.

Quasi-Transcendental: one of the modes or layers of the **transcendental**, sometimes also referred to as the empirical-transcendental or sensible-transcendentals. It is interested in how **sensing-transcendentals** are always experienced from within some *Stiftung*/**tradition** or other, which necessarily impart a particular style to how that transcendental mode of sensing affects the **experiencing** of people within those traditions. In this book, this concept is crucial to showing that transcendental structures are not **transcendent**, but remain always rooted in experience and in the particularities of history, culture, and so on.

Religion: a component of our **experience**. Traditionally, it has been understood as a particular thing, separable from other, non-religious things. In this book, it is argued that there is also a **transcendental** component to religion, meaning that religion is not just a thing or collection of things but also includes transcendental effects on **experiencing** that shape how experiencers experience many things that would not have traditionally been considered to be "religion." In that sense, the religious dimension of our experience cannot be reduced to things or nouns (religion) but must also include transcendental effects including a distinct type of **sensing-**

transcendental (called **religiosity**), and distinct types of religious *Stiftung(en)*/ **traditions**.

Religiosity: a distinct type of **sensing-transcendental** that opens a way of engaging the world in a uniquely religious way. In this book, the general sense of this religious way of sensing the world was described as giving us an **experience** of the connectivity of the world (and **subjectivity**) in its **material-spirituality**. As a **transcendental** structure, religiosity is only ever encountered in the particular style characteristic of different *Stiftungen*/**traditions**, such as "loving" the world (in Catholicism), "detaching" from the world (in certain forms of Buddhism), and so on. Nevertheless, seeing those as different styles of religiosity helps us open the door for new types of cross-cultural conversations in religion.

Sensing-Transcendental: one of the three levels or layers of **transcendental** analysis discussed in this book, alongside the **quasi-transcendental** and the **ultra-transcendental**, the sensing-transcendental refers to the ways we have of experiencing or engaging the world that result in distinct types of *Empfindnisse* or sensings. Examples of such distinct types of sensings include visibility, tactility, aurality, linguisticality, sociality, and more. This book argues for another, distinctly religious, mode of sensing the world: **religiosity**.

Spirit: a dimension of **material-spirituality** that includes both the meaningfulness embedded in phenomena and a force at work shaping **subjectivity**. Because the spirit that flows through subjectivity is the same as that which is meaningfully embedded in phenomena, it reveals how the **transcendental** is not **transcendent**: because spirit shapes how we experience, it has transcendental effects. And because spirit is embedded in phenomena, the transcendental effects it has on subjectivity arise from within **experience**, not from outside or beyond it.

Spirituality: the force that **spirit** exercises on **subjectivity** as a kind of animating force shaping the **experiencing** of various experiencers. Spirituality is expressed in a wide variety of ways in **experience**, including in the various modes of **sensing-transcendentals** and the way they influence each other in particular ways according to the **quasi-transcendental** *Stiftungen* or **traditions** by which any particular experiencer encounters them.

***Stiftung(en)*:** a **quasi-transcendental** element indicating how **subjectivity** is shaped and formed by history. It suggests a purpose or project that perdures through time, shaping subjectivity in accordance with that purpose. Usually translated into philosophical English as "institution," this book prefers to translate it as **tradition**, to maintain the sense of historicity and meaning-making inherent in the concept. In general, it refers to the way that being part of a particular type of community shapes subjectivity in particular ways.

Subjectivity: in its most basic sense, subjectivity is the capacity to have unitary **experience**. It is a process, a way of engaging the world by unifying the diverse **transcendental** modes (e.g., the various **sensing-transcendentals**, differing temporal experiences, etc.) into one ongoing, temporal project of experience. It has often been conflated historically with the Subject, as an individual entity. However, that has often led to the sense that subjectivity is ahistorical and **transcendent**—a point that this book is at pains to argue against. Instead, subjectivity must be understood as being generated differently in different **quasi-transcendental** contexts, thereby calling into question both the possibility and the desirability of transcendent, ahistorical thinking.

Tradition: a project or purpose pursued through time for a particular effect. In this book, we distinguish between the empirical effects of tradition and the **quasi-transcendental** effects of tradition. For the quasi-transcendental effects of tradition, see *Stiftung(en)*.

Transcendent: something that is outside of or beyond the world of **experience**. Some relation to transcendence has often been taken as an essential element of religion, for example, in many of the key figures of **phenomenology of religion**. However, this has been criticized as an overly monotheistic and Abrahamic understanding of religion by many people in the **critical philosophy of religion**. In this book, the transcendent is sharply distinguished from the **transcendental**, which is shown to arise within experience and therefore to not be transcendent.

Transcendental: the conditions of experiencing that are operative in our experience. In that sense, the transcendental refers to *how* we experience, rather than simply to *what* we experience. These conditions make experience possible, not simply in the logical sense (as in Kant), but as the actual conditions shaping how we experience a particular phenomenon. There are three distinct levels of transcendental analysis: the **sensing-transcendentals**, which give us distinct ways of engaging the world; **quasi-transcendental** *Stiftung*/**traditions**, which are the particular, historically conditioned style with which we take up the sensing-transcendentals; and the **ultra-transcendental**, which provides the impetus behind the distinct sensing-transcendentals.

Transcendental Phenomenology: the use of **phenomenology** to study **transcendental** structures, that is, to study the "how" of our **experiencing**. It is especially prominent in **philosophical phenomenology**.

Ultra-Transcendental: one of the three levels or layers of **transcendental** analysis discussed in this book, alongside the **quasi-transcendental** and the **sensing-transcendental**, the ultra-transcendental refers to an understanding of where sensing-transcendentals arise from. For Kant, the Subject was understood to be the ultimate ground of the sensing-transcendentals, and hence was taken by some post-Kantians (i.e., idealists) to be the heart of **experience** itself. Husserl sometimes seems to go in that direction, but he has several insights that lead beyond that, to a more phenomenologically consistent account of experience. Articulating and developing those insights has been a main task of **philosophical phenomenology**, with major figures developing differing accounts of the ultra-transcendental: Heidegger thought Being was the ultra-transcendental context of experience; Merleau-Ponty thought it was Flesh; Derrida thought it was differance; Henry considered it to be Life; Marion took it to be givenness; and so on.

Notes

Introduction

1. The so-called "affective turn" in religion is perhaps beginning to address this absence, but its focus primarily on emotion, although a helpful addition to the study of religion, is not broad enough to account for the various ways that religion shapes our experiencing.
2. This is key to differentiating phenomenological accounts of the transcendental from Kantian ones; see the introduction to *Phenomenology and the Transcendental*, eds. Sara Heinämaa, Mirja Hartimo, and Timo Miettinen (Oxfordshire: Routledge, 2014);and Neal DeRoo, *Political Logic of Experience: Expression in Phenomenology* (New York: Fordham University Press, 2022).
3. I take the phrase "philosophical phenomenology" as distinguishing it from other uses of phenomenology from Dan Zahavi, "Applied Phenomenology: Why it is Safe to Ignore the Epoché," *Continental Philosophy Review* 54 (2019): 1–15.
4. For one example of this synonymous usage, see Timothy Fitzgerald, "A 'Critique' of Religion as a Cross-Cultural Category," *Method and Theory in the Study of Religion* 9, no. 2: 91–110, which has as the title of subsection 1.2 "The transcendent, transcendental values" (94), and continues to use transcendental as synonymous with transcendent (e.g., "Whether or not 'supernatural' entities or a transcendental location for the sacred are involved … "; 96).
5. Dominique Janicaud, "The Theological Turn of French Phenomenology," in *Phenomenology and the Theological Turn: The French Debate*, trans. Bernard G. Prusak (New York: Fordham University Press, 2000), 16–103.
6. For more on the ambiguity of current uses of spirituality, see K. Chindeu Nweke, "Between Religiosity and Spirituality: Christianity and the Reemergence of the Immanentist Spiritualities," *Theology Today* 75, no. 2 (2018): 233–46; and Philip Sheldrake, "Constructing Spirituality: The 'Politics' of Definitions and Historical Interpretations," *Religion and Theology* 23 (2016): 15–34. A helpful summary of the varying uses can be found in Christina M. Gschwandtner, "Faith, Religion and Spirituality: A Phenomenological and Hermeneutic Contribution to Parsing the Distinctions," *Religions* 12, no. 7 (2021): 476; https://doi.org/10.3390/rel12070476.
7. Edmund Husserl, *The Crisis of European Sciences and Transcendental Phenomenology*, trans. David Carr (1936; Evanston: Northwestern University Press, 1970), 270.

8 For an understanding of the various ways that spirituality is understood in the contemporary study of religion, please see, in addition to the works referenced in note 5, Philip Sheldrake, *A Brief History of Spirituality* (Malden: Blackwell Publishing, 2007); Sandra M. Schneiders, "A Hermeneutical Approach to the Study of Christian Spirituality," in *Minding the Spirit: The Study of Christian Spirituality*, ed. Elizabeth Dryer and Mark S. Burrows (Baltimore: The John Hopkins University Press, 2005), 49–60; John Macquarrie, "Spirit and Spirituality," in *Exploring Christian Spirituality: An Ecumenical Reader*, ed. Kenneth J. Collins (Grand Rapids: Baker Books, 2000), 63–73.

9 One thinks primarily of figures in the aforementioned "theological turn," such as Jean-Luc Marion, Michel Henry, Jean-Yves Lacoste, Claude Romano, Paul Ricoeur, and Jean-Louis Chrétien. But one could also consider perhaps those farther afield, like Richard Kearney and John D. Caputo. For the phenomenological nature of Kearney's work, see Neal DeRoo, "Carnal Sacrality: Phenomenology, the Sacred and Material Bodies in Richard Kearney," in *Anacarnation and Returning to the Lived Body with Richard Kearney*, ed. Brian Treanor and James L. Taylor (New York: Routledge, 2023), 69–85. For Caputo as a transcendental phenomenologist, see chapter 1 of his *Specters of God* (Bloomington: Indiana University Press, 2022); and Neal DeRoo, "Life and Transcendental Phenomenologies of Religion: Michel Henry and John D. Caputo," in *Hymns to Life*, ed. Steven Nemes and Steven DeLay (Cascade: Wipf and Stock, forthcoming).

10 Jean-Luc Marion, *Being Given: Toward a Phenomenology of Givenness*, trans. Jeffery L. Kosky (1997; Stanford: Stanford University Press, 2002); and *Reduction and Givenness: Investigation of Husserl, Heidegger, and Phenomenology*, trans. Thomas A. Carlson (Evanston: Northwestern University Press, 1998).

11 Jean-Luc Marion, *In Excess: Studies of Saturated Phenomena*, trans. Robyn Hoerner and Vincent Berraud (New York: Fordham University Press, 2004).

12 Michel Henry, *Phénoménologie de la Vie vol 1: De la phénoménologie* (Paris: Presses Universitaires de France, 2003); Michel Henry, *Phénoménologie de la Vie vol 2: De la subjectivité* (Paris: Presses Universitaires de France, 2011); Michel Henry, *Phénoménologie de la Vie vol 3: Du l'art et du politique* (Paris: Presses Universitaires de France, 2005); Michel Henry, *Phénoménologie de la Vie vol 4: Sur l'éthique et de la religion* (Paris: Presses Universitaires de France, 2004).

13 Claude Romano, *Event and World*, trans. Shane Mackinlay (New York: Fordham University Press, 2009); Claude Romano, *Event and Time*, trans. Stephen E. Lewis (New York: Fordham University Press, 2013); Claude Romano *There is*, trans. Michael B. Smith (New York: Fordham University Press, 2015).

14 Jean-Luc Marion, "God Without Being," rp. in *Phenomenology and Eschatology: Not yet in the Now*, ed. Neal DeRoo and John Panteleimon Manoussakis (1946; New York: Routledge, 2021), 193–213.

15 Jean-Louis Chrétien, *The Ark of Speech*, trans. Andrew Brown (Abingdon: Routledge, 2003); Jean-Louis Chrétien, *The Call and the Response*, trans. Anne A. Davenport (New York: Fordham University Press, 2004); Jean-Louis Chrétien, *Under the Gaze of the Bible*, trans. John Marson Dunaway (New York: Fordham University Press, 2014).

16 Jean-Yves Lacoste, *Experience and the Absolute: Disputed Questions on the Humanity of Man*, trans. Mark Raferty-Skehan (New York: Fordham University Press, 2004).

17 Christina M. Gschwandtner, *Degrees of Givenness: On Saturation in Jean-Luc Marion* (Bloomington: Indiana University Press, 2014), 181.

18 We will return to this question in Chapter five.

19 We will return to this question in Chapter six.

20 I call this the "critical" philosophy of religion insofar as it arises from what Fitzgerald calls "a vigorous critical debate among some scholars who happen to work in religion departments, [that] has opened up a forum precisely for critical expression within the community of scholars, and for analysis of the 'archaeology' of the 'religion' category"; Fitzgerald, "A 'Critique' of Religion," 97.

21 Various views on "religion" and its helpfulness as a category are explored in Aaron W. Hughes and Russell T. McCutcheon (eds.), *What is Religion?: Debating the Academic Study of Religion* (Oxford: Oxford University Press, 2021).

22 In what follows we will explore more about what is meant by "subjective." For now, let me say that "subjective capabilities" simply means something like "has an awareness of," and this awareness is a distinct part of what is experienced that adds something to that experience. For example, my experience of sitting in my office watching a fire burn in the fireplace is not simply the existence of a person sitting in a room (an "office") whose eyes are directed toward a fire burning in a fireplace. Of course, the experience is not about anything other than seeing the fire burning in the fireplace—but there is, precisely, a seeing of the fire, an experiencing of the fire (it's brightness, its warmth, its coziness, its being *gezellig*, etc.) that is neither reducible simply to the empirical elements (person, fire, room) nor something entirely other than those empirical elements. The point is (I hope) intuitively simple, even if its significance can be difficult to grasp. Intuitively, we recognize that a camera recording the fire burning in the fireplace does not see or experience it, even though it accurately records the empirical elements in their unfolding. We might see or experience something through the camera or through the recording it provides us, but the camera itself neither sees nor experiences—it simply records. This difference between human (and, perhaps, other-than-human) seeing and experiencing and machine recording is, broadly, what we are after by the term "subjective."

23 For the significance also of considering what does not count as religion for our understanding of religion, see Kevin Schilbrack, "What *isn't* Religion?," *The Journal of Religion* 93, no. 1 (2013): 291–318.

24 See John D. Caputo, *Radical Hermeneutics: Repetition, Deconstruction, and the Hermeneutic Project* (Bloomington: Indiana University Press, 1988); and John D. Caputo, *More Radical Hermeneutics: On not Knowing Who We Are* (Bloomington: Indiana University Press, 2000).

25 Martin Heidegger, *Being and Time*, trans. John Macquarrie and Edward Robinson (1927; Oxford: Blackwell Publishing, 1962) is especially noteworthy in this regard, but it is far from alone.

26 "The phenomenology of religion defines the methodology that is uniquely associated with religious studies as a distinct discipline studying 'religion' itself" and later "only phenomenology provides for the academic study of religions a distinct methodology, justifying its claim to be a field of study in its own right, *sui generis*"; James L. Cox, *A Guide to the Phenomenology of Religion: Key Figures, Formative Influences and Subsequent Debates* (London: T&T Clark, 2006), 3 and 4, respectively. For further arguments to this effect, see also James C. Livingston, *Anatomy of the Sacred: An Introduction to Religion*, 5th ed. (Upper Saddle River, NY: Prentice Hall, 2005), 27; and James L. Cox, *An Introduction to Phenomenology of Religion* (London: Bloomsbury, 2009).

27 Christina M. Gschwandtner, "What is Phenomenology of Religion? (Part I): The Study of Religious Phenomena," *Philosophy Compass* 12, no. 2 (2019), e12566. Available online: https://doi.org/10.1111/phc3.12566, page 2 of 13; see also Gschwandtner, "Faith, Religion and Spirituality."

28 Timothy Fitzgerald, *Discourse on Civility and Barbarity: A Critical History of Religion and Related Categories* (Oxford: Oxford University Press, 2007).

29 Gavin Flood, *Beyond Phenomenology: Rethinking the Study of Religion* (London: Cassell, 1999); Russel McCutcheon, *Manufacturing Religion: The Discourse on Sui Generis Religion and the Politics of Nostalgia* (Oxford: Oxford University Press, 2003); Tomoko Masuzawa, *The Invention of World Religions* (Chicago: University of Chicago Press, 2005); Timothy Fitzgerald, *Discourse on Civility and Barbarity*; Kevin Schilbrack, "Religions: Are There Any?" *Journal of the American Academy of Religion* 78, no. 4 (2010): 1112–38; Wendy Cadge, Peggy Levitt, and David Smilde, "De-Centering and Re-Centering: Rethinking Concepts and Methods in the Sociological Study of Religion," *Journal for the Scientific Study of Religion* 84, no. 2 (2016): 373–400; Torkel Brekke, *Fundamentalism: Prophecy and Protest in an Age of Globalization* (Cambridge: Cambridge University Press, 2012); Brent Nongbri, *Before Religion: A History of a Modern Concept* (New Haven, CT: Yale University Press, 2015).

30 Karen M. Barad, *Meeting the Universe Halfway: Quantum Physics and the Entanglement of Matter and Meaning* (Durham, NC: Duke University Press, 2007).

31 I discuss the phenomenological account of transcendentality and its embeddedness in empirical conditions at length in the fourth chapter of DeRoo, *The Political*

Logic of Experience. Those wanting a deeper phenomenological or philosophical explanation of the transcendental are asked to look there. Here, I will keep the account at the summary level, offering only what is needed to explain the account of religion that is to follow.

32 Edmund Husserl, *Analyses Concerning Passive and Active Synthesis: Lectures on Transcendental Logic*, trans. A.J. Steinbock (New York: Springer, 2001), 126.

33 For more on my phenomenological understanding of subjectivity, see the second chapter of *The Political Logic of Experience*.

34 See §36 of Edmund Husserl, *Ideas Pertaining to a Pure Phenomenology and to a Phenomenological Philosophy: Second Book: Studies in the Phenomenology of Constitution*, trans. Richard Rojcewicz and Andre Schuwer (New York: Springer, 1989). There is a helpful and extensive discussion of this term in Alia Al-Saji, "Bodies and Sensings: On the Uses of Husserlian Phenomenology for Feminist Theory," *Continental Philosophy Review* 43, no. 1 (2010): 13–37; and in the second chapter of DeRoo, *The Political Logic of Experience*.

35 Merleau-Ponty, perhaps more than any other phenomenologist, talks about the connections between these distinct modes of sensing; see, for example, Maurice Merleau-Ponty, *The Visible and the Invisible*, trans. Alphonso Lingis (Evanston: Northwestern University Press, 1969).

36 Edmund Husserl, *Cartesian Meditations: An Introduction to Phenomenology*, trans. Dorion Cairns (Norwell: Kluwer Academic Publishers, 1977); Maurice Merleau-Ponty, "Eye and Mind," in *The Primacy of Perception: And Other Essays on Phenomenological Psychology, the Philosophy of Art, History, and Politics*, trans. Carleton Dallery, ed. John Wild and James E. Edie (Evanston: Northwestern University Press, 1964), 159–90.

37 *Stiftung* is a German term that is often used to indicate something that was begun for a particular reason and exists through time so as to live out its given and instituting task (for example, the Klimt Stiftung exists to document the life, times, and work of Gustav Klimt). Often colloquially translated as "foundation," *Stiftung* is usually translated into philosophical English as "institution" (see Robert Vallier, "Institution: The Significance of Merleau-Ponty's 1954 Course at the Collège de France," *Chiasmi International* 7 (2005): 281–302; and Maurice Merleau-Ponty, *Institution and Passivity: Course Notes from the Collège de France (1954–1955)*, trans. Leonard Lawlor and Heath Massey (Evanston: Northwestern University Press, 2010)), because "foundation" has too many epistemological (and foundational) overtones in philosophy. However, in the context of conversations in religious studies, as in political conversations, I fear that "institution" has too many structural connotations that threaten to lose the historical and traditional character of *Stiftung* as something pursuing a particular purpose through time. As such, I will generally use the term "tradition" rather than *Stiftung*—although there are times

when I will simply use the German term directly, if I think even "tradition" risks misunderstanding.

38 See Renaud Barbaras, *The Being of the Phenomenon*, trans. Ted Toadvine and Leonard Lawlor (Bloomington: Indiana University Press, 2004).

39 Husserl will talk about the difference between the transcendental (in general) and the empirical as a "parallel"; Edmund Husserl, *Phänomenologische Psychologie: Vorlesungen Sommersemester*, trans. Walter Biemel (1925; The Hague: Martinus Nijhoff, 1962), 342–3; the Preface to Edmund Husserl, *Ideas Pertaining to a Pure Phenomenology and to a Phenomenological Philosophy: First Book: General Introduction to a Pure Phenomenology*, ed. Fred Kersten (The Hague: Martinus Nijhoff, 1983); and Husserl, *Cartesian Meditations* (§§ 14 and 57), which yields, as Derrida puts it, "a difference in fact distinguishing nothing, a difference separating no state, no experience, no determined signification—but a difference which, without altering anything, changes all the signs" (Jacques Derrida, *Voice and Phenomenon: Introduction to the Problem of the Sign in Husserl's Phenomenology*, trans. Leonard Lawlor [1967; Evanston: Northwestern University Press, 2010], 11).

40 For the distinction between "living through" and "living in," see Edmund Husserl, *Logical Investigations, vol. 1*, ed. Dermot Moran (New York: Routledge, 2001), 193; and Husserl, *Ideas II*, § 56h.

41 I examine the phenomenological notion of expression and its implications for how we experience at great length in DeRoo, *The Political Logic of Experience*, especially the first chapter.

42 See Jacques Derrida, *Of Spirit: Heidegger and the Question*, trans. Geoffrey Bennington and Rachel Bowlby (Chicago: University of Chicago Press, 1991); but also Jacques Derrida, "Force of Law: The 'Mystical' Foundation of Authority," in *Deconstruction and The Possibility of Justice*, ed. Drucilla Cornell, Michel Rosenfeld, and David Gray Carlson (New York: Routledge, 1992); and Jacques Derrida, *Specters of Marx: The State of the Debt, the Work of Mourning and the New International*, trans. Peggy Kamuf (New York: Routledge, 1994).

43 See not just the standard German usage of *geistig/geistlich*, but Heidegger's uses of them, as Derrida explicates in *Of Spirit*.

44 On spirit as illuminating subjectivity, see Edith Stein, *Endliches und ewiges Sein: Versuch eines Aufstiegs zum Sinn des Seins*, in *Gesamtausgabe*, vols. 11/12, ed. Andreas Uwe Müller (Freiburg: Herder, 2016); and Gerda Walther, *Phänomenologie der Mystik* (Olten: Walter Verlag, 1955); on spirit as putting subjectivity in contact with something beyond itself, see Walther, *Phänomenologie*, 119; on spirit as an outward movement from the subject, see Hedwig Conrad-Martius, *Metaphysical Conversations*, ed. and trans. Christina M. Gschwandtner (Boston, MA: DeGruyter, 2024), 108.

Chapter 1

1. While I do not wish to reduce this lived component to consciousness (at least without more fully exploring what is meant by "consciousness"), it is fair at this point to say that this lived component is not unrelated to "what it is like to be" me, in the sense that Nagel first gives to that phrase; see Thomas Nagle, "What is it Like to be a Bat?" *Philosophical Review* 83, no. 4 (1973): 435–50.
2. No one has done more to explore all the implications of affectivity as a phenomenological problem than Michel Henry; see *Essence of Manifestation* trans. G.J. Etzkorn (New York: Springer, 1973); *Philosophy and Phenomenology of the Body* trans. G.J. Etzkorn (New York: Springer, 1975); and his five-volume set, *Phénoménologie de la Vie*. Underappreciated as an account of affectivity is Derrida's notion of *différance*; see especially *Voice and Phenomenon*. This notion of affectivity is taking on more importance in the study of religion; see, for example, Donovan Schaefer, *Religious Affects: Animality, Evolution, and Power* (Durham, NC: Duke University Press, 2015). The transcendental approach to the study of religion that I am suggesting in this text therefore opens new doors to and for the affective study of religion.
3. See Joan W. Scott, "The Evidence of Experience," in *Critical Inquiry* 17, no. 4 (1991): 773–97.
4. For more on the distinction between these two "moments" or elements of experience and their implications for feminist thought, see the first chapter of Cressida J. Heyes, *Anaesthetics of Existence: Essays on Experience at the Edge* (Durham, NC: Duke University Press, 2020).
5. This so-called "hermeneutic as" is discussed most notably in Martin Heidegger's *Being and Time*, trans. J. Macquarrie and E. Robinson (1927; Oxford: Blackwell Publishing, 1962), para. 44. It also features pre-eminently in the later hermeneutic tradition; see, for example, Richard Kearney's work on poetic figuration in *Poétique du possible: phénoménologie herméneutique de la figuration* (Paris: Éditions Beauchesne, 1984).
6. Merleau-Ponty discusses this most explicitly in the later parts of *The Visible and the Invisible*, trans. A. Lingis (Evanston, IL: Northwestern University Press).
7. Maurice Merleau-Ponty, "Eye and Mind." In *The Primacy of Perception: And Other Essays on Phenomenological Psychology, the Philosophy of Art, History and Politics*, trans. C. Dallery, ed. J. Wild and J.E. Edie (Evanston, IL: Northwestern University Press, 1964), 159–90.
8. This monadological conception of subjectivity is a problem that Husserl addresses and tries to overcome, especially in Husserl's *Cartesian Meditations: An Introduction to Phenomenology*, trans. D. Cairns (Norwell, MA: Kluwer Academic Publishers, 1977)

9 Husserl, *Analyses Concerning Passive and Active Synthesis: Lectures on Transcendtal Logic*, trans. A.J. Steinbeck (New York: Springer, 2001), 126.

10 See, for example, Merleau-Ponty's discussion of the different modes of sensing as "little subjectivities," in *The Visible and the Invisible*, 141.

11 Merleau-Ponty's early attempts to explain this relation via the notion of background arises from his early engagements with gestalt psychology; see *The Structure of Behavior*, trans. Alden L. Fisher (Boston, MA: Beacon Books, 1967); and *Phenomenology of Perception*, 2nd ed. (1945) trans. Donald Landes (Evanston, IL: Northwestern University Press, 2010).

12 The notion of "horizons" is endemic to Husserl's discussion of phenomenology. Jean-Luc Marion raises the possibility of a phenomenology (or at least a phenomenon) without horizons in his notion of the "saturated phenomenon"; see Marion, *In Excess: Studies of Saturated Phenomena*, trans. R. Horner and V. Berraud (New York: Fordham University Press, 2004). This notion of the possibility of phenomenology without horizons was the main subject of the Marion's infamous debate with Derrida; see, for example, their contributions to John D. Caputo and Michael J. Scanlon (eds.), *God, the Gift and Postmodernism* (Bloomington: Indiana University Press, 1999).

13 Merleau-Ponty uses the language of "milieu" in some of his earlier works, including his *Phenomenology of Perception* and *Structure of Behavior*, but it takes on greater importance in his later works, including *Signs*, trans. Richard C. McCleary (Evanston, IL: Northwestern University Press, 1964); and *Nature: Course Notes from the College de France*, comp. Dominique Seglard, trans. Robert Vallier (Evanston, IL: Northwestern University Press, 2003).

14 Husserl, *Ideas Pertaining to a Pure Phenomenology and to a Phenomenological Philosophy: Second Book: Studies in the Phenomenology of Constitution*, trans. R. Rojcewicz and A. Schuwer (New York: Springer, 1989), 250–1. This concept is discussed in more detail in Sara Heinämaa, "Embodiment and Expressivity in Husserl's Phenomenology: From *Logical Investigations* to *Cartesian Meditations*," *SATS: Northern European Journal of Philosophy* 11 (2010): 1–15; and in the second chapter of DeRoo, *The Political Logic of Experience: Expression in Phenomenology* (New York: Fordham University Press, 2022).

15 See the infamous discussion that "the Earth does not move" in Edmund Husserl, "Fundamental Investigations on the Phenomenological Origin of the Spatiality of Nature," in *Shorter Works*, trans. Fred Kersten, ed. Peter McCormick and Frederick A. Elleston (South Bend, IN: University of Notre Dame Press, 1981), 222–33.

16 Michel Henry, *Barbarism*, trans. Scott Davidson (1987; London: Bloomsbury Academic Press, 2012), 45–8.

17 For a more thorough elaboration of this distinction, see DeRoo, "Embodying the World: The Spiritual Significance of the Earth," *Crossings: The Journal of the International Network for Philosophy of Religion* [forthcoming].

18 I have elsewhere characterized experience as the expressive intertwining of knowing, being, and doing; see DeRoo, *The Political logic of Experience*, chapter three.

19 This is not to ignore that others distinguished the material and the spiritual prior to Descartes. But in the Platonic and neo-Platonic nature of the distinction, the notion of participation complicates any attempt to distinguish them as radical ontological opposites. Similarly, in Aristotelian and Thomistic accounts, the hylomorphic nature of the distinction again complicates any attempt to view them as radical ontological distinctives: even if the two do different things, they always come together and require each other. Whether Descartes actually intended for the material and the immaterial to be radically distinguished is much contested by Descartes scholars including, most notably in the context of our transcendental phenomenological approach, Jean-Luc Marion, whose early work was in Descartes; see Jean-Luc Marion, *Descartes Grey Ontology: Cartesian Ontology and Aristotelian Thought in the Regulae*, trans. Sarah E. Donahue (South Bend, IN: St. Augustine Press, 2022); Jean-Luc Marion, *On Descartes' Metaphysical Prism: The Constitution and The Limits of Onto-theo-logy in Cartesian Thought*, trans. Jeffrey L. Kosky (Chicago, IL: University of Chicago Press, 1999); Jean-Luc Marion, *Cartesian Questions: Method and Metaphysics* (1991; Chicago, IL: University of Chicago Press, 1999); Jean-Luc Marion, *On the Ego and on God: Further Cartesian Questions*, trans. Christina M. Gschwandtner (New York: Fordham University Press, 2008); Jean-Luc Marion, *Cartesian Questions III: Descartes Beneath the Mask of Cartesianism*, trans. Stephen E. Lewis Jr. and Stephanie Rumpza (Redwood City, CA: Stanford University Press, forthcoming); and Jean-Luc Marion, *Sur la théologie blanche de Descartes* (Paris: Presses Universitaires de France, 1981). Whatever Descartes' intentions, he was received, especially perhaps among religious thinkers, as advocating a sharp and ontological dualism between materiality and immateriality, such that what was true of one (mutable, causally determined, made of parts) the opposite must be true of the other (immutable, free, simple). The impact of this on especially Protestant Christian conceptions of the soul–body relation are difficult to overstate.

20 Philip Sheldrake, *A Brief History of Spirituality* (Malden, MA: Blackwell Publishing, 2007), 5. It should be noted that Sheldrake is contesting this account of spirituality. But in doing so, he implicitly acknowledges it as an account of spirituality that needs addressing.

21 This notion of super-natural spirituality is dominant in many strands of Protestant Christianity, for example.

22 G.W.F. Hegel *Introduction to the Philosophy of History*, trans. Leo Rauch (Indianapolis, IN: Hackett, 1988), 20–1.

23 G.W.F. Hegel, *Phenomenology of Spirit*, trans. A.V. Miller (Oxford: Oxford University Press, 1977), 264.

24 On spirit as connecting subjectivity to a "source" beyond itself, see Walther, *Phänomenologie der Mystik* (Olten: Walter Verlag, 1955), 122. On spirit as that which illuminates the individual self, see Walter, *Phänomenologie der Mystik*; and Stein, *Endliches und ewiges Sein: Versuch eines Aufstiegs zum Sinn des Seins*. In *Gesamtausgabe*, vols. 11/12, ed. A.U. Müller (Freiburg: Herder, 2016). On spirit as a movement taking the subject outside itself, Conrad-Martius, *Metaphysical Conversations*, ed. and trans. C.M. Gschwandtner (Boston, MA: DeGruyter, 2024), 108.

25 See Robin Wall Kimmerer, *Braiding Sweetgrass: Indigenous Wisdom, Scientific Knowledge, and the Teachings of Plants* (Minneapolis, MN: Milkweed Editions, 2013); the first quote is from p. 56; the second two are from p. 55. For more on the verb-based nature of the Potawatomi language, see Robin Wall Kimmerer and Helen Whybrow, "Robin Wall Kimmerer on the Language of Animacy," *Orion* March/April 2017; accessed online: https://orionmagazine.org/article/robin-wall-kimmerer-language-animacy/.

26 Aristotle's *The* Metaphysics, trans. Hugh Lawson-Tancred (1998; London: Penguin Classics, 2012) and Heidegger's reading of it in his *Introduction to Metaphysics* 2nd ed., trans. Gregory Fried and Richard Polt (1935; New Haven, CT: Yale University Press, 2014).

27 See, for example, Nāgārjuna, *The Fundamental Wisdom of the Middle Way*, trans. Jay L. Garfield (Oxford: Oxford University Press, 1995); and John Clark, "On Being None with Nature: Nagarjuna and the Ecology of Emptiness," *Capitalism, Nature, Socialism* 19, no. 4 (2008): 6–29.

28 See Robin Wall Kimmerer, *Braiding Sweetgrass*, 56. Interestingly, Kimmerer attempts to connect this notion of animate being (*Yawe*) to Yahweh, the Hebraic name for the Judeo-Christian God, suggesting that, in both cases, what is at stake is the equation of being with life with having breath.

29 Although this number is almost certainly not in the 50s (see John Steckley, *White Lies about the Inuit* [Toronto: University of Toronto Press, 2007]), there are more than ten words corresponding to what we would call "snow" or "ice" in Lucien Schneider's *Ulirnaisugutiit: An Inuktitut–English Dictionary of Northern Quebec, Labrador and Eastern Arctic Dialects*, trans. Dermot Rolin F. Collis (Quebec City: Les Presses des l'Universite Laval, 1985).

30 It seems to me, this would not be the case only for humans and human-made objects: a bird's nest, for example, is inexorably marked by its having been produced by and for a bird. Hence, this seems to attribute a level of subjectivity to birds as well, though we cannot pursue this question further.

31 See Anne-Christine Hornborg, *Mi'kmaq Landscapes: From Animism to Sacred Ecology* (New York: Routledge, 2021). My thanks to Benjamin Strachan for bringing this example to my attention. This idea is also explored, in the context of

the British colonization of Ireland in Brian Friel, *Translations* (London: Faber and Faber Plays, 1981).

32 Several recent accounts of "new materialisms" support this point; see, for example, the views collected in Diana Coole and Samantha Frost (eds.), *New Materialisms: Ontology, Agency and Politics* (Durham, NC: Duke University Press, 2010). Some of these concerns have begun to come into the realm of religion; see, for example, Clayton Crockett and Jeffery W. Robbins, *Religion, Politics and the Earth: The New Materialism* (New York: Palgrave Macmillan, 2012).

33 Kenneth J. Collins (ed.), *Exploring Christian Spirituality: An Ecumenical Reader* (Grand Rapids, MI: Baker Books, 2000), 10.

34 Walter Principe, "Toward Defining Spirituality," in *Exploring Christian Spirituality: An Ecumenical Reader*, ed. Kenneth J. Collins (Grand Rapids, MI: Baker Books, 2000), 43–61.

35 Sheldrake, *Brief History*.

36 Nweke, "Between Religiosity and Spirituality: Christianity and the Reemergence of the Immanentist Spiritualities." *Theology Today* 75, no. 2 (2018): 233–46.

37 James H. Leuba, *A Psychological Study of Religion* (New York: Macmillan Company, 1912); see appendix on 339–63.

38 Sheldrake, *Brief History*, 1–2.

39 Principe, "Toward Defining Spirituality," 48.

40 Sandra M. Schneiders, "Spirituality in the Academy," in *Exploring Christian Spirituality: An Ecumenical Reader*, ed. Kenneth J. Collins, 249–70 (Grand Rapids, MI: Baker Books, 2000), 251

41 John Macquarrie, "Spirit and Spirituality," *Exploring Christian Spirituality: An Ecumenical Reader*, ed. Kenneth J. Collins (Grand Rapids, MI: Baker Books, 2000), 63–73, at 63.

42 See, for example, Henry, *Barbarism*, xv, which describes culture as "the auto-revelation of life in its self-growth." For a more extended discussion of Henry on culture and its relation to Life, see my "Spiritual Life and Cultural Discernment: Renewing Spirituality through Henry," in *Michel Henry's Practical Philosophy*, ed. Michael R. Kelly, Brian Harding and Jeffrey Hanson (London: Bloomsbury, 2022), 45–65.

43 Henry, *Barbarism*, 47 and xv, respectively.

44 The uses of culture in religious studies seem to draw more broadly on either anthropological understandings (which are therefore inherently empirical) or on broadly Foucauldian accounts, which bear a much more complicated relationship to phenomenological understandings than can be outlined here (although we will return to it briefly in the conclusion of this book). For now, I think it is not overly contentious to acknowledge that Foucault's thought would not be described as engaging in transcendental phenomenology and hence can rightly be taken as both

distinct from Henry's account and as not necessarily pointing to the various types of effect (ultra-transcendental, sensing-transcendental, and quasi-transcendental) that we are hoping to elucidate in what follows.

45 We will return to this question in more detail—and with more tools at our disposal to deal with it more adequately—in Chapter five.

Chapter 2

1 Schilbrack, "What *Isn't* Religion?" *The Journal of Religion* 93, no. 1 (2013): 291–318.
2 Richard Kearney, *Touch: Recovering our Most Vital Sense* (New York: Columbia University Press, 2021).
3 Merleau-Ponty, *The Visible and the Invisible*, trans. A. Lingis (Evanston, IL: Northwestern University Press, 1969).
4 Michel Henry, *Barbarism*, trans. S. Davidson (1987; London: Bloomsbury Academic Press, 2012), 47. For more on the relation between spirituality and various cultural forms in Henry, see also DeRoo, "Spiritual Life and Cultural Discernment: Renewing Spirituality through Henry." In *Michel Henry's Practical Philosophy*, ed. M.R. Kelly, B. Harding, and J. Hanson (London: Bloomsbury, 2022), 45–65.
5 Thinking aesthetics in terms of beauty has a long line in Western thought, beginning at least from Plato (most notably in his *Hippias Major*). For a summary and overview of this tradition, see the section "Philosophical Conceptions of Beauty," in Crispin Sartwell, "Beauty," *The Stanford Encyclopedia of Philosophy* (Fall 2024 Edition), ed. Edward N. Zalta & Uri Nodelman. https://plato.stanford.edu/archives/fall2024/entries/beauty/.
6 On harmony as the key to aesthetics, see Hans Rookmaaker, "Ontwerp ener aesthetica op grondslag der wisjbegeerte der wetsidee," *Philosophia Reformata* 11, nos. 3 and 4 (1946): 141–62. Rookmaaker is drawing on and developing Herman Dooyeweerd's take on aesthetics as harmony in his *New Critique of Theoretical Thought, Volume 2: The General Theory of the Modal Spheres*, trans. David H. Freeman and H. De Jongste (1964; Jordan Station: Paideia Press, 1984), 346–8. Dooyeweerd himself claims to be building on the work of the classicist aestheticist Nicholas Boileau-Despréaux (1636–1711).
7 See Calvin C. Seerveld, "Modal Aesthetics," in *Hearing and Doing: Philosophical Essays Dedicated to H. Evan Runner* (Toronto: Wedge, 1979), 263–94.
8 And the appeal to ethicality helps highlight a certain normativity to all of these approaches. They are not "optional" in the sense of things a Subject could (or could not) choose to do, depending on the whim of the Subject. Rather, subjectivity is compelled to engage the world in these ways, insofar as an experiencer is able

to access that mode subjectively (e.g., insofar as someone is able to see and not just be seen). That is, we do not *choose* to see or not see (except by closing our eyes, turning off the lights, etc.)—we simply engage the world visibly. Similarly, we simply encounter the world as just (or not). There seems to be an implicit normativity to all these things that is part of our experiencing of the world. For how such norms are grounded in a homeworld and hence can be different for different people from different communities, see DeRoo, *Political Logic of Experience: Expression in Phenomenology* (New York: Fordham University Press, 2022) and Anthony J. Steinbock, *Home and Beyond: Generative Phenomenology after Husserl* (Evanston, IL: Northwestern University Press), 1995. For an explanation of such normativity even for perception, see Maxime Doyon, *Phenomenology and the Norms of Perception* (Oxford: Oxford University Press, 2025).

9. This possibility will be called into question in parts of this chapter, and will then be explored more fully in chapter three.
10. Wendy Doniger O'Flaherty, *Dreams, Illusion, and Other Realities* (Chicago, IL: University of Chicago Press, 1986), 119.
11. "Chandogya Upanishad," in *Upanishads: A New Translation*. trans. Patrick Olivelle (Oxford: Oxford University Press, 2008), 152.
12. Jean-Luc Marion's Catholic understanding of revelation trades heavily on this idea, that what we receive in divine revelation is a new way of experiencing the world. See Jean-Luc Marion, *Givenness and Revelation*, trans. Stephen E. Lewis (Oxford: Oxford Academic Press, 2016). For an analysis of revelation in terms of a new mode of sensing the world, see Neal DeRoo, "Thinking Revelation as Expression in and Through Phenomenology," *Journal for Continental Philosophy of Religion* 6 (2024): 31–50.
13. For example: "Love your neighbour as yourself" (Mark 12:31. *The Holy Bible* New International Version) or "By this everyone will know that you are my disciples, if you love one another" (John 13:35. *The Holy Bible* New International Version).
14. We will not pursue this further here, but we can see already that one reason for the difference in vision is that the painter's vision is more aesthetically attuned, whereas the scientist's vision is more theoretically attuned. That is, the different modes of sensing always intertwine with the other modes of sensing in different ways, ways that can be typical of certain traditions and/or certain time periods. We will return to this point in Chapters three and four.
15. I say "possible" because we presented only a very brief outline of the religious mode of sensing found in some religious traditions. Further investigation might yield greater similarity than we expect—or perhaps greater differences.
16. Robin Wall Kimmerer's discussion of the verb-based languages of Indigenous North American Peoples is an obvious counter-point; see Kimmerer, *Braiding Sweetgrass: Indigenous Wisdom, Scientific Knowledge, and the Teachings of Plants*

(Minneapolis, MN: Milkweed Editions, 2013), particularly the chapter entitled "Learning the Grammar of Animacy."

17 We cannot simply say "people," because it is not only people who experience: animals also do, and perhaps some plants. And I prefer not to say "Subjects," as that term has been poorly used in Western philosophy as a reification of subjectivity, and has therefore led to many philosophical confusions. Hence, I will simply use the somewhat awkward term "experiencers."

18 This experience was recounted by several people in relation to Taylor Swift's "The Era Tour" concerts; see, for a partial example; Hannah Lovaglio, "What Taylor Swift's Eras Tour Taught Me About Church," *The Presbyterian Outlook*, 2023: https://pres-outlook.org/2023/07/what-taylor-swifts-eras-tour-taught-me-about-church/; Melodie Roschman, "When Taylor Swift Took Me to Church," in *Spectrum Magazine*, 2023: https://spectrummagazine.org/culture/when-taylor-swift-took-me-church/; and Steph Copley, "I Found Religion…At a Taylor Swift Concert: My Transcendent Experience at Arrowhead Stadium," *It Was Never a Dress*, 2023: https://copleysteph.substack.c om/p/i-found-religion-at-a-taylor-swift.

19 Of course, the question of the etymology of the term religion is heavily contested, tracing at least back to Sarah F. Hoyt's classic essay "The Etymology of Religion," *The Journal of the American Oriental Society* 32, no. 3 (1912): 126–9. For some of these issues in linguistics, see Émile Benveniste, *Indo-European Language and Society*, trans. Elizabeth Palmer (London: Faber and Faber, 1973); see also Jacques Derrida's gloss on this in "Faith and Knowledge: Two Sources of 'Religion' at the Limits of Reason Alone," in *Religion* trans. David Webb (Redwood City, CA: Stanford University Press, 1998), 1–78. I do not mean here to imply a particular position in that debate. I simply want to indicate the feasibility of the account of religiosity I am offering within already extant understandings of the term religion without, I hope, merely repeating those extant understandings and the problems that have arisen alongside them.

20 An experience partially described in Brian Treanor, *Melancholic Joy: On Life Worth Living* (London: Bloomsbury, 2021).

21 For the notion of a flow state, see Mihály Csíkszentmihályi, *Beyond Boredom and Anxiety: Experiencing Flow in Work and Play* (San Francisco, CA: Jossey-Bass, 1975).

22 See Christina M. Gschwandtner's critique of Marion's account of religious experience via his notion of the "saturated phenomena" on just this score in her *Degrees of Givenness: On Saturation in Jean-Luc Marion* (Bloomington: Indiana University Press, 2014).

23 For a provisional phenomenological account of this relation, see Neal DeRoo, "A Phenomenology of Image-Bearing: Spirituality, Humanity, and the 'Supra-' Relation," in *Image, Phenomenon and Imagination in the Phenomenology of Religious Experience*, ed. Martin Nitsche and Olga Louchakova-Schwartz (Prague: Libri Nigri, 2020), 167–91.

24 See Edmund Husserl, *The Crisis of European Sciences and Transcendental Phenomenology*, trans. D. Carr (1936; Evanston, IL: Northwestern University Press, 1970), 270. Husserl elsewhere speaks also of "supra-national" (ibid. 275 and 289) and "supra-personal" (Edmund Husserl, *Zur Phänomenologie der Intersubjektivität: Zweiter Teil: 1921–1928*, ed. Iso Kern [The Hague: Martinus Nijhoff, 1973], 199) relationships.

25 See Herman Dooyeweerd, *New Critique of Theoretical Thought, Volume 1: The Necessary Presuppositions of Philosophy*, trans. D.H. Freeman and W.S. Young (Philadelphia, PA: The Reformed and Presbyterian Publishing Company, 1953–1958), 70.

26 1 John 4:8; *The Holy Bible* New International Version.

27 I would also contend that, for the majority of religious people, religiosity functions primarily via supra-relations rather than super-relations. But that is a claim that exceeds what I can argue for in this chapter.

28 This concern is summarized most notably in Schilbrack, "What *Isn't* Religion?"

29 The relation between the account of religiosity and "functional" definitions of religion is nuanced. Technically, religiosity is not a "function" but a mode of sensing the world in a unique way. At the same time, one could interpret that mode of sensing exclusively in terms of the "function" it plays in human living. Whether this can be done without loss is not immediately evident to me. For more on the distinction between substantive and functional definitions, see, for example, Melford Spiro, "Religion: Problems of Definition and Explanation," in *Anthropological Approaches to the Study of Religion*, ed. Michael Banton (London: Tavistock, 1966).

30 Schilbrack, "What *Isn't* Religion?" 291.

31 Fitzgerald, "A 'Critique' of Religion as a Cross-Cultural Category," *Method and Theory in the Study of Religion* 9, no. 2 (1997): 91–110, at 105.

32 Martin Reisebrodt, *The Promise of Salvation: A Theory of Religion*, tr. Steven Rendall (Chicago: University of Chicago Press, 2010), xi.

33 Peter Berger, *The Sacred Canopy: Elements of a Sociological Theory of Religion* (New York: Doubleday, 1967), 175.

Chapter 3

1 The aesthetic, qua mode of sensing, is not found simply in artworks, nor is it accessible only to those with training in the "fine arts." The notion of the aesthetic as a "philosophy of art" is no longer talking about the aesthetic as a mode of sensing the world, but something else entirely.

2 Daniel A. Cox, "Rise of Conspiracies Reveals An Evangelical Divide in the GOP," *Survey Center on American Life* (February 12, 2021). www.americansurveycenter.org/rise-of-conspiracies-reveal-an-evangelical-divide-in-the-gop/.

3. See J. Aaron Simmons, "Religious but not Spiritual: A Constructive Proposal," *Religions* 12, no. 6 (2021): 433; https://doi.org/10.3390/rel12060433.
4. Howard Lavine, James Ron, and Richard L. Wood, "Why Are White Evangelicals Anti-Human Rights?" *Open Global Rights* (December 21, 2020). www.openglobalrights.org/why-are-white-evangelicals-anti-human-rights/#:~:text=Although%2056%25%20of%20respondents%20told,of%20police%20racism%20and%20violence%2C.
5. Most notably Kristin Kobes-Du Mez, *Jesus and John Wayne: How White Evangelicals Corrupted a Faith and Fractured a Nation* (New York: Liveright, 2020). But see also Gwenda Blair, "How Norman Vincent Peale Taught Donald Trump to Worship Himself," *Politico Magazine* October 6, 2015; www.politico.com/magazine/story/2015/10/donald-trump-2016-norman-vincent-peale-213220/. For more on the influence of Norman Vincent Peale for American religious life in general, see Carol V.R. George, *God's Salesman: Norman Vincent Peale and the Power of Positive Thinking* (Oxford: Oxford University Press 1993); and Christopher Lane, *Surge of Piety: Norman Vincent Peale and the remaking of American Religious Life* (New Haven, CT: Yale University Press 2016). I thank Mark Griffiths for bringing this connection between Trump and Norman Vincent Peale to my attention.
6. One could do a similar analysis talking about how evangelical Christians inhabit their sexuality very differently than do adherents of tantric traditions of Buddhism and Hinduism.
7. This example suggests that there is something about being trained in the "style" or tradition of jazz music that changes how people are able to hear certain sounds, which partially explains why those trained in jazz can appreciate sounds and noises that often strike those untrained or unfamiliar with jazz as atonal or grating. Thanks to Benjamin Strachan for this example. For more on the relationship between phenomenology and jazz music, see Bruce Ellis Benson, *The Improvisation of Musical Dialogue: A Phenomenology of Music* (Cambridge: Cambridge University Press, 2003).
8. See, for example, Talal Asad, *Genealogies of Religion: Discipline and Reasons of Power in Christianity and Islam* (Baltimore, MD: Johns Hopkins University Press, 1993); Tomoko Masuzawa, *The Invention of World Religions* (Chicago, IL: University of Chicago Press, 2005); and Richard King, *Orientalism and Religion: Postcolonial Theory, India, and the "Mystic East"* (New York: Routledge, 1999).
9. Asad, *Genealogies of Religion*, 28.
10. Ibid., 54.
11. Charles Taylor, *A Secular Age* (Cambridge, MA: Harvard University Press, 2007).
12. See Gianni Vattimo, *After Christianity*, trans. Luca D'Isanto (New York: Columbia University Press, 2002); and, John D. Caputo and Gianni Vattimo, *After the Death of God*, ed. Jeffrey W. Robbins (New York: Columbia University Press, 2007).

For more on secularism as the outgrowth and culmination of Christianity, see P.D. Bubbio, "Secularisation and Kenosis in Gianni Vattimo's *Kehre*," *SOPHIA* (2024). https://doi.org/10.1007/s11841-024-01037-7

13 A point made also about those who currently identify as "spiritual but not religious" in J. Aaron Simmons, "Religious, but not Spiritual".

14 See, for example, Asad, *Genealogies of Religion*, 45: "This modest view of religion (which would have horrified the early Christian Fathers or Medieval churchmen) is a product of the only legitimate space allowed to Christianity by post-Enlightenment society, the right to individual belief."

15 Ibid., 45–6.

16 Ibid., 28.

17 Taylor, *A Secular Age*; these concepts are initially introduced and explained on pages 27–42.

18 Asad, *Genealogies of Religion*, 45.

19 For some summaries and accounts of this "material turn," see Sonia Hazard, "The Material Turn in the Study of Religion," *Religion and Society* 4, no. 1 (2013): 21 pages. https://doi.org/10.3167/arrs.2013.040104; Peter J. Bräunlein, "Thinking Religion Through Things: Reflections on the Material Turn in the Scientific Study of Religion\s," *Method & Theory in the Study of Religion* 28, no. 4/5 (2016): 365–99; and Kevin Schilbrack, "The Material Turn in the Academic Study of Religions," *The Journal of Religion* 99, no. 2 (2019), https://doi.org/10.1086/701868, which is a review of David Chidester, *Religion: Material Dynamics* (Berkeley: University of California Press, 2018) and David Morgan, *Images at Work: The Material Culture of Enchantment* (New York: Oxford University Press, 2018).

20 This turn is most famously articulated in Donovan O. Schaefer, *Religious Affects: Animality, Evolution, Power* (Durham, NC: Duke University Press, 2015). One finds evidence of it across religious studies (and various other humanities and social sciences), for example in Karen Bray and Stephen D. Moore (eds.), *Religion, Emotion, Sensation: Affect Theories and Theologies* (New York: Fordham University Press, 2019); Cornel W. Du Toit, "Emotion and the Affective Turn: Towards an Integration of Cognition and Affect in Real Life Experience," *HTS Toelogiese Studies/Theological Studies* 70, no. 1 (2014): 9 pages, http://dx.doi.org/10.4102/hts.v70i1.2692; and Yannick Fer, "An Affective (U-)Turn in the Sociology of Religion? Religious Emotions and Native Narratives," in *Bringing Back the Social into the Sociology of Religion*, ed. Veronique Altglas and Matthew Wood (Leiden: Brill, 2018); https://doi.org/10.1163/9789004368798.

21 Though these complications are much less prevalent in the phenomenological philosophy of religion.

22 A point made, in very different ways, by Alvin Plantinga and by Anselm; see, for example, Alvin Plantinga, *God and Other Minds: A Study of the Rational*

Justification of Belief in God (Ithaca, NY: Cornell University Press, 1967); Alvin Plantinga, "Is Belief in God Properly Basic?" *Noûs* 16, no. 1 (1981): 41–51; Alvin Plantinga, "Reason and Belief in God," *Faith and Rationality: Reason and Belief in God*, ed. by Alvin Plantinga and Nichola Wolterstorff (London: Notre Dame University Press, 1983): 16–93; and Anselm of Canterbury, "Proslogion," in *The Major Works* ed. Brian Davies and G.R. Evans (London: Oxford University Press, 1998), 82–104.

23 He takes the name barbarism from the end of Husserl's "Vienna Lecture": "There are only two escapes from the crisis of the European existence: the downfall of Europe in its estrangement from its own rational sense of life, its fall into hostility toward the spirit and into *barbarity*; or the rebirth of Europe from the spirit of philosophy through a heroism of reason that overcomes naturalism once and for all"; Edmund Husserl, "The Vienna Lecture," in *The Crisis of European Sciences and Transcendental Phenomenology* trans. David Carr (Evanston, IL: Northwestern University Press, 1970), 269–99; 299.

24 Michel Henry, *Barbarism*, trans. D. Davidson (1987; London: Bloomsbury Academic Press, 2012), 17.

25 Ibid., 40.

26 Ibid., 47.

27 Ibid., xv.

28 Gadamer describes this as a "prejudice against prejudices"; see Gadamer, *Truth and Method*, sSecond revised edition, trans. Joel Weisenheimer and Donald G. Marshall (London and New York: Continuum, 2004), 273–7.

29 Gloria Anzaldúa, for one, laments how her commitment to *nepantla* spirituality is something that the vast majority of (secular) scholars "resist"; see Gloria Anzaldúa, *Interviews/Entrevistas*, ed. AnaLouise Keating (New York: Routledge, 2000), 7. Furthermore, Christopher D. Tirres discusses Anzaldúa's relation to religion and spirituality in "Spiritual Activism and Practice: Gloria Anzaldúa's Mature Spirituality," *The Pluralist* 14, no. 1 (2019): 119–40.

30 Fitzgerald, "A 'Critique' of Religion as a Cross-Cultural Category." *Method and Theory in the Study of Religion* 9, no. 2 (1997): 91–110, at 91–2.

31 Ibid., 101–3.

32 Ibid., 93.

33 This is, of course, not to say that no one can reject the idea that malls have a religious dimension to them. Someone certainly could—but the nature of that rejection has to either: (a) be based on something more than the assumptions of one's own tradition; or (b) be clearly explained as "from the perspective of this religious tradition, with these assumptions, one should not claim that malls are religious."

34 See DeRoo, *Political Logic of Experience: Expression in Phenomenology* (New York: Fordham University Press, 2022), on the often infinitesimal nature of generative change.

35 For a discussion of this, see Véronique Altglas, "Westernization and Easternization of Religion," *The SAGE Encyclopedia of the Sociology of Religion* (2024). https://doi.org/10.4135/9781529714401.n513; accessed online January 13, 2025.

36 For more on expression as a "logic of experiencing," see DeRoo, *Political Logic of Experience*.

37 The phrase is crucial to the reasoning behind the system of residential schools that emerged in North American in the later part of the nineteenth century. It was first used in a speech entitled "The Advantage of Mixing Indians with Whites" given by Captain Richard Henry Pratt at the National Conference of Charities and Correction in Denver, Colorado in 1892. The text of that speech is available online: https://carlisleindian.dickinson.edu/teach/kill-indian-him-and-save-man-r-h-pratt-education-native-americans. For more on this phrase and its impacts, see Ward Churchill, *Kill the Indian, Save the Man: The Genocidal Impact of American Indian Residential Schools* (San Francisco, CA: City Light Books, 2004).

38 Alvin Plantinga, "Advice to Christian Philosophers," *Faith and Philosophy: Journal of the Society of Christian Philosophers* 1, no. 3 (1984): 253–71.

39 Elaine Coburn, "Indigenous Research as Resistance," *Socialist Studies/Études socialistes* 9, no. 1 (Spring 2013): 52–63. See also her edited volume *More Will Sing Their Way to Freedom: Indigenous Resistance and Resurgence* (Winnipeg: Fernwood Publishing, 2015). For more on the relation between Indigenous thought and its necessary grounding the lives of Indigenous people, see also Glenn Coulthard's development of the notion of grounded normativity in *Red Skin, White Masks: Rejecting the Colonial Politics of Recognition* (Minneapolis, MN: University of Minnesota Press, 2014).

40 There are certainly resonances here of the "nothing about us without us" approach concerning oppressed or under-represented groups; see James I. Charlton, *Nothing About Us Without Us: Disability, Oppression and Empowerment* (Irvine: University of California Press, 2000).

41 An argument I make more explicitly in chapter four of *Political Logic of Experience*.

42 As the history of scholars associated with the Institute for Christian Studies (ICS) attests. The work done around the ICS has contributed to the creation or reform of various universities, day schools, a labor union, trade guilds (including the Christian Farmer's Federation of Ontario), and public advocacy groups (such as Citizens for Public Justice, in Canada, and the Center for Public Justice, in the United States), to name a few.

Chapter 4

1 See, for example, Schilbrack, "What *Isn't* Religion?" *The Journal of Religion* 93, no. 1 (2013): 291–318; Fitzgerald, "A 'Critique' of Religion as a Cross-Cultural Category."

Method and Theory in the Study of Religion 9, no. 2 (1997): 91–110; and Melford Spiro, "Religion: Problems of Definition and Explanation," in *Anthropological Approaches to the Study of Religion*, ed. Michael Banton (London: Tavistock, 1966).

2. On givenness as a mode of phenomenality, see Jean-Luc Marion, *Being Given: Toward a Phenomenology of Givenness*, trans. J.L. Kosky (1997; Stanford, CA: Stanford University Press, 2002); and Jean-Luc Marion, *Reduction and Givenness: Investigation of Husserl, Heidegger, and Phenomenology*, trans. T.A. Carlton (Evanston, IL: Northwestern University Press, 1998).

3. See, for example, Schilbrack's debates with McCutcheon, summarized in Kevin Schilbrack, "A Metaphysics for the Study of Religion: A Critical Reading of Russel McCutcheon," *Critical Research on Religion* 8, no. 1 (2020): 87–100. https://doi.org/10.1177/2050303219900229.

4. As Asad suggests in his *Genealogies of Religion: Discipline and Reasons of Power in Christianity and Islam* (Baltimore, MD: Johns Hopkins University Press, 1993). For more on Asad's view of secularism, see his *Formations of the Secular: Christianity, Islam, Modernity* (Stanford, CA: Stanford University Press, 2003).

5. James H. Cone, *The Cross and the Lynching Tree* (Maryknoll, NY: Orbis Books, 2011).

6. Richard Kearney's "Epiphanies of the Everyday: Toward a Micro-Eschatology," in *After God: Richard Kearney and the Religious Turn in Continental Philosophy*, ed. John Panteleimon Manoussakis (New York: Fordham University Press, 2006), 3–20, would be a primary example in contemporary Continental philosophy of religion. This could, perhaps, be extended to the entire "liturgical" or "sacramental" approach to materiality—a point which we will return to next chapter.

7. Which still would not make it true that all phenomena are religious phenomena; it would simply mean the phenomenon of believing "all phenomena cannot be religious phenomena" might itself be a religious phenomenon.

8. Some examples we cited include: Hannah Lovaglio, "What Taylor Swift's Eras Tour Taught Me About Church," *The Presbyterian Outlook*, 2023: https://pres-outlook.org/2023/07/what-taylor-swifts-eras-tour-taught-me-about-church/; Melodie Roschman, "When Taylor Swift Took Me to Church," *Spectrum Magazine*, 2023: https://spectrummagazine.org/culture/when-taylor-swift-took-me-church/; and Steph Copley, "I Found Religion … At a Taylor Swift Concert: My Transcendent Experience at Arrowhead Stadium," *It Was Never a Dress*, 2023: https://copleysteph.substack.com/p/i-found-religion-at-a-taylor-swift.

9. For an argument to this effect, see Michele Augusto Riva and Giancarlo Cesana, "The Charity and the Care: The Origin and Evolution of hospitals." *European Journal of Internal Medicine* 24, no. 1 (2013): 1–4.

10. See, for example, Derrida on the theological roots of the political notion of sovereignty in Jacques Derrida, *Rogues: Two Essays on Reason*, trans. Pascale-Anne Brault and Michael Naas (Redwood City, CA: Stanford University Press, 2005).

11 James K. A. Smith, *Desiring the Kingdom: Worship, Worldviews, and Cultural Formation* (Ada, MI: Baker Academic, 2009).
12 As Jonathan Z. Smith, says: "'Religion' [...] is a term created by scholars for their intellectual purposes and therefore is theirs to define"; see Jonathan Z. Smith, "Religion, Religions, Religious," in *Critical Terms for Religious Studies*, ed. Mark Taylor (Chicago, IL: University of Chicago Press, 1998): 269–284, at 281.

Chapter 5

1 See, for example, Talal Asad, *Genealogies of Religion: Discipline and Reasons of Power in Christianity and Islam* (Caltimore, MD: Johns Hopkins University Press, 1993); Talal Asad, "The Construction of Religion as an Anthropological Category" in *Religion in Today's World: Global Issues, Sociological Perspectives*, ed. Melissa Wilcox (New York: Routledge, 2013); and Timothy Fitzgerald, "A 'Critique' of Religion as a Cross-Cultural Category." Method and Theory in the Study of Religion 9, no. 2 (1997):91–110.
2 I note physical "or symbolic" here to clearly indicate that twentieth-century attempts to locate religion in language or symbolic representation tend to still fall primarily into this traditional materialist camp: the material part of the conditions (the particular sounds or markings on a page that give us a word) taken on religious significance only through their transmutation into the spiritual [*geistig*], that is, into meanings, concepts, and so on.
3 Fitzgerald, "A 'Critique' of Religion," 93.
4 Ibid., 101–2.
5 Ibid., 103.
6 For a summary of some of these movements and the philosophical assumptions involved, see Bräunlein, "Thinking Religion Through Things: Reflections on tge Material Turn in the Scientific Study of Religion\s." *Method & Theory in the Study of Religion* 28, nos. 4/5 (2016): 365–99.
7 See, for example, Kearney's chapter on "sacramental imagination" in *Anatheism: Returning to God After God* (New York, Columbia University Press), 85–100.
8 In his earlier work, Marion seems to suggest saturated phenomena are distinct (and atypical) experiences. In some of his later work, especially "The Banality of Saturation," Marion suggests that saturation is not exclusively the mark of distinct phenomena but can perhaps be characteristic of phenomenality itself. We will get to a certain interpretation of what that might mean below. For more on this transition, see Shane MacKinlay, *Interpreting Excess: Jean-Luc Marion, Saturated Phenomena, and Hermeneutics* (New York: Fordham University Press, 2010); see esp. 58–9.

9 See Jean-Luc Marion, *In Excess: Studies of Saturated Phenomena*, trans. R. Horner and V. Berraud (New York: Fordham University Press, 2004).
10 See, for example, Jean-Luc Marion, "Evidence and Bedazzlement," in *Prolegomena to Charity*, trans. Stephen Lewis (New York: Fordham University Press, 2002), 53–70.
11 It is worth noting that Marion claims (for example in "The Banality of Saturation") that such saturated experiences happen quite often, although we simply aren't able to "bear" them. The distinction between experiences we have and experiences we "bear" is phenomenologically important but is perhaps not relevant enough for the current conversation to be worth considering here. Regardless, we will return to how Marion gets out of the conundrum described here in a moment.
12 See, Jean-Luc Marion, *Revelation Comes from Elsewhere*, trans. Stephen E. Lewis and Stephanie Rumpza (Redwood City, CA: Stanford University Press, 2024).
13 Kearney, "Epiphanies of the Everyday: Toward a Micro-Eschatology" in *After God: Richard Kearney and the Religious Turn in Continental Philosophy*, ed. J. Panteleimon Manoussakis (New York: Fordham University Press, 2006), 3–20.
14 For a description of this account of sacrality in Kearney's work, see DeRoo, "Carnal Sacrality: Phenomenology, the Scared ad Material Bodies in Richard Kearney." In *Anacarnation and Returning to the Lived Body with Richard Kearney*, ed. B. Treanor and J.L. Taylor (New York: Routledge, 2023), 69–85.
15 See Richard Kearney, *Touch: Recovering our Most Vital Sense* (New York: Columbia University Press, 2021); and Richard Kearney and Brian Treanor (eds.), *Carnal Hermeneutics* (New York: Fordham University Press, 2015).
16 See, for example, Kearney, *Anatheism: Returning to God After God* (New York: Columbia University Press, 2010), 86. Kearney draws the pots and pans language predominantly from Teresa of Avila; see Teresa of Avila, *Collected Works* 3, trans. Kieran Kavanagh and Otilio Rodriguez (Washington, DC: ICS, 1985),5.8.
17 Kearney draws the "cries in the streets" language predominantly from James Joyce; see, *Anatheism*, 104–10.
18 Richard Kearney, "Imagination, Anatheism and the Sacred: A Dialogue with James Wood," in Kearney and Zimmerman (eds.), *Reimagining the Sacred: Richard Kearney Debates God* (New York: Columbia University Press, 2016), 19–45; 35.
19 I draw the name here especially from John D. Caputo's account; see *The Weakness of God: A Theology of the Event* (Bloomington: Indiana University Press, 2006). In Caputo's usage (found also in Vattimo, Nancy, Crockett, Robbins, and others in this tradition), the notion of event seems to follow a broadly Deleuzian direction. This is, perhaps, in contrast to the way "event" is used in Marion, Romano, and others in a more phenomenological register.
20 On religion as a kind of energy, see Jean-Luc Nancy, *Dis-Enclosure: The Deconstruction of Christianity*, trans. Bettina Bergo, Gabriel Malenfant, and Michael B. Smith (New York: Fordham University Press, 2008); Jean-Luc Nancy,

"Atheistic Experience" in *Atheism, Faith and Experience*, ed. Claude Roman and Robyn Horner (London: Bloomsbury, 2020); and Clayton Crockett and Jefferey W. Robbins, *Religion, Politics and the Earth: the New Materialism* (New York: Palgrave Macmillan, 2012).

21 John D. Caputo, *The Insistence of God: A Theology of the Perhaps* (Bloomington: Indiana University Press, 2015).
22 John D. Caputo, *What Would Jesus Deconstruct: The Good News of Postmodernism for the Church* (Grand Rapids, MI: Baker Academic, 2007).
23 John D. Caputo, *On Religion* (New York: Routledge, 2001), 32–6.
24 See J. Aaron Simmons and Stephen Minister (eds.), *Reexamining Deconstruction and Determinate Religion: Toward a Religion with Religion* (Pittsburgh, PA: Duquesne University Press, 2012).
25 A distinction that seems to parallel our distinction between religion's effects on transcendental modes of sensing and its quasi-transcendental effects on religious traditions.
26 See the first chapter of Caputo's *On Religion* and John D. Caputo, *What to Believe?: Twelve Brief Lessons in Radical Theology* (New York: Columbia University Press, 2023), 77–8 for some gestures in this direction, even though the majority of his work remains explicitly within the Christian tradition.
27 For this notion of force in relation to deconstruction, see Derrida, "Force of Law: The 'Mystical' Foundation of Authority" in *Acts of Religion*, ed. Gil Anidjar (New York and London: Routledge, 2002), 228–298.
28 See, for example, Jean-Luc Nancy, "The Surprise: Of the Event," in *Hegel after Derrida*, ed. Stuart Barnett (London and New York: Routledge, 1998).
29 Caputo, *On Religion*, 24–5; Caputo, *What to Believe?*, 3–14.
30 See Caputo, *What to Believe?*, 15–32.
31 For a reading of the event-al approach in this vein, see James K.A. Smith's critique of Derrida's notion of religion in "Re-Kanting Postmodernism," *Faith and Philosophy* 17, no. 4 (2000): 558–71; for a broader analysis of this approach in the Christian tradition, see James K. A. Smith's *The Fall of Interpretation: Philosophical Foundations for a Creational Hermeneutics* (Lisle: InterVarsity Press: 2000).
32 See, Nancy, *Dis-Enclosure*, 25; Robyn Horner summarizes this account of the event in her *The Experience of God: A Phenomenology of Revelation* (Cambridge: Cambridge University Press, 2022), 135–42.
33 Jean-Luc Marion, *Revelation Comes from Elsewhere*.
34 See Marion, "God Without Being." Reprinted in *Phenomenology and Eschatology: Not yet in the Now*, ed. N. DeRoo and J. Panteleimon Manoussakis (1946; New York: Routledge, 20210), 193–213.
35 Jean Grondin, "In any Event? Critical Remarks on the Recent Fascination with the Notion of Event," in *Being Shaken: Ontology and the Event*, ed. Michael Marder and Santiago Zabala (London and New York: Palgrave MacMillan, 2014), 65.

36 We will return to this "as much as possible" question next chapter, when we examine more closely the relationship between thinking from a particular tradition and thinking across traditions.
37 Fitzgerald, "A 'Critique' of Religion," 92–3.
38 A point acknowledged and discussed in Christina M. Gschwandtner, *Ways of Living Religion: Philosophical investigations into Religious Experience* (Cambridge: Cambridge University Press, 2024).

Chapter 6

1 This seems to be Fitzgerald's main problem with the transcendence-assumption; see "A 'Critique' of Religion," particularly pages 101–3; see also Timothy Fitzgerald, "Japanese Religion as Ritual Order," *Religion* 23 (1993): 315–41; Timothy Fitzgerald, "Ritual, Politics, and Soteriology in Ambedkar Buddhism," *Indian Journal of Buddhist Studies* 5 (1994): 25–44; and Timothy Fitzgerald, "Things, Thoughts, and People Out of Place," Review of Mark R. Mullins et al., *Religion and Society in Modern Japan*, in *Japanese Journal of Religious Studies* 22 (1995): 201–17.
2 "Modernization as the superficial imitation of western institutions appears to have brought religions into existence in various non-western cultures" (Fitzgerald, "A 'Critique' of Religion," 99). See also Fitzgerald, "Hinduism and the World Religion Fallacy," *Religion* 20 (1990): 101–18; Helen Hardacre, "The Shinto Priesthood in Early Meiji Japan: Preliminary Inquiries," *History of Religions* 27, no. 3 (1998): 294–320; Talal Asad, *Genealogies of Religion: Discipline and Reasons of Power in Christianity and Islam* (Baltimore, MD: Johns Hopkins University Press, 1993); Tomoko Masuzawa, *The Invention of World Religions* (Chicago, IL: University of Chicago Press, 2005).
3 For more on the notion of expression as it functions in (transcendental) phenomenology, see my *Political Logic of Experience*.
4 See Paul Ricoeur, *Living Up to Death*, trans. David Pellauer (Chicago, IL: University of Chicago Press, 2009), 15. See also Ricoeur, *Critique and Conviction: Conversations with François Azouvi and Marc de Launay*, trans. Kathleen Blamey (New York: Columbia University Press, 1998), 145; Ricoeur, "Religious Belief: The Difficult Path of the Religious." in *A Passion for the Possible: Thinking with Paul Ricoeur*, ed. B. Treanor and H.I. Venema (New York: Fordham University Press, 2010), 27–39; 38; and Christina M. Gschwandtner, "Faith, Religion and Spirituality: A Phenomenological and Hermeneutic Contribution to Parsing the Distinctions," *Religions* 12, no. 7 (2021): https://doi.org/10.3390/rel12070476; section 4.3.
5 I explore this question at length in *Political Logic of Experience*. See also Thomas Szanto and Dermot Moran (eds.), *Phenomenology of Sociality: Discovering the*

We (New York: Routledge, Taylor & Francis Group, 2016); and Timo Miettinen, "Transcendental Social Ontology," in *Phenomenology and the Transcendental*, ed. Sara Heinämaa, Mirja Hartimo, and Timo Miettinen (New York: Routledge, 2014), 147–71.

6. See Neal DeRoo, "The Everyday Power of Liturgy: On the Significance of the Transcendental for a Phenomenology of Liturgy," *Religions* 12, no. 8 (2021): 633; https://doi.org/10.3390/rel12080633 for an example of this. Much of the rest of this section is heavily indebted to material from that article.

7. For an excellent example of this, see Christina M. Gschwandtner, *Welcoming Finitude: Toward a Phenomenology of the Orthodox Liturgy* (New York: Fordham University Press, 2019).

8. Think back to our discussion in Chapter three of how the tradition of white evangelicalism impacted things like views on conspiracy theories and human rights in statistically significant ways.

9. For more on the notion of grounded normativity, see Glen Coulthard and Leanne Betasamosake Simpson, "Grounded Normativity/Place-Based Solidarity," *American Quarterly* 68, no. 2 (June 2016): 249–55, and a more in-depth development in Glen Sean Coulthard, *Red Skin, White Masks: Rejecting the Colonial Politics of Recognition* (Minneapolis, MN: University of Minnesota Press, 2014).

10. For one account of how this type of grounded normativity emerges in Nishinaabeg intelligence and culture, see Leanne Betasamosake Simpson, "Land as Pedagogy: Nishnaabeg Intelligence and Rebellious Transformation," in *Decolonization: Indigeneity, Education and Society* 3, no. 3 (2014): 1–25; and Simpson, *As we Have Always Done: Indigenous Freedom through Radical Resistance* (Minneapolis, MN: University of Minnesota Press, 2020).

11. See Alvin Plantinga, "Advice to Christian Philosophers," *Faith and Philosophy: Journal of the Society of Christian Philosophers* 1, no. 3 (1984): 253–71, for an account of what a Christian philosophy might entail.

12. Michel Henry, *I am the Truth: Toward a Philosophy of Christianity*, trans. Susan Emanuel (Redwood City, CA: Stanford University Press, 2000), 1.

13. See especially chapter 3, "This Truth Called Life," in Henry's *I am the Truth*, 33–52.

14. See, for example, Henry's discussions of the divinity of Christ in chapter 5, "The Phenomenology of Christ," *I am the Truth*, 69–93.

15. See especially chapter 10, "The Christian Ethic," in Henry's *I am the Truth*, 171Ą90.

16. See chapter 12, "The Word of God, Scripture," in Henry's *I am the Truth*, 215–33; and Michel Henry, *Words of Christ*, trans. Christina M. Gschwandtner (Grand Rapids, MI: Wm. B. Eerdmans Publishing Co., 2002).

17. See, for example, Joseph Rivera, *The Contemplative Self after Michel Henry* (Notre Dame, IN: University of Notre Dame Press, 2015).

18. It must be noted that Rivera seems to misunderstand a good portion of the phenomenology at work in Henry, and thereby seems to read Henry's account as if

it were a theological account, which it is not. For a criticism of Rivera on this score, see Neal DeRoo, "Eschatology, Expression and Spirituality: A Response to Rivera," *Syndicate*. https://syndicate.network/symposia/philosophy/the-contemplative-self-after-michel-henry/.

19 The category of the "in-itself" seems to have little room in phenomenology, which is instead interested in phenomena which are necessarily entangled, and therefore never exist strictly in-themselves.

20 See Michel Henry, *Barbarism*, trans. S. Davidson (1987; London: Bloomsbury Academic Press, 2012). On *Stiftung* as a mode of being in transcendental phenomenology, see Renaud Barbaras, *The Being of the Phenomenon*, trans. T. Toadvine and L. Lawlor (Bloomington: Indiana University Press, 2004), especially page 58.

21 For more on this distinction, see Jonathan Z. Smith, "Religion, Religions, Religious." In *Critical Terms for Religious Studies*, ed. M. Taylor (Chicago, IL: University of Chicago Press, 1998), 269–84.

Conclusion

1 Both of these examples were discussed in Chapter three; see Cox "Rise of Conspiracies"; and Lavine et al., "Why Are White Evangelicals Anti-Human Rights?"

2 For some analyses on these differences, see Howard Thurman, *Jesus and the Disinherited* (New York: Abingdon-Cokesbury Press, 1949); James H. Cone, *The Cross and the Lynching Tree* (Maryknoll, NY: Orbis Books, 2011); and Esau McCaulley, *Reading While Black: African American Biblical Interpretation as an Exercise in Hope* (Lisle, IL: InterVarsity Press, 2020).

3 Although subjectivity is required for experience as we have outlined it in this book, it is not necessarily the case that only humans can engage the world subjectively. We know other organisms engage the world subjectively via some of the transcendental modes of sensing, like visibility, tactility, and so on. It seems quite likely that some organisms engage the world subjectively via sociality (herd, pack, and communal animals) and linguisticality (whales, dolphins), as well, so it is not just the "empirical senses" that other organisms can engage with subjectively.

4 See my *Political Logic of Experience* for a more in-depth account of expressivity as the logic of how experience works.

5 "Lévinas is arguably not developing a phenomenology of religion or investigating religious phenomena, but employing religiously inflected language in order to call philosophy to recognize its responsibility to ethics as first philosophy and to confront its tendency to totalitarianism"; Christina M. Gschwandtner, "What

is Phenomenology of Religion? (Part II): The Phenomenology of Religious Experience," *Philosophy Compass* 14, no. 2 (2019): e12567, https://doi.org/10.1111/phc3.12567.

6 See Alvin Plantinga, *God and Other Minds: A Study of the Rational Justification of Belief in God* (Ithaca, NY: Cornell University Press,1967); Plantinga, "Is Belief in God Properly Basic?" *Noûs* 16, no. 1 (1981): 410–51; and Plantinga, "Reason and Belief in God." In *Faith and Rationality: Reason and Belief in God*, ed. A. Plantinga and N. Wolterstoff (London: Notre Dame University Press, 1983), 16–93.

7 Alvin Plantinga, "Advice to Christian Philosophers." Faith and Philosophy: Journal of the Society of Christian Philosophers 1, no. 3 (1984): 253–71 at 255.

8 See Richard Rorty, *Contingency, Irony, Solidarity* (Cambridge: Cambridge University Press, 1989).

Bibliography

Al-Saji, Alia. "Bodies and Sensings: On the Uses of Husserlian Phenomenology for Feminist Theory." *Continental Philosophy Review* 43, no. 1 (2010): 13–37.

Altglas, Véronique. "Westernization and Easternization of Religion." *The SAGE Encyclopedia of the Sociology of Religion* (2024): https://doi.org/10.4135/9781529714401.n513; accessed online January 13, 2025.

Anselm of Canterbury. "Proslogion." In *The Major Works*, edited by Brian Davies and G.R. Evans, 82–104. London: Oxford University Press, 1998.

Anzaldúa, Gloria. *Interviews/Entrevistas*, edited by AnaLouise Keating. New York: Routledge, 2000.

Aristotle. *The Metaphysics*, translated by Hugh Lawson-Tancred. 1998. London: Penguin Classics, 2012.

Asad, Talal. "The Construction of Religion as an Anthropological Category." In *Religion in Today's World: Global Issues, Sociological Perspectives*, edited by Melissa Wilcox. New York: Routledge, 2013.

Asad, Talal. *Formations of the Secular: Christianity, Islam, Modernity*. Stanford, CA: Stanford University Press, 2003.

Asad, Talal. *Genealogies of Religion: Discipline and Reasons of Power in Christianity and Islam*. Baltimore, MD: Johns Hopkins University Press, 1993.

Avila, Teresa of. *Collected Works* Volume 3, translated by Kieran Kavanagh and Otilio Rodriguez. Washington, DC: Institute of Carmelite Studies, 1985.

Barad, Karen M. *Meeting the Universe Halfway: Quantum Physics and the Entanglement of Matter and Meaning*. Durham, NC: Duke University Press, 2007.

Barbaras, Renaud. *The Being of the Phenomenon*, translated by Ted Toadvine and Leonard Lawlor. Bloomington: Indiana University Press, 2004.

Benson, Bruce Ellis. *The Improvisation of Musical Dialogue: A Phenomenology of Music*. Cambridge: Cambridge University Press, 2003.

Benveniste, Émile. *Indo-European Language and Society*, translated by Elizabeth Palmer. London: Faber and Faber, 1973.

Berger, Peter. *The Sacred Canopy: Elements of a Sociological Theory of Religion*. New York: Doubleday, 1967.

Betasamosake Simpson, Leanne. *As we Have Always Done: Indigenous Freedom through Radical Resistance*. Minneapolis: University of Minnesota Press, 2020.

Betasamosake Simpson, Leanne. "Land as Pedagogy: Nishnaabeg Intelligence and Rebellious Transformation." *Decolonization: Indigeneity, Education and Society* 3, no. 3 (2014): 1–25.

Blair, Gwenda. "How Norman Vincent Peale Taught Donald Trump to Worship Himself," *Politico Magazine*, October 6, 2015; www.politico.com/magazine/story/2015/10/donald-trump-2016-norman-vincent-peale-213220/.

Bray, Karen, and Stephen D. Moore (eds.). *Religion, Emotion, Sensation: Affect Theories and Theologies*. New York: Fordham University Press, 2019.

Bräunlein, Peter J. "Thinking Religion Through Things: Reflections on the Material Turn in the Scientific Study of Religion\s." *Method & Theory in the Study of Religion* 28, nos. 4/5 (2016): 365–99.

Brekke, Torkel. *Fundamentalism: Prophecy and Protest in an Age of Globalization*. Cambridge: Cambridge University Press, 2012.

Bubbio, P.D. "Secularisation and Kenosis in Gianni Vattimo's *Kehre*." *SOPHIA* (2024). https://doi.org/10.1007/s11841-024-01037-7.

Cadge, Wendy, Peggy Levitt, and David Smilde. "De-Centering and Re-Centering: Rethinking Concepts and Methods in the Sociological Study of Religion." *Journal for the Scientific Study of Religion* 84, no. 2 (2016): 373–400.

Caputo, John D. *The Insistence of God: A Theology of the Perhaps*. Bloomington: Indiana University Press, 2015.

Caputo, John D. *More Radical Hermeneutics: On not Knowing Who We Are*. Bloomington: Indiana University Press, 2000.

Caputo, John D. *On Religion*. New York: Routledge, 2001.

Caputo, John D. *Radical Hermeneutics: Repetition, Deconstruction, and the Hermeneutic Project*. Bloomington: Indiana University Press, 1988.

Caputo, John D. *Specters of God: An Anatomy of the Apophatic Imagination*. Bloomington: Indiana University Press, 2022.

Caputo, John D. *The Weakness of God: A Theology of the Event*. Bloomington: Indiana University Press, 2006.

Caputo, John D. *What to Believe?: Twelve Brief Lessons in Radical Theology*. New York: Columbia University Press, 2023.

Caputo, John D. *What Would Jesus Deconstruct: The Good News of Postmodernism for the Church*. Grand Rapids, MI: Baker Academic, 2007.

Caputo, John D. and Michael J. Scanlon (eds.). *God, the Gift and Postmodernism*. Bloomington: Indiana University Press, 1999.

Caputo, John D., and Gianni Vattimo. *After the Death of God*, edited by Jeffrey W. Robbins. New York: Columbia University Press, 2007.

"Chandogya Upanishad." In *Upanishads: A New Translation*, translated by Patrick Olivelle. Oxford: Oxford University Press, 2008.

Charlton, James I. *Nothing About Us Without Us: Disability, Oppression and Empowerment*. Irvine: University of California Press, 2000.

Chidester, David. *Religion: Material Dynamics*. Berkeley: University of California Press, 2018.

Chrétien, Jean-Louis. *The Ark of Speech*, translated by Andrew Brown. Abingdon: Routledge, 2003.

Chrétien, Jean-Louis. *The Call and the Response*, translated by Anne A. Davenport. New York: Fordham University Press, 2004.

Chrétien, Jean-Louis. *Under the Gaze of the Bible*, translated by John Marson Dunaway. New York: Fordham University Press, 2014.

Churchill, Ward. *Kill the Indian, Save the Man: The Genocidal Impact of American Indian Residential Schools*. San Francisco, CA: City Light Books, 2004.

Clark, John. "On Being None with Nature: Nagarjuna and the Ecology of Emptiness." *Capitalism, Nature, Socialism* 19, no. 4 (2008): 6–29.

Coburn, Elaine. "Indigenous Research as Resistance." *Socialist Studies/Études socialistes* 9 no. 1 (Spring 2013): 52–63.

Coburn, Elaine (ed.). *More Will Sing Their Way to Freedom: Indigenous Resistance and Resurgence*. Winnipeg: Fernwood Publishing, 2015.

Collins, Kenneth J. (ed.). *Exploring Christian Spirituality: An Ecumenical Reader*. Grand Rapids, MI: Baker Books, 2000.

Cone, James H. *The Cross and the Lynching Tree*. Maryknoll, NY: Orbis Books, 2011.

Conrad-Martius, Hedwig. *Metaphysical Conversations*, edited and translated by Christina M. Gschwandtner. Boston, MA: DeGruyter, 2024.

Coole, Diana, and Samantha Frost (eds.). *New Materialisms: Ontology, Agency and Politics*. Durham, NC: Duke University Press, 2010.

Copley, Steph. "I Found Religion ... At a Taylor Swift Concert: My Transcendent Experience at Arrowhead Stadium." *It Was Never a Dress*, 2023: https://copleysteph.substack.com/p/i-found-religion-at-a-taylor-swift.

Coulthard, Glen Sean. *Red Skin, White Masks: Rejecting the Colonial Politics of Recognition*. Minneapolis: University of Minnesota Press, 2014.

Coulthard, Glen Sean, and Leanne Betasamosake Simpson. "Grounded Normativity/Place-Based Solidarity." *American Quarterly* 68, no. 2 (June 2016): 249–55.

Cox, Daniel A. "Rise of Conspiracies Reveals An Evangelical Divide in the GOP." *Survey Center on American Life* (February 12, 2021). www.americansurveycenter.org/rise-of-conspiracies-reveal-an-evangelical-divide-in-the-gop/.

Cox, James L. *A Guide to the Phenomenology of Religion: Key Figures, Formative Influences and Subsequent Debates*. London: T&T Clark, 2006.

Cox, James L. *An Introduction to Phenomenology of Religion*. London: Bloomsbury, 2009.

Crockett, Clayton, and Jeffery W. Robbins. *Religion, Politics and the Earth: The New Materialism*. New York: Palgrave Macmillan, 2012.

Csíkszentmihályi, Mihály. *Beyond Boredom and Anxiety: Experiencing Flow in Work and Play*. San Francisco, CA: Jossey-Bass, 1975.

DeRoo, Neal. "Carnal Sacrality: Phenomenology, the Sacred and Material Bodies in Richard Kearney." In *Anacarnation and Returning to the Lived Body with Richard Kearney*, edited by Brian Treanor and James L. Taylor, 69–85. New York: Routledge, 2023.

DeRoo, Neal. "Embodying the World: The Spiritual Significance of the Earth." *Crossings: The Journal of the International Network for Philosophy of Religion* (forthcoming).

DeRoo, Neal. "The Everyday Power of Liturgy: On the Significance of the Transcendental for a Phenomenology of Liturgy." *Religions* 12, no. 8 (2021); https://doi.org/10.3390/rel12080633.

DeRoo, Neal. "Eschatology, Expression and Spirituality: A Response to Rivera." *Syndicate*. https://syndicate.network/symposia/philosophy/the-contemplative-self-after-michel-henry/.

DeRoo, Neal. "Life and Transcendental Phenomenologies of Religion: Michel Henry and John D. Caputo." In *Hymns to Life*, edited by Steven Nemes and Steven DeLay. Cascade, OR: Wipf and Stock, forthcoming.

DeRoo, Neal. "A Phenomenology of Image-Bearing: Spirituality, Humanity, and the 'Supra-' Relation." In *Image, Phenomenon and Imagination in the Phenomenology of Religious Experience*, edited by Martin Nitsche and Olga Louchakova-Schwartz, 167–91. Prague: Libri Nigri, 2020.

DeRoo, Neal. *Political Logic of Experience: Expression in Phenomenology*. New York: Fordham University Press, 2022.

DeRoo, Neal. "Spiritual Life and Cultural Discernment: Renewing Spirituality through Henry." In *Michel Henry's Practical Philosophy*, edited by Michael R. Kelly, Brian Harding, and Jeffrey Hanson, 45–65. London: Bloomsbury, 2022.

DeRoo, Neal. "Thinking Revelation as Expression in and through Phenomenology." *Journal for Continental Philosophy of Religion* 6 (2024): 31–50.

Derrida, Jacques. "Faith and Knowledge: Two Sources of 'Religion' at the Limits of Reason Alone." In *Religion*, translated by David Webb, 1–78. Redwood City, CA: Stanford University Press, 1998.

Derrida, Jacques. "Force of Law: The 'Mystical' Foundation of Authority." In *Deconstruction and The Possibility of Justice*, edited by Drucilla Cornell, Michel Rosenfeld, and David Gray Carlson. New York: Routledge, 1992.

Derrida, Jacques. *Of Spirit: Heidegger and the Question*, translated by Geoffrey Bennington and Rachel Bowlby. Chicago, IL: University of Chicago Press, 1991.

Derrida, Jacques. *Rogues: Two Essays on Reason*, translated by Pascale-Anne Brault and Michael Naas. Redwood City, CA: Stanford University Press, 2005.

Derrida, Jacques. *Specters of Marx: The State of the Debt, the Work of Mourning and the New International*, translated by Peggy Kamuf. New York: Routledge, 1994.

Derrida, Jacques. *Voice and Phenomenon: Introduction to the Problem of the Sign in Husserl's Phenomenology*, translated by Leonard Lawlor. 1967. Evanston, IL: Northwestern University Press, 2010.

Doniger O'Flaherty, Wendy. *Dreams, Illusion, and Other Realities*. Chicago, IL: University of Chicago Press, 1986.

Dooyeweerd, Herman. *New Critique of Theoretical Thought, Volume 1: The Necessary Presuppositions of Philosophy*, translated by D. H. Freeman and W. S. Young. Philadelphia, PA: The Reformed and Presbyterian Publishing Company, 1953–1958.

Dooyeweerd, Herman. *New Critique of Theoretical Thought, Volume 2: The General Theory of the Modal Spheres*, translated by David H. Freeman and H. De Jongste. 1964. Jordan Station: Paideia Press Ltd., 1984.

Doyon, Maxime. *Phenomenology and the Norms of Perception*. Oxford: Oxford University Press, 2025.

Du Toit, Cornel W. "Emotion and the Affective Turn: Towards an Integration of Cognition and Affect in Real Life Experience." *HTS Toelogiese Studies/Theological Studies* 70, no. 1 (2014): 9 pages, http://dx.doi.org/10.4102/hts.v70i1.2692.

Fer, Yannick. "An Affective (U-)Turn in the Sociology of Religion? Religious Emotions and Native Narratives." In *Bringing Back the Social into the Sociology of Religion*, edited by Veronique Altglas and Matthew Wood. Leiden: Brill, 2018; https://doi.org/10.1163/9789004368798.

Fitzgerald, Timothy. "A 'Critique' of Religion as a Cross-Cultural Category." *Method and Theory in the Study of Religion* 9, no. 2. (1997): 91–110.

Fitzgerald, Timothy. *Discourse on Civility and Barbarity: A Critical History of Religion and Related Categories*. Oxford: Oxford University Press, 2007.

Fitzgerald, Timothy. "Hinduism and the World Religion Fallacy." *Religion* 20 (1990): 101–18.

Fitzgerald, Timothy. "Japanese Religion as Ritual Order." *Religion* 23 (1993): 315–41.

Fitzgerald, Timothy. "Ritual, Politics, and Soteriology in Ambedkar Buddhism." *Indian Journal of Buddhist Studies* 5 (1994): 25–44.

Fitzgerald, Timothy. "Things, Thoughts, and People Out of Place, Review of Mark R. Mullins et al., *Religion and Society in Modern Japan*." *Japanese Journal of Religious Studies* 22 (1995): 201–17.

Flood, Gavin. *Beyond Phenomenology: Rethinking the Study of Religion*. London: Cassell, 1999.

Friel, Brian. *Translations*. London: Faber and Faber Plays, 1981.

Gadamer, Hans-Georg. *Truth and Method*, second revised edition, translation revised by Joel Weisenheimer and Donald G. Marshall. London and New York: Continuum, 2004.

George, Carol V. R. *God's Salesman: Norman Vincent Peale and the Power of Positive Thinking*. Oxford: Oxford University Press 1993.

Grondin, Jean. "In any Event? Critical Remarks on the Recent Fascination with the Notion of Event." In *Being Shaken: Ontology and the Event*, edited by Michael Marder and Santiago Zabala. London and New York: Palgrave MacMillan, 2014.

Gschwandtner, Christina M. *Degrees of Givenness: On Saturation in Jean-Luc Marion*. Bloomington: Indiana University Press, 2014.

Gschwandtner, Christina M. "Faith, Religion and Spirituality: A Phenomenological and Hermeneutic Contribution to Parsing the Distinctions." *Religions* 12, no. 7 (2021): https://doi.org/10.3390/rel12070476.

Gschwandtner, Christina M. *Ways of Living Religion: Philosophical investigations into Religious Experience*. Cambridge: Cambridge University Press, 2024.

Gschwandtner, Christina M. *Welcoming Finitude: Toward a Phenomenology of the Orthodox Liturgy*. New York: Fordham University Press, 2019.

Gschwandtner, Christina M. "What is phenomenology of religion? (Part I): The Study of Religious Phenomena." *Philosophy Compass* 12, no. 2 (2019), e12566. https://doi.org/10.1111/phc3.12566.

Gschwandtner, Christina M. "What is Phenomenology of Religion? (Part II): The Phenomenology of Religious Experience." *Philosophy Compass* 14, no. 2 (2019): e12567. https://doi.org/10.1111/phc3.12567.

Hardacre, Helen. "The Shinto Priesthood in Early Meiji Japan: Preliminary Inquiries." *History of Religions* 27, no. 3 (1998): 294–320.

Hazard, Sonia. "The Material Turn in the Study of Religion." *Religion and Society* 4, no. 1 (2013): 21 pages. https://doi.org/10.3167/arrs.2013.040104.

Hegel, G. W. F. *Introduction to the Philosophy of History*, translated by Leo Rauch. Indianapolis, IN: Hackett, 1988.

Hegel, G. W. F. *Phenomenology of Spirit*, translated by A. V. Miller. Oxford: Oxford University Press, 1977.

Heidegger, Martin. *Being and Time*, translated by John Macquarrie and Edward Robinson. 1927. Oxford: Blackwell Publishing, 1962.

Heidegger, Martin. *Introduction to Metaphysics*, 2nd ed., translated by Gregory Fried and Richard Polt. 1935. New Haven, CT: Yale University Press, 2014.

Heinämaa, Sara. "Embodiment and Expressivity in Husserl's Phenomenology: From *Logical Investigations* to *Cartesian Meditations*." *SATS: Northern European Journal of Philosophy* 11 (2010): 1–15.

Heinämaa, Sara Mirja Hartimo, and Timo Hartimo (eds.). *Phenomenology and the Transcendental*. AbingsdAAbingdon: Routledge, 2016.

Henry, Michel. *Barbarism*, translated by Scott Davidson. 1987. London: Bloomsbury Academic Press, 2012.

Henry, Michel. *Essence of Manifestation*, translated by G. J. Etzkorn. New York: Springer, 1973.

Henry, Michel. *I am the Truth: Toward a Philosophy of Christianity*, translated by Susan Emanuel. Redwood City, CA: Stanford University Press, 2000.

Henry, Michel. *Phénoménologie de la Vie vol 1: De la phénoménologie*. Paris: Presses Universitaires de France, 2003.

Henry, Michel. *Phénoménologie de la Vie vol 2: De la subjectivité*. Paris: Presses Universitaires de France, 2011.

Henry, Michel. *Phénoménologie de la Vie vol 3: Sur l'art et du politique*. Paris: Presses Universitaires de France, 2005.

Henry, Michel. *Phénoménologie de la Vie vol 4: Sur l'éthique et de la religion*. Paris: Presses Universitaires de France, 2004.

Henry, Michel. *Phénoménologie de la vie vol 5*. Paris: Universitaires de France, 2015.

Henry, Michel. *Philosophy and Phenomenology of the Body*, translated by G. J. Etzkorn. New York: Springer, 1975.

Henry, Michel. *Words of Christ*, translated by Christina M. Gschwandtner. Grand Rapids, MI: Wm. B. Eerdmans Publishing Co., 2002.

Heyes, Cressida J. *Anaesthetics of Existence: Essays on Experience at the Edge*. Durham, NC: Duke University Press, 2020.

Hornborg, Anne-Christine. *Mi'kmaq Landscapes: From Animism to Sacred Ecology*. New York: Routledge, 2021.

Horner, Robyn. *The Experience of God: A Phenomenology of Revelation*. Cambridge: Cambridge University Press, 2022.

Hoyt, Sarah F. "The Etymology of Religion." *The Journal of the American Oriental Society* 32, no. 3 (1912).

Hughes, Aaron W., and Russell T. McCutcheon (eds.). *What is Religion?: Debating the Academic Study of Religion*. Oxford: Oxford University Press, 2021.

Husserl, Edmund. *Analyses Concerning Passive and Active Synthesis: Lectures on Transcendental Logic*, translated by A. J. Steinbock. New York: Springer, 2001.

Husserl, Edmund. *Cartesian Meditations: An Introduction to Phenomenology*, translated by Dorion Cairns. Norwell, MA: Kluwer Academic Publishers, 1977.

Husserl, Edmund. *The Crisis of European Sciences and Transcendental Phenomenology*, translated by David Carr. 1936. Evanston, IL: Northwestern University Press, 1970.

Husserl, Edmund. "Fundamental Investigations on the Phenomenological Origin of the Spatiality of Nature." In *Shorter Works*, translated by Fred Kersten, edited by Peter McCormick and Frederick A. Elleston, 222–33. South Bend, IN: University of Notre Dame Press, 1981.

Husserl, Edmund. *Ideas Pertaining to a Pure Phenomenology and to a Phenomenological Philosophy: First Book: General Introduction to a Pure Phenomenology*, edited by Fred Kersten. The Hague: Martinus Nijhoff, 1983.

Husserl, Edmund. *Ideas Pertaining to a Pure Phenomenology and to a Phenomenological Philosophy: Second Book: Studies in the Phenomenology of Constitution*, translated by Richard Rojcewicz and Andre Schuwer. New York: Springer, 1989.

Husserl, Edmund. *Logical Investigations*, vol. 1, edited by Dermot Moran. New York: Routledge, 2001.

Husserl, Edmund. *Phänomenologische Psychologie: Vorlesungen Sommersemester*, translated by Walter Biemel. 1925. The Hague: Martinus Nijhoff, 1962.

Husserl, Edmund. "The Vienna Lecture." In *The Crisis of European Sciences and Transcendental Phenomenology*, translated by David Carr, 269–99. Evanston, IL: Northwestern University Press, 1970.

Husserl, Edmund. *Zur Phänomenologie der Intersubjektivität: Zweiter Teil: 1921–1928*, edited by Iso Kern. The Hague: Martinus Nijhoff, 1973.

Janicaud, Dominique. "The Theological Turn of French Phenomenology." In *Phenomenology and the Theological Turn: The French Debate*, translated by Bernard G. Prusaki, 16–103. New York: Fordham University Press, 2000.

Kearney, Richard. *Anatheism: Returning to God After God*. New York: Columbia University Press, 2010.

Kearney, Richard. "Epiphanies of the Everyday: Toward a Micro-Eschatology." In *After God: Richard Kearney and the Religious Turn in Continental Philosophy*, edited by John Panteleimon Manoussakis, 3–20. New York: Fordham University Press, 2006.

Kearney, Richard. "Imagination, Anatheism and the Sacred: A Dialogue with James Wood." In *Reimagining the Sacred: Richard Kearney Debates God*, edited by Richard Kearney and Jens Zimmerman. New York: Columbia University Press, 2016: 19–45.

Kearney, Richard. *Poétique du Possible: Phénoménologie Herméneutique de la Figuration*. Paris: Éditions Beauchesne, 1984.

Kearney, Richard. *Touch: Recovering our Most Vital Sense*. New York: Columbia University Press, 2021.

Kearney, Richard, and Brian Treanor (eds.). *Carnal Hermeneutics*. New York: Fordham University Press, 2015.

Kearney, Richard, and Jens Zimmerman (eds.). *Reimagining the Sacred: Richard Kearney Debates God*. New York: Columbia University Press, 2016.

King, Richard. *Orientalism and Religion: Postcolonial Theory, India, and the "Mystic East."* New York: Routledge, 1999.

Kimmerer, Robin Wall. *Braiding Sweetgrass: Indigenous Wisdom, Scientific Knowledge, and the Teachings of Plants*. Minneapolis, MN: Milkweed Editions, 2013.

Kimmerer, Robin Wall, and Helen Whybrow. "Robin Wall Kimmerer on the Language of Animacy." *Orion* March/April 2017; https://orionmagazine.org/article/robin-wall-kimmerer-language-animacy/.

Kobes-Du Mez, Kristin. *Jesus and John Wayne: How White Evangelicals Corrupted a Faith and Fractured a Nation*. New York: Liveright, 2020.

Lacoste, Jean-Yves. *Experience and the Absolute: Disputed Questions on the Humanity of Man*, translated by Mark Raferty-Skehan. New York: Fordham University Press, 2004.

Lane, Christopher. *Surge of Piety: Norman Vincent Peale and the Remaking of American Religious Life*. New Haven, CT: Yale University Press 2016.

Lavine, Howard, James Ron, and Richard L. Wood. "Why Are White Evangelicals Anti-Human Rights?" *Open Global Rights* (December 21, 2020). www.openglobalrights.org/why-are-white-evangelicals-anti-human-rights/#:~:text=Although%20 56%25%20of%20respondents%20told,of%20police%20racism%20and%20 violence%2C.

Leuba, James H. *A Psychological Study of Religion*. New York: Macmillan Company, 1912.

Livingston, James C. *Anatomy of the Sacred: An Introduction to Religion*, 5th ed. Upper Saddle River, NJ: Prentice Hall, 2005.

Lovaglio, Hannah. "What Taylor Swift's Eras Tour Taught Me About Church." *The Presbyterian Outlook*, 2023: https://pres-outlook.org/2023/07/what-taylor-swifts-eras-tour-taught-me-about-church/.

MacKinlay, Shane. *Interpreting Excess: Jean-Luc Marion, Saturated Phenomena, and Hermeneutics*. New York: Fordham University Press, 2010.

Macquarrie, John. "Spirit and Spirituality." In *Exploring Christian Spirituality: An Ecumenical Reader*, edited by Kenneth J. Collins, 63–73. Grand Rapids, MI: Baker Books, 2000.

Marion, Jean-Luc. *Being Given: Toward a Phenomenology of Givenness*, translated by Jeffery L. Kosky. 1997. Stanford, CA: Stanford University Press, 2002.

Marion, Jean-Luc. *Cartesian Questions: Method and Metaphysics*. 1991. Chicago, IL: University of Chicago Press, 1999.

Marion, Jean-Luc. *Cartesian Questions III: Descartes Beneath the Mask of Cartesianism*, translated by Stephen E. Lewis Jr. and Stephanie Rumpza. Redwood City, CA: Stanford University Press, 2025.

Marion, Jean-Luc. *Descartes Grey Ontology: Cartesian Ontology and Aristotelian Thought in the Regulae*, translated by Sarah E. Donahue. South Bend, IN: St. Augustine Press, 2022.

Marion, Jean-Luc. "Evidence and Bedazzlement." In *Prolegomena to Charity*, translated by Stephen Lewis, 53–70. New York: Fordham University Press, 2002.

Marion, Jean-Luc. *Givenness and Revelation*, translated by Stephen E. Lewis. Oxford: Oxford Academic Press, 2016.

Marion, Jean-Luc. "God Without Being." Reprinted in *Phenomenology and Eschatology: Not yet in the Now*, edited by Neal DeRoo and John Panteleimon Manoussakis, 193–213. 1946. New York: Routledge, 2021.

Marion, Jean-Luc. *In Excess: Studies of Saturated Phenomena*, translated by Robyn Hoerner and Vincent Berraud. New York: Fordham University Press, 2004.

Marion, Jean-Luc. *On Descartes' Metaphysical Prism: The Constitution and The Limits of Onto-theo-logy in Cartesian Thought*, translated by Jeffrey L. Kosky. Chicago, IL: University of Chicago Press, 1999.

Marion, Jean-Luc. *On the Ego and on God: Further Cartesian Questions*, translated by Christina M. Gschwandtner. New York: Fordham University Press, 2008.

Marion, Jean-Luc. *Reduction and Givenness: Investigation of Husserl, Heidegger, and Phenomenology*, translated by Thomas A. Carlton. Evanston, IL: Northwestern University Press, 1998.

Marion, Jean-Luc. *Revelation Comes From Elsewhere*, translated by Stephen E. Lewis and Stephanie Rumpza. Redwood City, CA: Stanford University Press, 2024.

Marion, Jean-Luc. *Sur la théologie blanche de Descartes*. Paris: Presses Universitaires de France, 1981.

Masuzawa, Tomoko. *The Invention of World Religions*. Chicago, IL: University of Chicago Press, 2005.

McCaulley, Esau. *Reading While Black: African American Biblical Interpretation as an Exercise in Hope*. Lisle, IL: InterVarsity Press, 2020.

McCutcheon, Russel. *Manufacturing Religion: The Discourse on Sui Generis Religion and the Politics of Nostalgia*. Oxford: Oxford University Press, 2003.

Merleau-Ponty, Maurice. "Eye and Mind." In *The Primacy of Perception: And Other Essays on Phenomenological Psychology, the Philosophy of Art, History, and Politics,* translated by Carleton Dallery, edited by John Wild and James E. Edie, 159–90. Evanston, IL: Northwestern University Press, 1964.

Merleau-Ponty, Maurice. *Institution and Passivity: Course Notes from the Collège de France (1954–1955)*, translated by Leonard Lawlor and Heath Massey. Evanston, IL: Northwestern University Press, 2010.

Merleau-Ponty, Maurice. *Nature: Course Notes from the College de France*, compiled by Dominique Seglard, translated by Robert Vallier. Evanston, IL: Northwestern university Press, 2003.

Merleau-Ponty, Maurice. *Phenomenology of Perception*, 2nd ed., translated by Donald Landes. 1945. Evanston, IL: Northwestern University Press, 2010.

Merleau-Ponty, Maurice. *Signs*, translated by Richard C. McCleary. Evanston, IL: Northwestern University Press, 1964.

Merleau-Ponty, Maurice. *The Structure of Behavior*, translated by Alden L. Fisher. Boston, MA: Beacon Books, 1967.

Merleau-Ponty, Maurice. *The Visible and the Invisible*, translated by Alphonso Lingis. Evanston, IL: Northwestern University Press, 1969.

Miettinen, Timo. "Transcendental Social Ontology." In *Phenomenology and the Transcendental*, edited by Sara Heinämaa, Mirja Hartimo, and Timo Miettinen, 147–71. New York: Routledge, 2014.

Morgan, David. *Images at Work: The Material Culture of Enchantment*. New York: Oxford University Press, 2018.

Nāgārjuna, *The Fundamental Wisdom of the Middle Way*, translated by Jay L. Garfield. Oxford: Oxford University Press, 1995.

Nagle, Thomas. "What is it Like to be a Bat?" *Philosophical Review* 83, no. 4 (1973): 435–50.

Nancy, Jean-Luc. "Atheistic Experience." In *Atheism, Faith and Experience*, edited by Claude Roman and Robyn Horner. London: Bloomsbury, 2020.

Nancy, Jean-Luc. *Dis-Enclosure: The Deconstruction of Christianity*, translated by Bettina Bergo, Gabriel Malenfant, and Michael B. Smith. New York: Fordham University Press, 2008.

Nancy, Jean-Luc. "The Surprise: Of the Event." In *Hegel after Derrida*, edited by Stuart Barnett. London and New York: Routledge, 1998.

Nongbri, Brent. *Before Religion: A History of a Modern Concept*. New Haven, CT: Yale University Press, 2015.

Nweke, K. Chindeu. "Between Religiosity and Spirituality: Christianity and the Reemergence of the Immanentist Spiritualities." *Theology Today* 75, no. 2 (2018): 233–46.

Plantinga, Alvin. "Advice to Christian Philosophers." *Faith and Philosophy: Journal of the Society of Christian Philosophers* 1, no. 3 (1984): 253–71.

Plantinga, Alvin. *God and Other Minds: A Study of the Rational Justification of Belief in God*. Ithaca, NY: Cornell University Press, 1967.

Plantinga, Alvin. "Is Belief in God Properly Basic?" *Noûs* 16, no. 1 (1981): 41–51.

Plantinga, Alvin. "Reason and Belief in God." In *Faith and Rationality: Reason and Belief in God*, edited by Alvin Plantinga and Nichola Wolterstorff, 16–93. London: Notre Dame University Press, 1983.

Pratt, Richard Henry. "The Advantage of Mixing Indians with Whites." Speech given at the National Conference of Charities and Correction in Denver, CO in 1892. The text of that speech is available online: https://carlisleindian.dickinson.edu/teach/kill-indian-him-and-save-man-r-h-pratt-education-native-americans.

Principe, Walter. "Toward Defining Spirituality." In *Exploring Christian Spirituality: An Ecumenical Reader*, edited by Kenneth J. Collins, 43–61. Grand Rapids, MI: Baker Books, 2000.

Reisebrodt, Martin. *The Promise of Salvation: A Theory of Religion*, translated by Steven Rendall. Chicago, IL: University of Chicago Press, 2010.

Ricoeur, Paul. *Critique and Conviction: Conversations with François Azouvi and Marc de Launay*, translated by Kathleen Blamey. New York: Columbia University Press, 1998.

Ricoeur, Paul. *Living Up to Death*, translated by David Pellauer. Chicago, IL: University of Chicago Press, 2009.

Ricoeur, Paul. "Religious Belief: The Difficult Path of the Religious." In *A Passion for the Possible: Thinking with Paul Ricoeur*, edited by Brian Treanor and Henry Isaac Venema. New York: Fordham University Press, 2010; pp. 27–39.

Riva, Michele Augusto, and Giancarlo Cesana. "The Charity and the Care: The Origin and Evolution of Hospitals." *European Journal of Internal Medicine* 24, no. 1 (2013): 1–4.

Rivera, Joseph. *The Contemplative Self after Michel Henry*. Notre Dame, IN: University of Notre Dame Press, 2015.

Romano, Claude. *Event and Time*, translated by Stephen E. Lewis. New York: Fordham University Press, 2013.

Romano, Claude. *Event and World*, translated by Shane Mackinlay. New York: Fordham University Press, 2009.

Romano, Claude. *There Is*, translated by Michael B. Smith. New York: Fordham University Press, 2015.

Rorty, Richard. *Contingency, Irony, Solidarity*. Cambridge: Cambridge University Press, 1989.

Roschman, Melodie. "When Taylor Swift Took Me to Church." *Spectrum Magazine*, 2023: https://spectrummagazine.org/culture/when-taylor-swift-took-me-church/.

Rookmaaker, Hans. "Ontwerp ener aesthetica op grondslag der wisjbegeerte der wetsidee." *Philosophia Reformata* 11, nos. 3 and 4 (1946): 141–62.

Sartwell, Cripin. "Beauty." In *The Stanford Encyclopedia of Philosophy*, edited by Edward N. Zalta and Uri Nodelman. Fall 2024. https://plato.stanford.edu/archives/fall2024/entries/beauty/.

Schaefer, Donovan. *Religious Affects: Animality, Evolution, and Power*. Durham, NC: Duke University Press, 2015.

Schilbrack, Kevin. "The Material Turn in the Academic Study of Religions." *The Journal of Religion* 99, no. 2 (2019). https://doi.org/10.1086/701868.

Schilbrack, Kevin. "A Metaphysics for the Study of Religion: A Critical Reading of Russel McCutcheon." *Critical Research on Religion* 8, no. 1 (2020): 87–100. https://doi.org/10.1177/2050303219900229.

Schilbrack, Kevin. "Religions: Are There Any?" *Journal of the American Academy of Religion* 78, no. 4 (2010): 1112–38.

Schilbrack, Kevin. "What *isn't* Religion?" *The Journal of Religion* 93, no. 1 (2013): 291–318.

Schneider, Lucien. *Ulirnaisugutiit: An Inuktitut-English Dictionary of Northern Quebec, Labrador and Eastern Arctic Dialects*, translated by Dermot Rolin F. Collis. Quebec City: Les Presses des l'Universite Laval, 1985.

Schneiders, Sandra M. "A Hermeneutical Approach to the Study of Christian Spirituality." In *Minding the Spirit: The Study of Christian Spirituality*, edited by Elizabeth Dryer and Mark S. Burrows, 49–60. Baltimore, MD: The John Hopkins University Press, 2005.

Schneiders, Sandra M. "Spirituality in the Academy." In *Exploring Christian Spirituality: An Ecumenical Reader*, edited by Kenneth J. Collins, 249–70. Grand Rapids, MI: Baker Books, 2000.

Scott, Joan W. "The Evidence of Experience." *Critical Inquiry* 17, no. 4 (1991): 773–97.

Seerveld, Calvin C. "Modal Aesthetics." In *Hearing and Doing: Philosophical Essays Dedicated to H. Evan Runner*, 263–94. Toronto: Wedge, 1979.

Sheldrake, Philip. *A Brief History of Spirituality*. Malden, MA: Blackwell Publishing, 2007.

Sheldrake, Philip. "Constructing Spirituality: The 'Politics' of Definitions and Historical Interpretations." *Religion and Theology* 23 (2016): 15–34.

Simmons, J. Aaron. "Religious but not Spiritual: A Constructive Proposal." *Religions* 12, no. 6 (2021); https://doi.org/10.3390/rel12060433.

Simmons, J. Aaron, and Stephen Minister (eds.). *Reexamining Deconstruction and Determinate Religion: Toward a Religion with Religion*. Pittsburgh, PA: Duquesne University Press, 2012.

Smith, James K. A. *Desiring the Kingdom: Worship, Worldviews, and Cultural Formation*. Ada, MI: Baker Academic, 2009.

Smith, James K. A. *The Fall of Interpretation: Philosophical Foundations for a Creational Hermeneutics*. Lisle, IL: InterVarsity Press: 2000.

Smith, James K. A. "Re-Kanting Postmodernism." *Faith and Philosophy* 17, no. 4 (2000): 558–71.

Smith, Jonathan Z. "Religion, Religions, Religious." In *Critical Terms for Religious Studies*, edited by Mark Taylor, 269–84. Chicago, IL: University of Chicago Press, 1998.

Spiro, Melford. "Religion: Problems of Definition and Explanation." In *Anthropological Approaches to the Study of Religion*, edited by Michael Banton. London: Tavistock, 1966.

Steckley, John. *White Lies about the Inuit*. Toronto: University of Toronto Press, 2007.

Stein, Edith. *Endliches und ewiges Sein: Versuch eines Aufstiegs zum Sinn des Seins*. In *Gesamtausgabe*, vols. 11/12, edited by Andreas Uwe Müller. Freiburg: Herder, 2016.

Steinbock, Anthony J. *Home and Beyond: Generative Phenomenology after Husserl.* Evanston, IL: Northwestern University Press, 1995.

Szanto, Thomas, and Dermot Moran (eds.). *Phenomenology of Sociality: Discovering the We.* New York: Routledge, Taylor & Francis Group, 2016.

Taylor, Charles. *A Secular Age.* Cambridge, MA: Harvard University Press, 2007.

Thurman, Howard. *Jesus and the Disinherited.* New York: Abingdon-Cokesbury Press, 1949.

Tirres, Christopher D. "Spiritual Activism and Practice: Gloria Anzaldúa's Mature Spirituality." *The Pluralist* 14, no. 1 (2019): 119–40.

Treanor, Brian. *Melancholic Joy: On Life Worth Living.* London: Bloomsbury, 2021.

Vallier, Robert. "Institution: The Significance of Merleau-Ponty's 1954 Course at the Collège de France." *Chiasmi International* 7 (2005): 281–302.

Vattimo, Gianni. *After Christianity*, translated by Luca D'Isanto. New York: Columbia University Press, 2002.

Walther, Gerda. *Phänomenologie der Mystik.* Olten: Walter Verlag, 1955.

Zahavi, Dan. "Applied Phenomenology: Why it is Safe to Ignore the Epoché." *Continental Philosophy Review* 54 (2019): 1–15.

Index

aesthetics 39–40, 61, 177n.1
   harmony 174n.6
   beauty 174n.5
aestheticality 39–41, 61, 175n.14
affective turn 69, 163n.1, 179n.20
affectivity 2, 132, 169n.2
Al-Saji, Alia 167n.34
Anselm of Canterbury 179–80n.22
anthropology (of religion) 53–4
Aristotle 31, 171n.19
   The Metaphysics 172n.26
Asad, Talal 6, 65, 67, 68, 78, 158
   Genealogies of Religion 179n.14
Augustine 24–5

Barad, Karen 9
Being, Epochs of 12
Berger, Peter 53
Black Lives Matter movement 59–60
Buddhism 42, 43, 57–8, 72, 79, 93, 134, 161, 178n.6
   Maya 41, 50–1, 90

Caputo, John D. 108–10, 185n.26; *see also* Event(-al) Religious Experience
   Specters of God 164n.9
   The Weakness of God A Theology of the Event 184n.19
Catholicism 5, 6, 85, 106, 109, 117, 127, 129, 151, 175n.12
Charlton, James I. 181n.40
Christianity 6, 42, 44, 50, 59–60, 62–6, 76, 85, 89, 93, 98, 132–3; *see also* Catholicism; *and* love in Christianity
   Christ 187n.14
   eucharist 5, 103, 127–8, 129, 137
   philosophy 131, 150–1
   post-Enlightenment 66–7, 179n.14
   Protestant Reformation 86
   Protestantism 96, 127, 171n.19, 171n.21

secular[ized] 81, 83, 90, 96, 99, 101
the Trinity 57, 142
Nicene formulation 85, 143
Churchill, Ward 181n.37
Coburn, Elaine 78, 181n.39
Collins, Kenneth 34
colonialism 6, 20, 36, 71, 73, 74, 77, 78, 121–2, 152, 156
   British colonization of Ireland 172–3n.31
   North American colonization 33; *see also* residential schools, North American Indian.
comparative study of religion 38, 58, 85
Cone, James 88
Conrad-Martius, Hedwig 168n.44
consciousness 158, 169n.1
conspiracy theories 59, 187n.8
Constitution, United States of America 96–7
Coulthard, Glenn 181n.39, 187n.9
Cox, James L. 166n.26
critical philosophy of religion 6–9, 14, 149, 150, 158, 160, 162
culture 34, 35–6, 53, 70, 103–4, 143, 159, 160, 173n.42, 173n.44

Daoism 58, 90
   Dao 73–4, 94, 130
Decolonial Critique 64, 71
deconstruction 109–10, 185n.27
Derrida, Jacques 16, 110, 168n.39, 168n.43, 176n.19, 182n.10, 185n.27, 185n.31
   différance 12, 162, 169n.2
Descartes, Rene 171n.19
   Cartesianism 28, 30, 103
Dooyeweerd, Herman 40, 50, 174n.6
Doyon, Maxime 174–5n.8

Eliade, Mircea 2, 3, 8
Empfindnisse 11, 25, 26, 161

embedded phenomenon 9–15, 54, 87, 114, 126, 159, 161; *see also* entangled phenomenon
embodiment 36, 85, 126, 171n.14
empirical-transcendental 12, 160;
empirical religious studies 3, 20, 23, 69, 82, 83, 103, 117, 136, 138; *see also* affective turn; *and* material turn.
entangled phenomenon 9, 12–13, 59, 81, 82, 97, 140, 188n.19
Epochē 37, 113, 159, 160
ethicality 40–1, 48, 115, 174–5n.8
event(-al) religious experience 19, 102, 108–110, 111–17, 185n.31
experience 1–3, 7–11, 13, 14, 16–17, 20, 23–9, 31, 37–44, 47–9, 58, 61, 65, 70–1, 74, 81–3, 88–90, 92–5, 102, 105–8, 111, 114–17, 119, 125–7, 137–49, 154, 159–162, 165n.22, 168n.41, 169n.4, 171n.18, 188n.4
experienced 7, 25, 57, 93, 112, 124, 126, 130, 144–7, 154, 157, 158–60
experiencing 1–2, 4, 8–9, 11–13, 15, 17–21, 37, 39–40, 45, 47–9, 61, 71–2, 83, 87, 89, 98–9, 106–8, 110–18, 126, 135–8, 144–5, 147, 154–7, 158–62, 163n.1, 181n.36
expression 14–17, 20, 33, 36, 54, 63, 76, 85, 99, 122–4, 131, 134–7, 140, 146–8, 153, 154, 168n.41, 171n.18, 181n.36, 186n.3, 188n.4

Falque, Emmanuel 3, 151, 160
fire, experience of 144, 165n.22
Fitzgerald, Timothy 72, 103–4, 112, 118
"A 'Critique' of Religion as a Cross-Cultural Category" 163n.3, 165n.20, 186n.1, 186n.2
Foucault, Michel 70, 145, 147, 173–4n.44

Gadamer, Hans-Georg 180n.28
Generativity 10, 16, 28–9, 31, 32, 33, 51, 62, 116, 124–5, 146–8, 159, 180n.34
Gestalt Psychology 170n.11
Grondin, Jean 113
grounded normativity 131, 181n.39, 187n.9, 187n.10; *see also* Simpson, Leanne Betasamosake; *and* Coulthard, Glenn.

Gschwandtner, Christina M. 5, 163n.6
Welcoming Finitude: Toward a Phenomenology of the Orthodox Liturgy 187n.7
Degrees of Giveness 176n.22

Hegel, G.W.F 30, 159
Heidegger, Martin 160, 162; *see also* Being, Epochs of
Being and Time 166n.25, 169n.5
Introduction to Metaphysics 2nd ed. 172n.26
Heinämaa, Sara 163n.2, 170n.14
Henry, Michel 28, 39, 40, 134, 162, 164n.9, 169n.2, 173–4n.44, 187–8n.18; *see also* Life in Michel Henry.
Barbarism [1987] 18, 36, 133, 173n.42, 174n.4
barbarism 70–1, 180n.23
I am the Truth: Toward a Philosophy of Christianity 132–3, 187n.14
hermeneutics 8, 24, 169n.5
Hinduism 44, 62, 178n.6
Brahman 26, 50, 51, 73, 143
Tat Tvam Asi 41, 42, 50
Ātman 42, 50
Horner, Robyn 185n.32
Husserl, Edmund 3, 11, 25, 27, 28, 37, 50, 159, 160, 162, 168n.40, 170n.15, 177n.24
Cartesian Meditations 168n.39, 169n.8
Horizons 170n.12
Ideas Pertaining to a Pure Phenomenology and to a Phenomenological Philosophy Second Book Studies in the Phenomenology of Constitution 167n.34
Lifeworld 28, 84
"The Vienna Lecture" 180n.23

impressionist painting 61, 85; *see also* Monet, Claude.
intentionality 2
intersectionality as academic methodology 5, 6
intersectionality of traditions 61, 63, 66, 74–9, 81, 84, 89, 122, 141

Institute for Christian Studies (Toronto) 181n.42
Inuit language 31, 61, 172n.29
Islam 42, 45, 85, 86, 89, 95, 119, 156–7
   Allah 26, 114, 130, 135, 143
   Mohammed 106
   Sufi mysticism 90

Janicaud, Dominique 3; *see also* phenomenology, theological turn in.
jazz music 61, 178n.7
Joyce, James 184n.17
Judaism 42, 44, 150
   Kabbalahic mysticism 90

Kant, Immanuel 2, 10–12, 26–7, 28, 144, 147, 162, 163n.2
Kearney, Richard 112, 164n.9, 184n.14
   Poétique du possible phénoménologie herméneutique de la figuration 169n.5
   'Epiphanies of the Everyday: Toward a Micro-Eschatology' 107, 182n.6
   Anatheism 183n.7, 184n.16
Kimmerer, Robin Wall 31, 172n.25
   Braiding Sweetgrass 172n.28, 175n.16
Klimt, Gustav 167n.37

Lacoste, Jean-Yves 3, 5, 164n.9
Leibniz, Gottfried Wilhelm 27
Levinas, Emmanuel 3, 150–1, 160, 189n.5
Life in Michel Henry 5, 12, 36, 70–1, 132, 173n.42
linguisticality 11, 12, 37–9, 45, 61, 96, 117, 135, 140, 159, 161, 188n.3
Livingston, James C. 166n.26
love in Christianity 42, 50, 62, 63, 84, 90, 94–5, 175n.13

MacKinlay, Shane 183n.8
Macquarrie, John 35, 164n.8
Marion, Jean-Luc 3, 112, 160, 162, 164n.9, 184n.19; *see also* sacramental religious experience.
   on Descartes 171n.19
   giveness 5, 12, 111, 182n.2
   love 106, 107, 117, 151–2
   revelation 106, 111, 115, 151, 175n.12

saturated phenomena 5, 105–7, 170n.12, 176n.22, 183n.8, 184n.11
material turn 69, 103, 179n.19
material-spirituality 3–4, 16–17, 23, 27–30, 32–9, 47, 60–1, 82, 84, 87, 114–15, 139, 141, 143–4, 146–7, 159, 161
McCutcheon, Russel 6, 158, 182n.3
Merleau-Ponty, Maurice 25, 39, 160, 162, 170n.11, 170n.13
   flesh 12
   The Visible and the Invisible 167n.35, 169n.6, 170n.10
   Institution and Passivity: Course Notes from the Collège de France (1954–1955) 167n.37
   "eye and mind" 26, 43–4, 51, 58
Milieu 27–9, 35, 170n.13
Mi'kmaq Tradition 33
Monet, Claude 93–4
mystical experience 19, 24, 49, 93, 105, 119

Nāgārjuna 31, 172n.27
Nagel, Thomas 169n.1
new materialism 173n.32
Nweke, Chinedu 34, 163n.6

ontological distinction 28, 87, 146–7, 171n.19
Otto, Rudolph 2, 3, 8, 26, 151–2

phenomenality 9, 47–8, 104, 105, 141, 182n.2, 183n.8
phenomenological distinction 28, 87, 109, 147
phenomenology of religion 2, 3, 8, 9, 20, 109, 114, 137, 158–60, 162, 166n.26, 189n.5
phenomenology, theological turn in 3, 151, 160, 164n.9
philosophical phenomenology 2, 23–4, 102, 129, 158, 160, 162, 163n.3
philosophical phenomenology of religion 5, 6, 15, 102, 105, 108, 158, 160
philosophy of religion 5, 20, 71, 90, 104, 117, 149–53, 158; *see also* critical philosophy of religion
   analytic philosophy of religion 149; *see also* Plantinga, Alvin

Continental Philosophy of Religion 149, 182n.6; *see also* Caputo, John D.; *and* Falque, Emmanuel; *and* Gschwandtner, Christina M.; *and* Kearney, Richard; *and* Marion, Jean-Luc; *and* Romano, Claude
Plantinga, Alvin 78, 79, 150, 179–80n.22
  "Advice to Christian Philosophers" 187n.11
Principe, Walter 34–5
productivity 31–2, 35–8, 82, 87; *see also* generativity.
Potawatomi language 31

quasi-transcendental 12–15, 19, 28, 59, 62, 63, 124, 127, 129, 130, 132, 134, 138, 141, 154, 160–2
quasi-transcendental effects 36, 58, 60, 65, 66, 69, 75, 81, 82, 84–5, 87, 93–4, 122, 128, 155, 162

Red Cross 88
Reformational philosophy 174n.6, 181n.42; *see also* Dooyeweerd, Herman; *and* Institute for Christian Studies (Toronto); *and* Seerveld, Cal
religiosity 17–20, 39–41, 43, 45–56, 61–64, 66, 74, 82, 89, 92–5, 109, 110–11, 115–17, 123, 125, 129, 130, 134–7, 140, 147–8, 155, 157, 161, 176n.19, 177n.27, 177n.29
religious effects 15, 18–19, 72, 81–3, 84, 88–9, 91–4, 118, 140, 147–9, 155
religious experience 5, 8, 19, 49, 82, 93, 101–3, 106, 107–8, 111, 114, 116–20, 135, 139, 140, 145, 146, 147, 160, 176n.22; *see also* event(-al) religious experience; *and* sacramental religious experience
religious materialism 102–4, 107
religious studies 1–3, 5, 8, 37, 81, 137, 146, 158, 173–4n.44; *see also* empirical religious Studies; *and* comparative studies of religion.
  cross-cultural 20, 55, 121–3, 138
religious phenomena 5, 14–15, 19, 38, 57, 61, 65, 72, 75, 81–3, 91, 93, 94, 97–9, 110, 122–9, 134–5, 137–9, 140, 143, 149, 152–5, 182n.7
religious dimension of experience 4, 18, 19, 38, 49, 53, 83, 87–92, 96, 97, 101, 108, 111, 115–19, 140, 142–3, 147, 148, 180n.33
religious[ly-inflected] phenomenon 74–5
residential schools, North American Indian 76, 181n.37
Ricoeur, Paul 125, 164n.9, 186n.4
Romano, Claude 5, 164n.9, 184n.19
Rumi [Jalāl al-Dīn Muḥammad Rūmī] 24–5

Sacramental Religious Experience 19, 101–2, 106–8, 111–12, 116, 182n.6
Schaefer, Donovan 169n.2, 179n.20
Schilbrack, Kevin 6, 158, 182n.3
  "What *isn't* Religion?" 165n.23, 177n.28
Schneiders, Sandra M. 35
secular assumptions 64–5, 69, 71, 73, 75, 78, 92, 96, 119
secularism 18, 64–7, 68–70, 74, 90, 156, 157; *see also* secular assumptions.
  in academia 71, 76–7
Seerveld, Cal 174n.7
sensing-transcendental 11, 26, 159–62, 173–4n.44; *see also* aestheticality; *and* ethicality; *and* linguisticality; *and* religiosity; *and* sociality; *and* tactility; *and* visibility
Sheldrake, Philip 34
  A Brief History of Spirituality 171n.20
Simpson, Leanne Betasamosake 187n.9, 187n.10
Smith, James K.A. 185n.31
  mall as religious phenomenon 98, 116
Smith, Jonathan Z. 6, 158
  "Religion, Religions, Religious" 188n.21
sociality 11, 12, 38, 60–3, 115, 140, 161, 188n.3
solipsism 102, 126
spirit 3, 16, 30–3, 40, 70, 161, 168n.44, 172n.24
  spiritual force [*Geistlich*] 16, 30–2, 34, 110

spiritual product 31–3
spirituality 3–4, 30–5, 114, 159, 161, 163n.6, 164n.8, 171n.20, 171n.21, 174n.4, 180n.29
spiritual-sensuous 27; *see* material-spirituality
Stiftung(en) 12, 36, 51, 62, 81, 85, 141, 159–62, 167n.37, 188n.20
Stein, Edith 168n.44
Steinbock, Anthony J. 174–5n.8
style 11–12, 20, 35, 38, 43–4, 55, 62, 66, 84–5, 94, 130–3, 139, 142, 161–2, 178n.7
subjectivity 10–11, 16–19, 26–33, 47, 50, 61, 66, 70, 82–7, 92, 95, 102, 116, 130, 141, 158–62, 167n.33, 168n.44, 169n.8, 172n.24, 172n.30, 174–5n.8, 176n.17, 188n.3
  subjective access 89, 146
  subjective capabilities 7, 15, 77, 165n.22
Swift, Taylor 92, 176n.18, 182n.8

tactility 11, 25, 28, 39, 60–1, 115, 140, 159, 161
Taylor, Charles 78
  A Secular Age 65
  disenchanted world 66–8, 70, 119
  buffered self 66–8, 70, 119
Teresa of Avila 184n.16
tradition 12–15, 17–18, 26, 30, 34–6, 44, 46, 51, 55, 57–63, 66, 68–9, 84–7, 89, 93–5, 98–9, 107, 109, 117, 122–4, 128–31, 136, 138, 141–3, 148, 152–3, 159–62, 167–8n.37

transcendence 10, 14, 17–18, 20, 36–7, 51–2, 66–9, 71, 101–115, 121–3, 143, 158, 160, 162, 163n.4, 186n.1
transcendental conditions 10, 12, 15, 70
transcendental analysis 10, 13, 14, 127, 161–2
transcendental phenomenology 2–3, 5, 8–10, 14, 24, 25, 27, 39, 129, 162, 173n.44, 188n.20
transcendental phenomenology of religion 3, 14–21, 124, 133, 137

ultra-transcendental 11–17, 27–8, 35–6, 47, 70, 102, 159, 161–2
  Earth as ultra-transcendental condition 28–9

Vallier, Robert 167n.37
Van der Leeuw, Gerardus 2, 3, 8, 159
Vattimo, Gianni 65, 67, 178–9n.12, 184n.19
verb-based structure, indigenous Canadian languages 31, 172n.25, 175–6n.16
visibility 11–12, 17, 25, 27–9, 37–40, 42–3, 45, 48–9, 53, 89, 115, 134–5, 159, 161

Walther, Gerda 168n.44, 172n.24
White evangelicalism 59–60, 109, 140–2, 178n.5, 187n.8, 188n.1

Yahweh 172n.28

Zahavi, Dan 163n.3